The Practical Guide to Using

GENERATIVE AI IN PHOTOSHOP

COLIN SMITH

The Practical Guide to Using Generative AI in Photoshop
Colin Smith

Editor: Jocelyn Howell
Project manager: Lisa Brazieal
Marketing manager: Koryn Olage
Layout and type: William Hartman
Front cover design: Aren Straiger

ISBN: 979-8-88814-217-2
1st Edition (1st printing)
© 2025 Colin Smith

Rocky Nook Inc.
1010 B Street, Suite 350
San Rafael, CA 94901
USA

Distributed in the UK and Europe by Publishers Group UK
Distributed in the U.S. and all other territories by Publishers Group West

Library of Congress Control Number: 2023952311

*For the creators, the curious, the catalysts. Make change,
with intention, with passion, and always for the better.*

CONTENTS

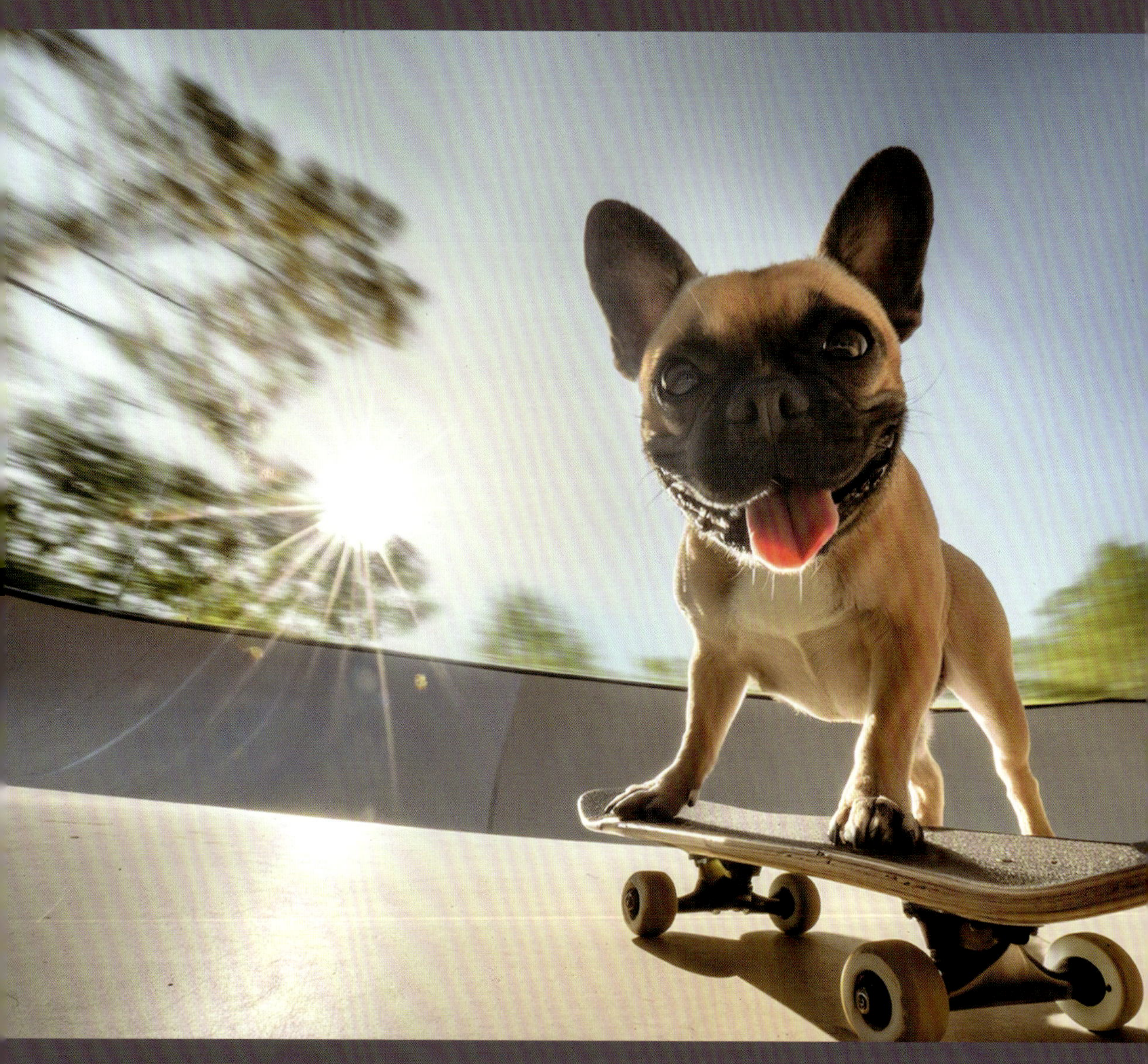

GENERATIVE AI

In this first essential chapter, we will lay a foundation. You will learn what Generative AI is and how to build an effective text prompt that will help you get better results from your generated art. We will generate some images from scratch to help you understand how everything works. This chapter is unique because here we look at the basics of Generative AI, and only in this chapter do we generate from scratch. The rest of the book is devoted to practical applications of AI generation to be used on your own photography and work.

What Is Generative AI?

If you are looking for a book that gets into the mathematics and science of how Generative AI works, this isn't that book. If you are looking for a practical guide that shows you exactly how to use Generative AI in Photoshop to help you save time and accomplish almost magical things with your images, welcome! Keep reading.

Generative AI is artificial intelligence capable of generating pictures, text, videos, etc., usually from a text prompt. All of this is made possible by the computer model, which simulates different things based on its training or learning. In this book we are focusing on images.

Generative AI came into the mainstream quite recently when Chat GPT was released. You type in a question, and Chat GPT responds by generating text answers. This fascinated people and the adoption rate was unprecedented—it took just two months to reach 100 million users.

This well-documented statistic is interesting, particularly when you consider the time it took for other technologies to reach 100 million users:

- Telephone: 75 years to reach 100 million users

- Mobile phones: 16 years to reach 100 million users

- Internet: 7 years to reach 100 million users

- Twitter: 5 years to reach 100 million users

- WhatsApp: 3.5 years to reach 100 million users

- Instagram: 2.5 years to reach 100 million users

- TikTok: 9 months to reach 100 million users

Shortly after this, popular AI image generators began to appear, starting with DALL-E, Stable Diffusion, and Midjourney. With these programs, all you have to do is type in a text prompt and suddenly images based on those text prompts appear. This is known as *Text to Image*. Adobe has been using AI for several years with its Sensei model—for example, Select Subject and Neural Filters. With the exception of the Neural Filters, Sensei wasn't generating images as much as it was understanding them and helping with things like selections. The Neural Filters were generating, but in a very low-key way; I suspect Adobe, unsure how its userbase would respond, was being cautious.

But all of this changed in March 2023 when Adobe debuted Firefly. Firefly is the Adobe generative AI model. Firefly was fully trained on the millions of Adobe Stock images and images in the Creative Commons only. This makes Firefly safe for commercial work and addresses some of the ethical concerns people had.

However, it's recently come to light that some Midjourney images had made their way into Adobe Stock and were also used in the training. An Adobe spokesman said, "Every image submitted to Adobe Stock, including a very small subset of images generated with AI, goes through a rigorous moderation process to ensure it does not include IP, trademarks, recognizable characters or logos, or reference artists' names." It's believed about 5% of these images are AI generated.

AI Changes the Landscape

We won't go into a long conversation about the ethics and impact of Generative AI on artists, but we can't completely ignore this important conversation either. There are many places online where you can engage in healthy (or not so healthy) debate about these topics.

I'm not sure who said it first, but Harvard Business School Professor Karim Lakhani is credited for saying, "People won't be replaced by AI, they will be replaced by people using AI." Like it or not, I think this is very true.

In our history and development, we have gone through many changes. The Stone Age, Iron Age, industrial age, machine age, atomic age, information age, etc. When Jethro Tull invented the seed drill in 1701, it increased food production and brought economic prosperity. I'm sure it wasn't great for the farm workers who were replaced.

Or consider the invention of textile and weaving machines, which gave rise to the famed Luddites who, in fear of losing their jobs and under the leadership of Ned Ludd, went about attacking factories and smashing the machines with sledge hammers in the early 1800s. Rumor has it Ned Ludd from Sherwood never actually existed. A Luddite is now a synonym for a technophobe.

There has always been great debate at the beginning of every major change. It's called progress. With every step of progress there are winners and losers. Let's face it, the toothpaste is out of the tube and it isn't going back in. In my opinion, the best way to deal with progress is to embrace it and learn to use it for your advantage. You can fight it, but you won't win, and you will wear yourself out trying. Human life expectancy has also increased with each of these major changes.

No matter where you are with these changes, I respect your position—whether you are super excited about AI, or reluctantly dragging yourself along, that's okay.

Let me quickly sum up my mental journey on this: When I first heard about Generative AI, I was excited. When I first used it, I was horrified. The next day, when I used it again, I started to see the limitations and understand that there are things AI can assist with and things only a human can do. After using these tools on a daily basis for almost two years, they have found their way into my daily workflows. I see Generative AI as a tool, just as I see any other tools. Yes, it's a very powerful tool, and I wouldn't want to go back to not having these tools.

I still find myself being just as creative as before, and Generative AI helps me. The way I use Generative AI in Photoshop saves me a lot of time by allowing me to avoid tedious work. Faster selections, quickly patching up images, expanding backgrounds, changing the orientation of images, seamlessly joining scans, removing difficult things from images, adding small touches without spending hours searching stock libraries, adding reflections—on and on. I don't generally use Generative Fill to create cats flying through space in retro cars while eating rainbow-colored bananas, but that could be fun. I use Generative AI as a practical tool to support my creativity, and I intend on showing you how to do so in this book.

If you are reading this book, I take it that you are one of the people willing to embrace progress and use it to your advantage.

How Does Generative AI Work in Photoshop?

From here on out, we will focus on using Generative AI. In a nutshell, you make a selection around the area where you want to remove, change, or generate pixels, then enter some words in the form of a text prompt, and Photoshop generates unique images that have never been generated before.

Primary Way You Will Use Text Prompts

In the next chapter, we will be focusing on generating images using Generative Fill in Photoshop, and we will look at these tools more in depth then. For now, I would like to introduce you to the main place you will be entering text prompts.

Go to Window > Contextual Task Bar to open a context-sensitive Task Bar. Only when a selection has been made will you see the Generative Fill option (**FIGURE 1.1**).

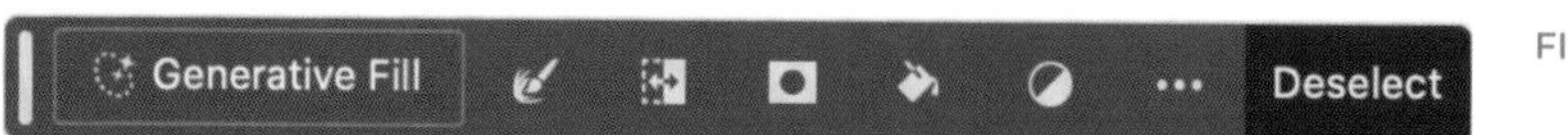

FIGURE 1.1

When you click Generative Fill, a text box will appear. This is where you will type your text prompt (**FIGURE 1.2**). You will then click the Generate button to convert the text into an image.

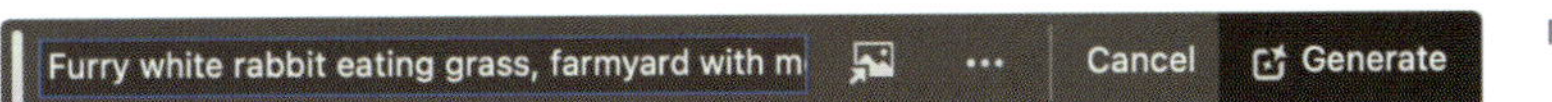

TIP For a complex text prompt, it might be easier to write the prompt into a text editor and then paste it into the Text field.

Once the image is generated, the text prompt will appear in the Properties panel (**FIGURE 1.3**). This is the best place to modify the text prompt and work with it until the perfect image is generated. When you have modified the text prompt, click Generate to update your image and add more variations.

Whenever you click on a different Generative Layer, the prompt will be updated to reflect the prompt that generated that selected layer.

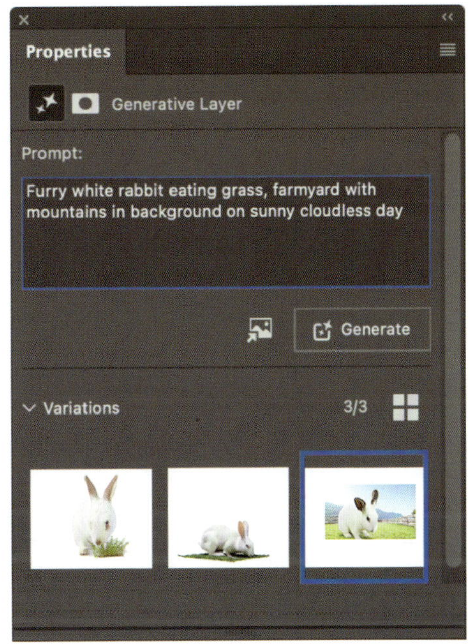

FIGURE 1.3

Generate Image

For this first section, we will use Generate Image to create images from scratch so you can see how prompts work without any other influence. However, the emphasis of this book is primarily on using Generative AI to assist with your workflow as you edit your own images and photos, and less about generating brand-new images from scratch. We will be mainly using Generative Fill after this chapter.

To use Generate Image, you need an open document, so either create a new document or open an existing one. If you work in an existing document, a new layer will be created. This can be useful for making backgrounds.

We will start with a blank document.

1.   Choose File > New.

2. Choose your document size (**FIGURE 1.4**). This will be highly dependent on your needs. In this case, I chose 3000px by 2400px.

3. Click on the Generate Image button, which can be found in the Task Bar or at the bottom of the Tools panel (**FIGURE 1.5**), or choose Edit > Generate image.

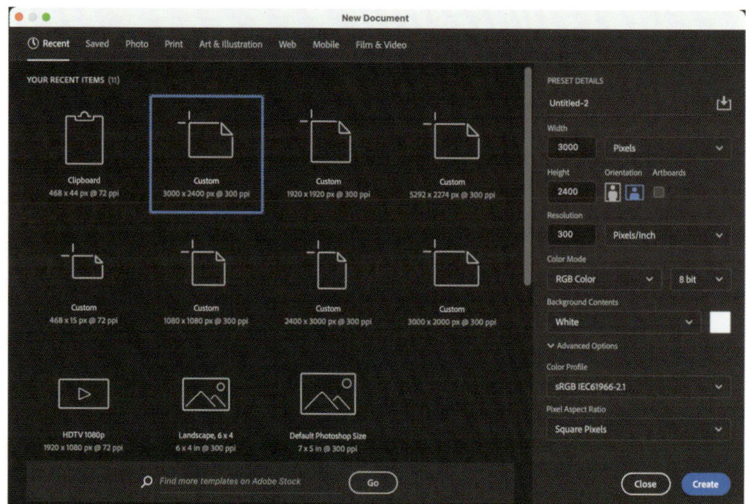

FIGURE 1.4

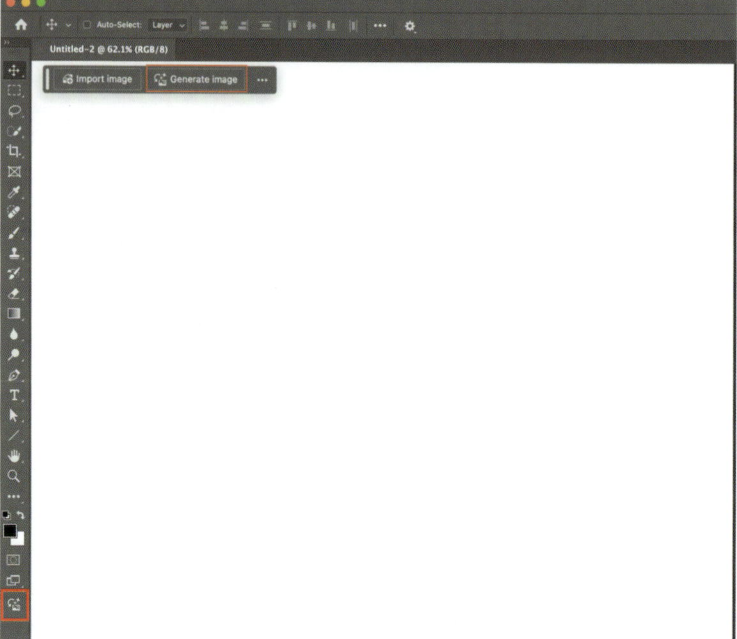

FIGURE 1.5

You will see a window with several features (**FIGURE 1.6**). Right now, the important ones are:

1. A description box: This is where you will enter your text prompt.

2. Content Type: Choose between Art and Photo. For the majority of this book, we will be using Photo, but you can create different art styles if you prefer.

3. Reference Image: You can influence the style of the image by uploading a reference image. The image generated will take on the art style (not the subject matter) of the reference image. In Generative Fill (next chapter), it will be influenced by the literal subject matter.

4. Effects: If you want to generate according to different effects, styles, mediums, and art movements, choose them from here. There are some photographic options as well as art options to choose from. It's also worth noting that you can use these words in your prompts, so take a look at what's available.

5. Prompt Inspiration: The right side of the panel is a gallery of prompt inspiration. Click on any of these thumbnails to see the text prompt associated with the image. This is a great learning tool.

To use Generate Image, at a minimum, enter your text prompt, choose a Content type, and click Generate.

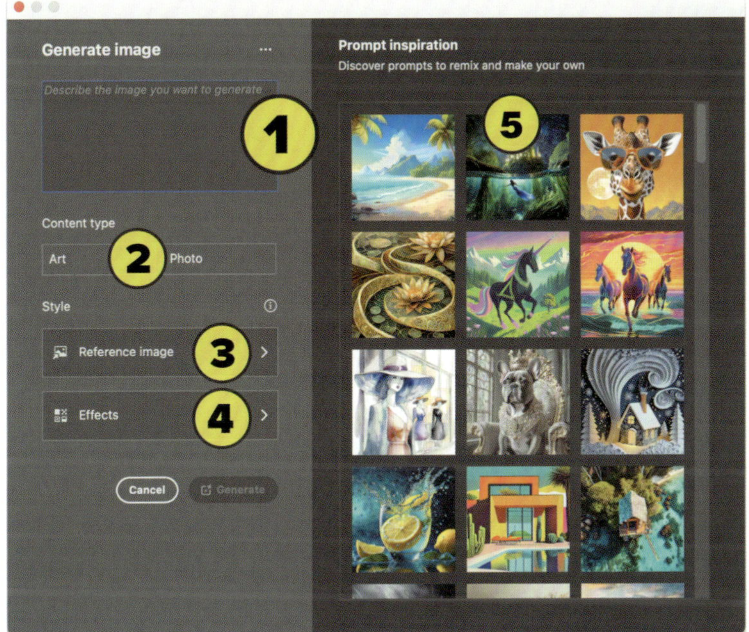

FIGURE 1.6

You will see a progress bar while you wait for the generated image to appear. During that time, the prompt is sent to the Adobe computers via the internet, the image is processed and generated in the cloud, and then it is sent back to Photoshop. You will see the generated image appear in your document window (**FIGURE 1.7**).

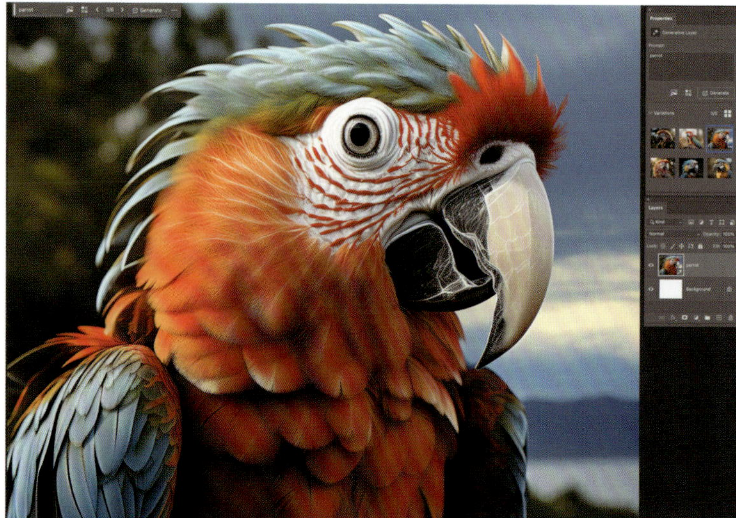

FIGURE 1.7

Have a look at the Properties panel (**FIGURE 1.8**).

1. You will see your prompt at the top of the panel. You can modify it here and click Generate to generate a new image.

2. If you want to open the Content Type panel, click the center button below the Prompt field.

3. Whenever you generate an image, there will be three variations to choose from. Simply click a thumbnail to select a different variation. Each time you click Generate, three more variations will be generated. These variations and prompts are unique to each layer. These special layers are called Generative Layers and can be modified at any time, even after other layers have been generated.

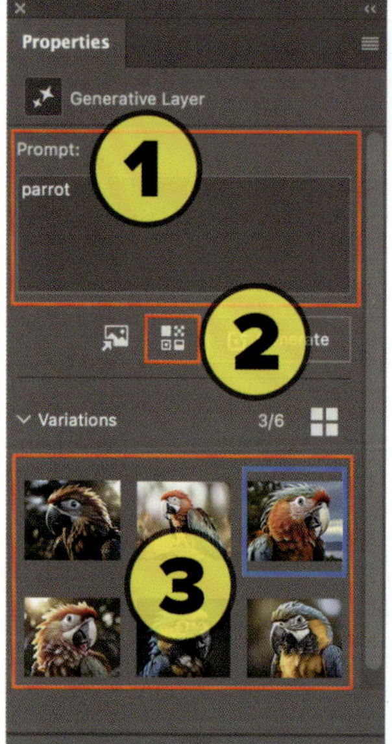

FIGURE 1.8

Click a different variation to change the image (**FIGURE 1.9**).

Text Prompts

When using Generative AI in Photoshop, the quality of your results is determined by how well you craft your text prompts. As you will find in the next chapter, the shape of your selection plays a large part too.

Throughout the majority of this book, we will be working with existing photos, but Photoshop can generate images from scratch. You can select your entire document and enter a prompt into Generative Fill, but a better way to generate images from scratch is to use Generate Image. Generate Image uses the Adobe Firefly engine along with the tool ported into Photoshop. The tools are not identical, but they are quite similar.

In this section, we will talk about text prompts. This is how you tell Photoshop what you want it to generate. There are a few things you should and shouldn't do. Photoshop (powered by the Adobe Firefly AI model) uses text prompts in a similar way to other text-to-image generators such as Midjourney and DALL-E. However, there are also some things that are different and specific to Photoshop and Firefly. Let's explore them now.

How to Write an Effective Text Prompt

Writing prompts is an art as well as a science. The first rule of thumb is to keep your prompt as specific and clear as possible. Start simple and add to the prompt as you need to.

Here we'll walk through how to build up a prompt. You won't use all of these elements in every prompt, and I would encourage you to use just what you need, nothing more. Use your creativity and eventually you will develop your own style of creating prompts that works for you.

Most text-to-image generators have a gallery that allows you to see the text prompts used. I encourage you to learn and glean inspiration from other people's text prompts, but try to come up with your own and not just copy existing ones.

Adobe suggests a minimum of three words for an effective prompt. We will build our prompt up one concept at a time so you can see how the prompts affect the generated image. However, when you write a prompt, you won't generate a new image every time you add a word or phrase like we do here; you will finish your prompt first, then generate and modify as you need to.

1. What is it (**FIGURE 1.10**)? Introduce the object. Is it a bird, a car, a pair of shoes? What kind of bird, car, or shoes? If it doesn't matter, don't add anything.

   `"parrot"`

2. Describe the object (**FIGURE 1.11**). Add properties of the object. What color is it? What material is it made out of?

   `"blue parrot"`

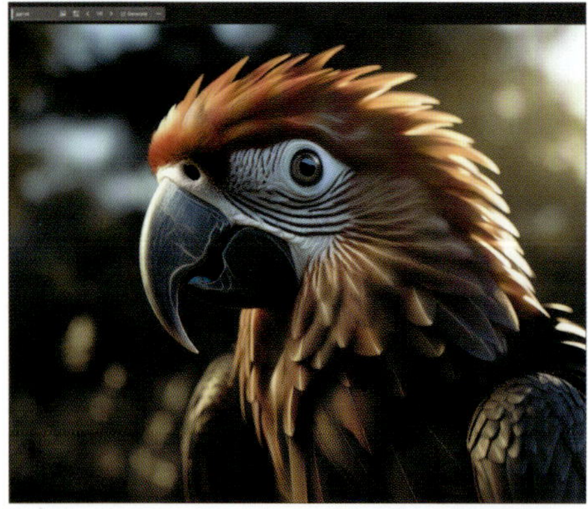

FIGURE 1.10

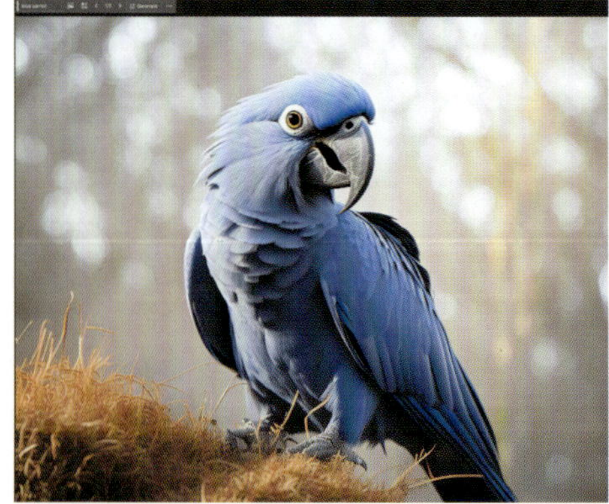

FIGURE 1.11

3. What is it doing? Is the bird flying or standing? Often, the context of the image surrounding the selection will answer this. If the context doesn't provide clues, you can prompt with the text (**FIGURE 1.12**).

    "blue parrot singing"

4. Are their secondary objects, props (**FIGURE 1.13**)?

    "blue parrot singing standing on perch"

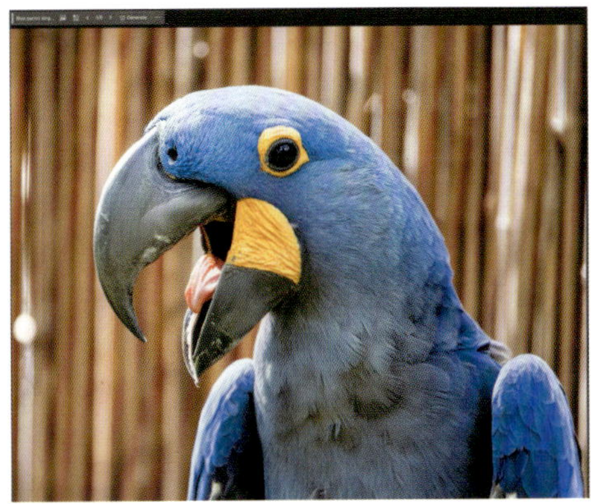

FIGURE 1.12

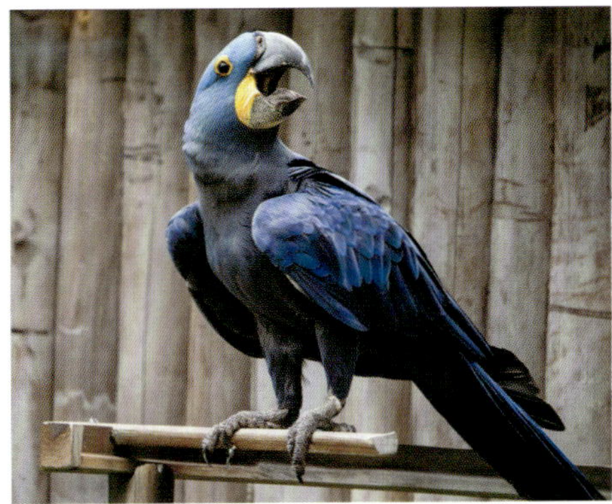

FIGURE 1.13

5. Where is this (**FIGURE 1.14**)? Is there a specific location? Is the parrot in a house, at the beach, in a rain forest?

    "blue parrot singing standing on perch, by beach"

6. Are there more details on the setting? Maybe a specific type of beach or forest or house (**FIGURE 1.15**)?

    "blue parrot singing standing on perch, by Hawaiian beach"

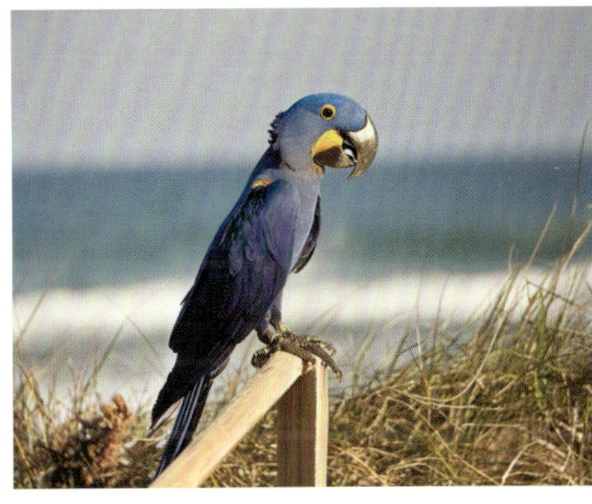

FIGURE 1.14

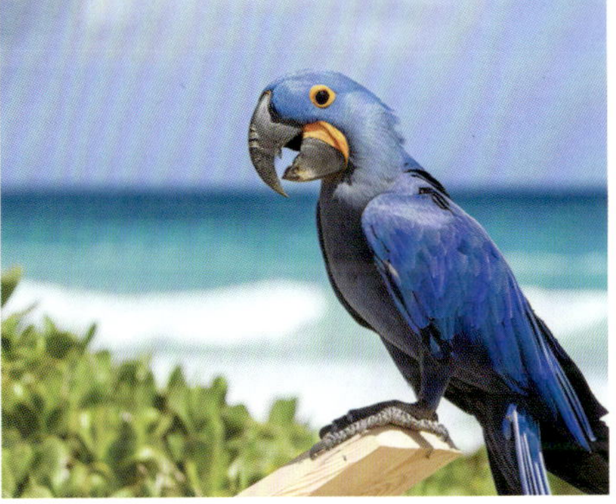

FIGURE 1.15

7. What time is it? Can you include a specific time of day or night (**FIGURE 1.16**)? You can also define lighting direction and color here: top lighting, front lighting, lit from left, etc. Lit from left with blue-colored light, or incandescent lighting, etc., will also work.

   `"blue parrot singing standing on perch, by Hawaiian beach, during sunset"`

Do You Need Commas?

Separating parts of the prompt with commas will help you add more detail to the different parts of the image separately. This is helpful, for example, when you want to include details about both the subject and the background.

8. Let's say we want to build out the background of our bird image (**FIGURE 1.17**):

   `"blue parrot singing standing on perch, by Hawaiian beach, with big waves and palm trees, during sunset"`

9. This list is by no means exhaustive. There are other things you can include in your prompt, including and not limited to:

10. Add some emotion. Describe the feeling of the scene: dreamy, surprised, excited, whimsical, elegant. This can add a lot of life to the image, sometimes in unexpected ways.

11. What is the weather or atmosphere like? Is it clear, foggy, cloudy, snowing, raining?

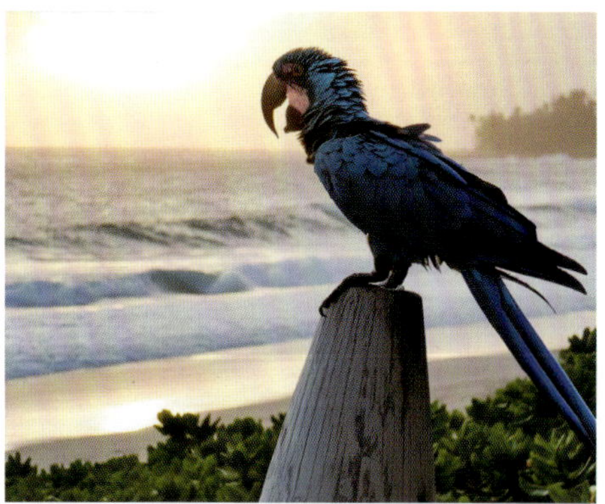

FIGURE 1.16

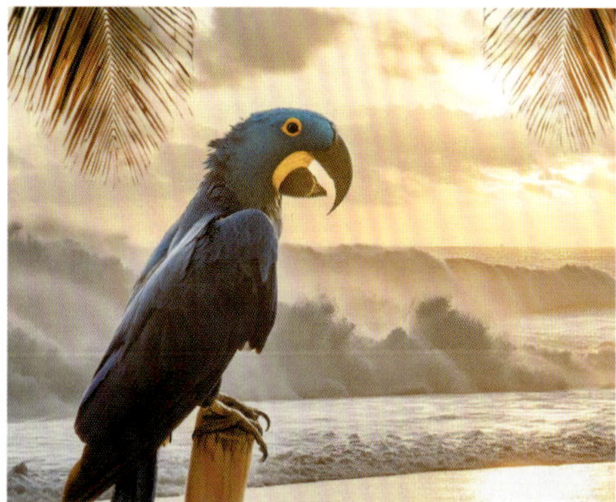

FIGURE 1.17

Based on what we just learned, we could start with a placeholder prompt. Something like:

```
object + properties, verb, props, location, time, emotion, weather
```

This will give us a good start. Replace the placeholder words with your specific words, remove the ones that aren't necessary, and maybe add one or two of your own to personalize your starter prompt. Remember, we can also generate an image with just a single word.

Extending the Prompt

Let's look at additional descriptive words we can use to make our images more interesting, or specific to certain styles.

- Style? Is there a specific style to the image? Maybe a particular era or art movement.

- Rendering styles? Wide-angle, fisheye, macro, tilt shift, shallow depth of field, bokeh, long exposure, grainy film.

If you look under Effects in Generate Image, or on firefly.adobe.com, you will find there are additional options you can choose from. You can click the buttons to add these to your prompts, or you can simply draw inspiration from them and type in the words.

I encourage you to explore these options and see which ones work for you. We will explore two of the categories here, starting with Movements.

Movements

Movements are different popular art movements through time, such as Art Nouveau, followed by Art Deco. This is where some art history knowledge comes in handy. Some people say there is no skill in writing prompts, but they are quite wrong.

Using the default placeholder prompt we designed…

```
object + properties, verb, props, location, time, weather, emotion
```

…let's generate an image that tells something of a story (**FIGURE 1.18**).

```
tall policeman, frantically running, in rainy city street,
mid-morning, searching
```

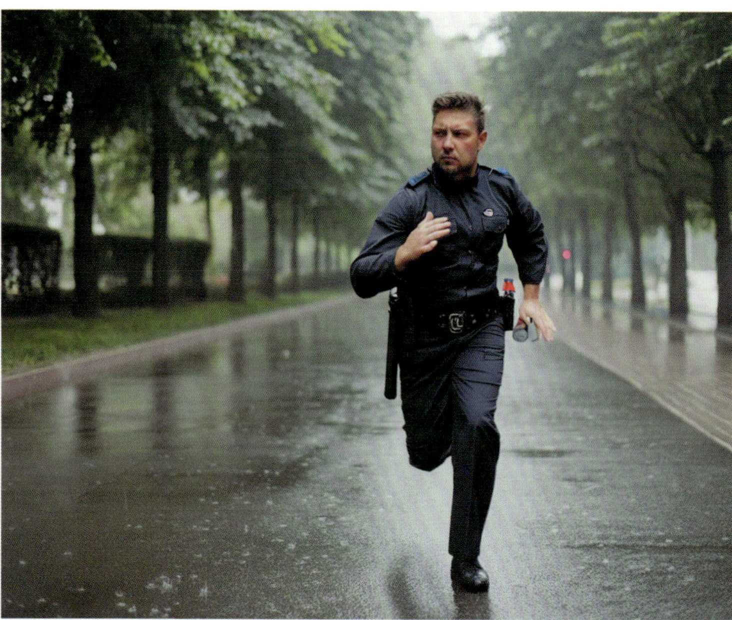

FIGURE 1.18

Now let's try using the same prompt, but add Steampunk from Movements (**FIGURES 1.19 AND 1.20**). Steampunk is a style that fuses the Victorian-era style and advanced technology that is powered by the resources of the time, mainly steam powered—think H. G. Wells or Jules Verne's writings.

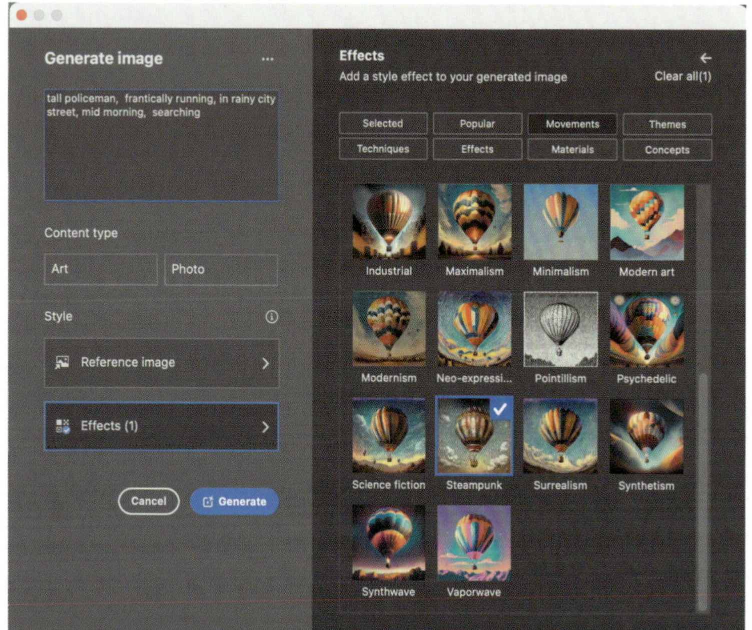

FIGURE 1.19

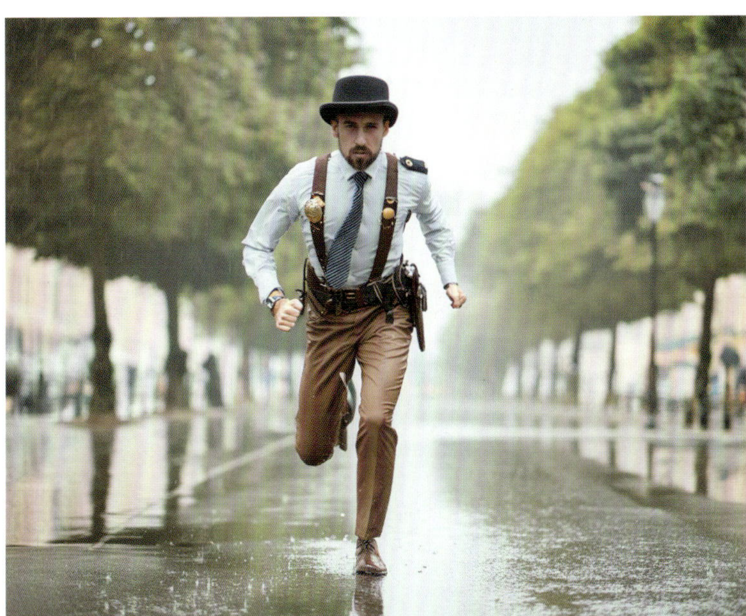

Let's once again use the same prompt, but choose Cyberpunk instead of Steampunk (**FIGURES 1.21 AND 1.22**). Cyberpunk is a gothic, futuristic style featuring a lot of blue and pink neon and cybernetics—think *The Fifth Element* or *Blade Runner*.

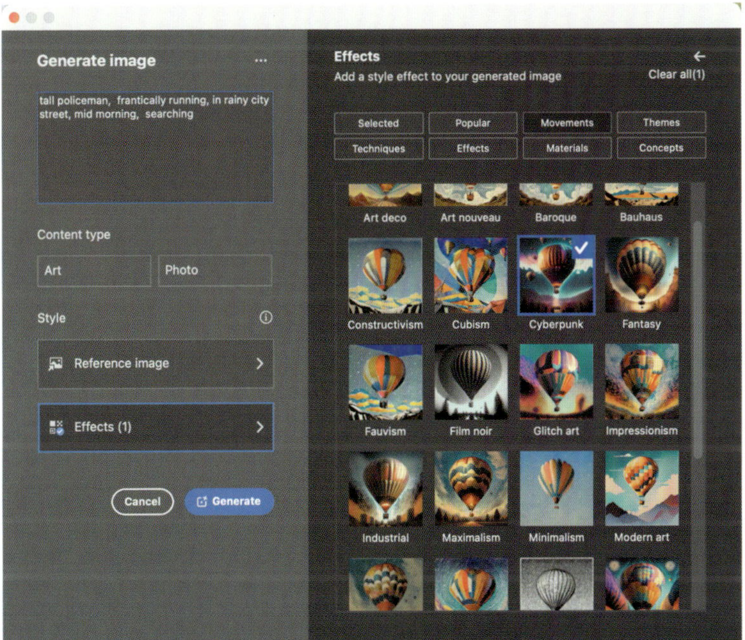

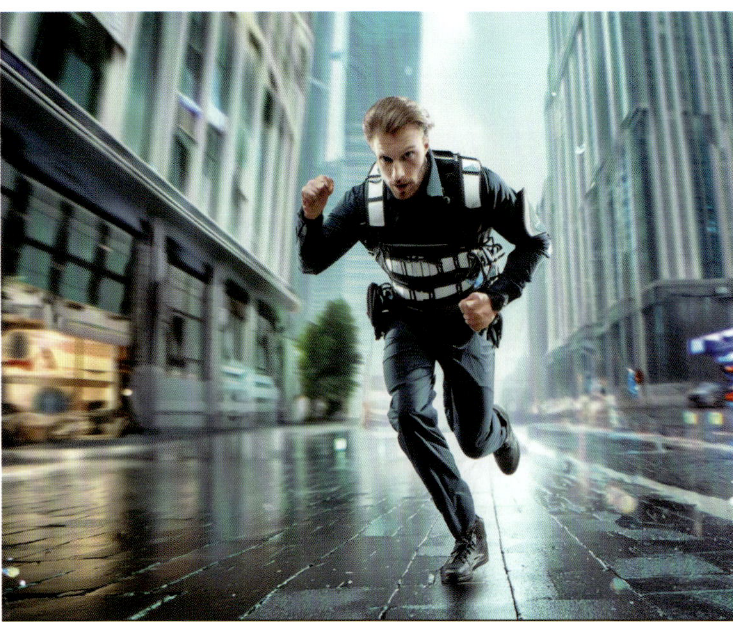

As you can see, the influences of a movement can greatly influence the style of the image generated. When you are applying a particular style, you are saying a lot, with fewer words.

Effects

The effects are a way of applying photographic techniques, among other things, to your images. Think of things like fisheye, bokeh, antique photo, tilt-shift, long exposure. Even though not all of these terms are available as buttons, it doesn't matter, as you will soon see.

We are using the following prompt:

```
excited french bulldog, extreme skateboarding, skate park,
warm sunny day
```

FIGURE 1.23 shows the unmodified result.

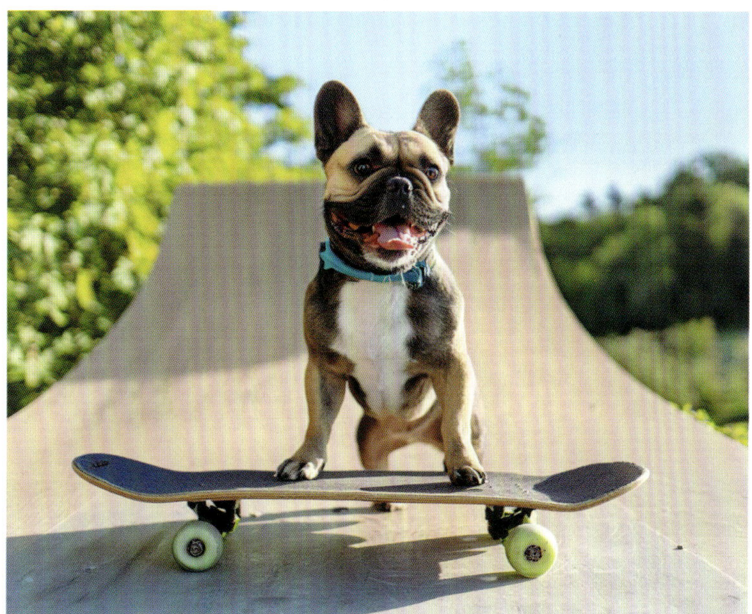

This time, we will choose Effects and apply Fisheye (**FIGURE 1.24**).

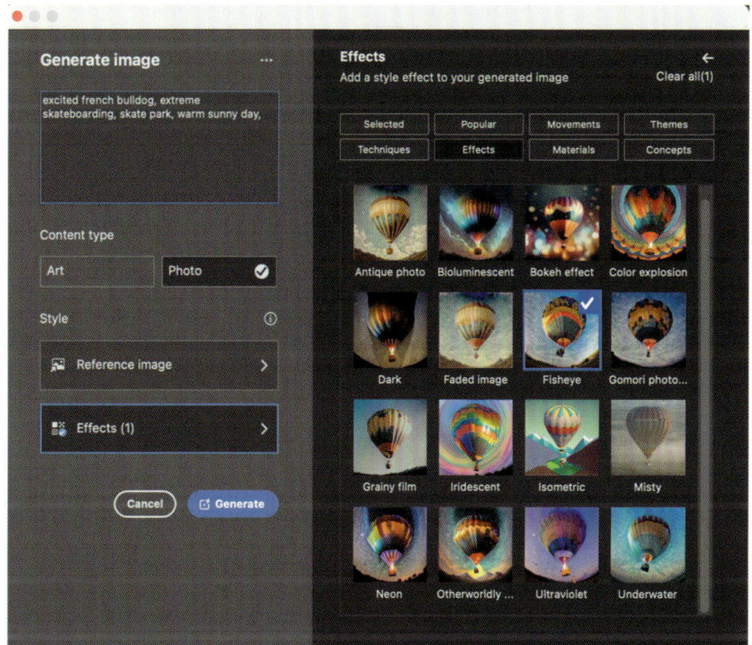

FIGURE 1.24

If you've seen many pictures of Frenchies, you'll know that the fisheye lens is a popular choice to capture the personality and hilarity of this adorable dog (**FIGURE 1.25**).

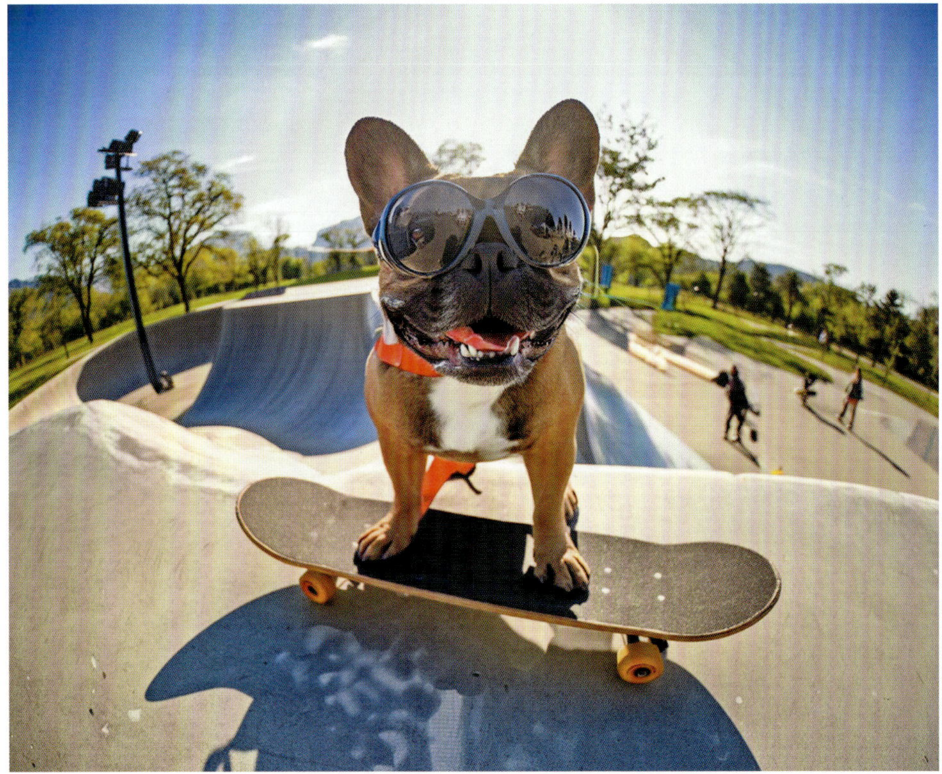

FIGURE 1.25

Okay, so what do you do if the effect you want to use isn't available from the menu? It doesn't matter one bit. You will get the same result by adding the word to the prompt. Firefly understands many more styles than those available in the Effects menu. The styles listed are just designed to help you write your prompt.

Add "long exposure" to the prompt text (**FIGURE 1.26**), and now you get an image with some motion blur to imply that a longer exposure time was used (**FIGURE 1.27**).

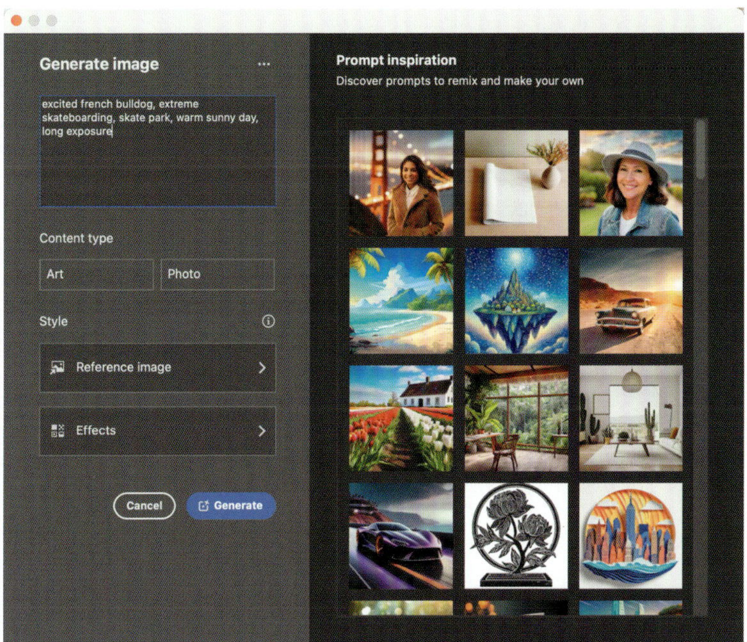

FIGURE 1.26

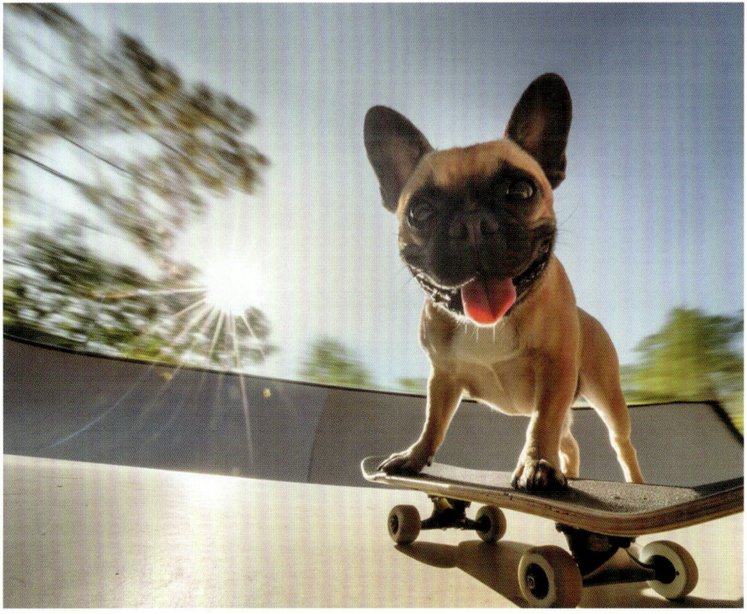

FIGURE 1.27

Use a Reference Image in Generate Image

We are going to take a quick peek into Reference Images for Generate Image. This will give you an idea of the capabilities of Generative AI. We won't go in depth on digital art, as the focus of these pages is enhancing your photography.

Just to appease the cat people, I generated an image of a cat with the following prompt (**FIGURE 1.28**):

```
bewildered happy cat curled up on wooden desk, playing with
wires, tangled in wires in front of lots of vintage electronic
dials and switches and gizmos, screens and meters
```

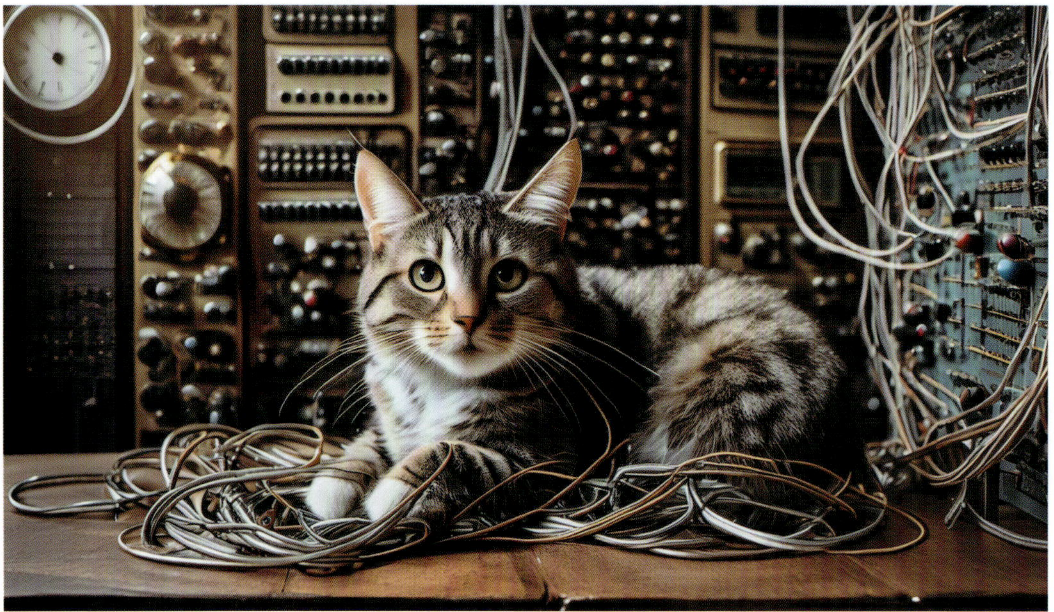

FIGURE 1.28

This time, we will generate with the exact same prompt, but use a reference image to see how it affects the result.

1. Create a new document. I set the dimensions at 1920px x 1080px.

2. Click on Generate Image in the Task Bar.

3. Enter the text prompt.

4. Click on Reference Image. You will now see a gallery of images.

5. Click the thumbnail with the cyan and magenta neon ring (**FIGURE 1.29**).

6. Click Generate.

You can clearly see the influence on the style of the image (**FIGURE 1.30**).

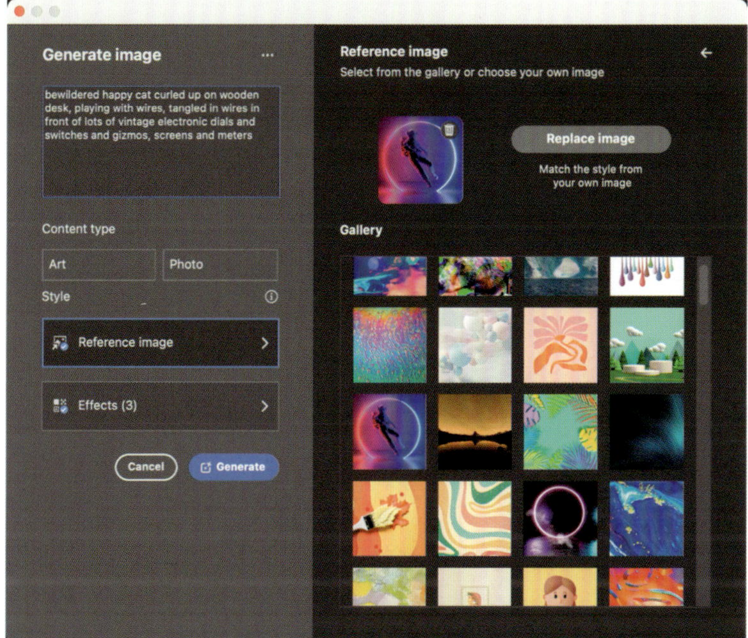

FIGURE 1.29

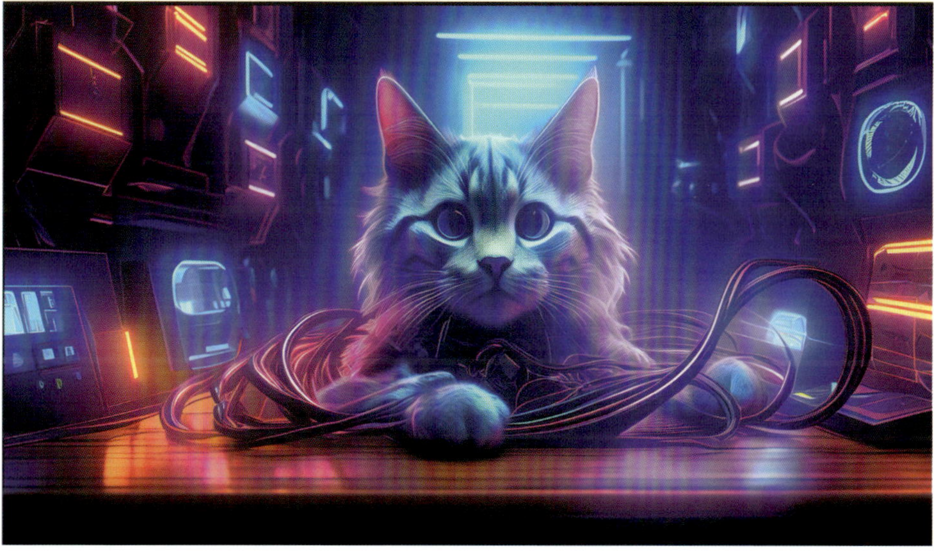

FIGURE 1.30

Let's try it again.

1. Click on Generate Image in the Task Bar.

2. Enter the same text prompt as before.

3. Click on Reference Image.

4. Click on Choose Image (**FIGURE 1.31**).

5. This time, I'll use a quick pencil sketch I made (**FIGURE 1.32**).

6. Click Generate.

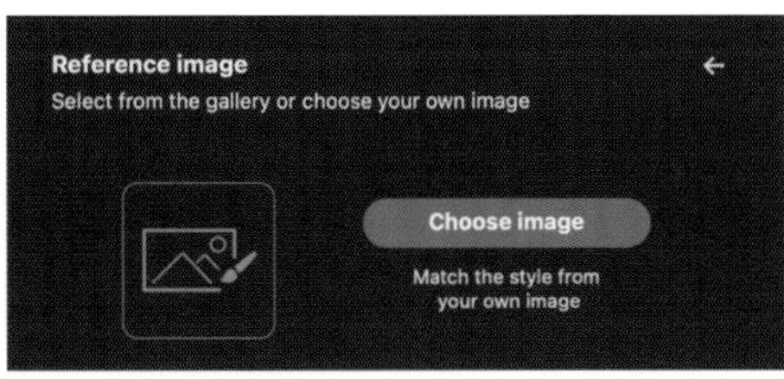

FIGURE 1.31

Now the cat took on the style of the pencil sketch (**FIGURE 1.33**).

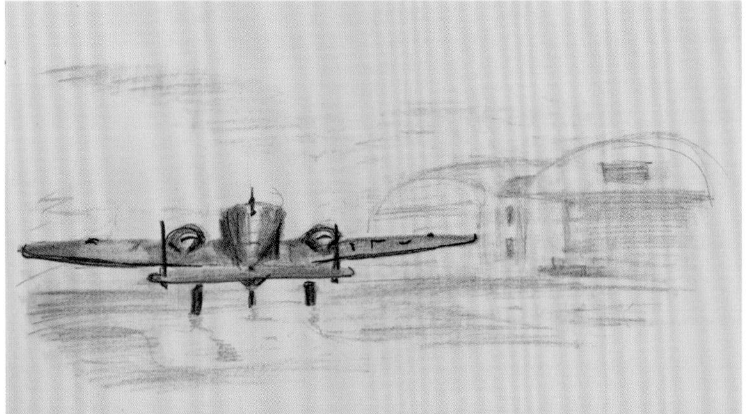

FIGURE 1.32

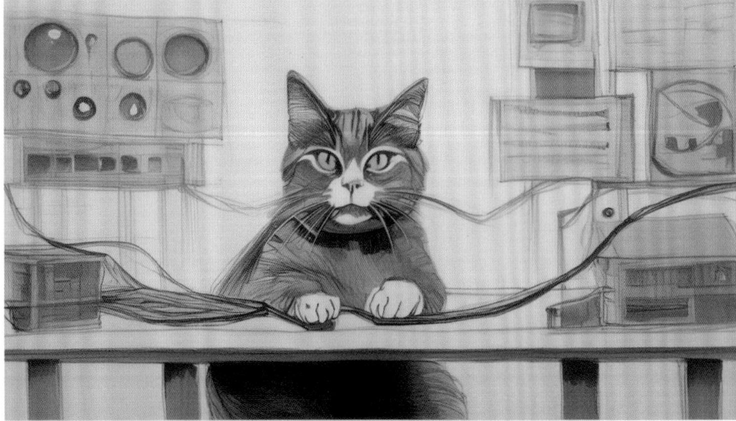

FIGURE 1.33

Let's use a different reference image of another sketch I made. This time it is very abstract ink line art (**FIGURE 1.34**).

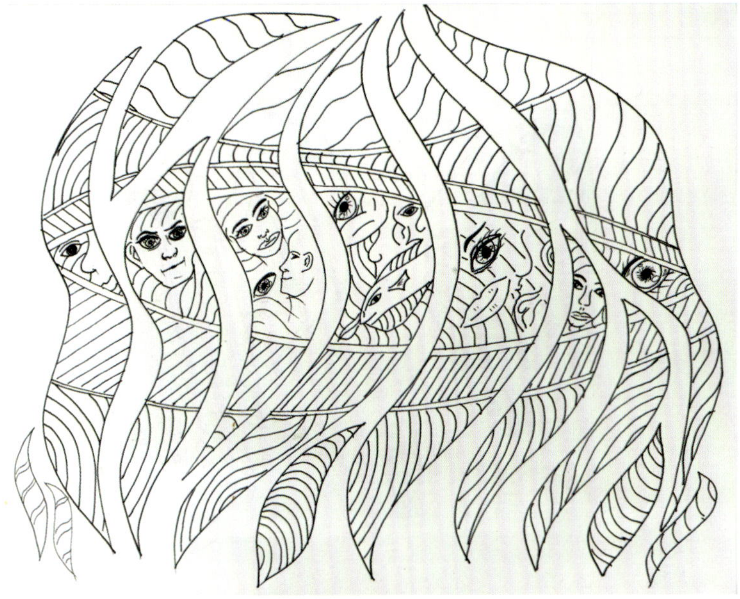

FIGURE 1.34

Notice we get an image generated in line art that is also a little abstract (**FIGURE 1.35**).

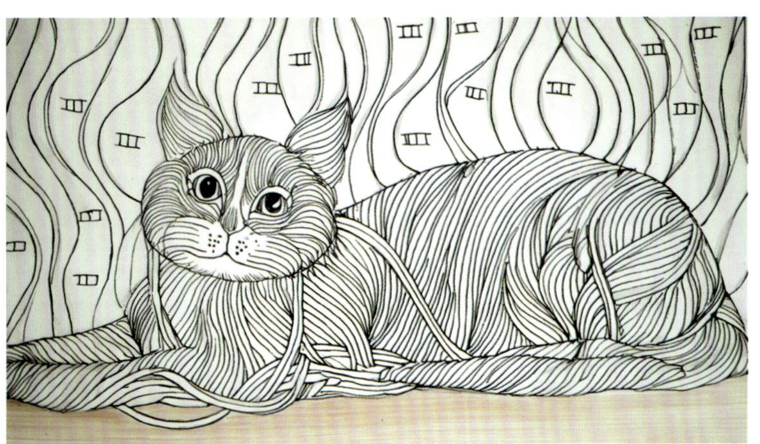

FIGURE 1.35

This time, let's use a photographic reference image of a cat (**FIGURE 1.36**).

Now we have a similar-looking cat—it even has a yellow collar—but it's still taking the expression and pose from the prompt (**FIGURE 1.37**).

> bewildered happy cat curled up on
> wooden desk, playing with wires,
> tangled in wires in front of lots of
> vintage electronic dials and switches
> and gizmos, screens and meters

I encourage you to experiment with the reference images.

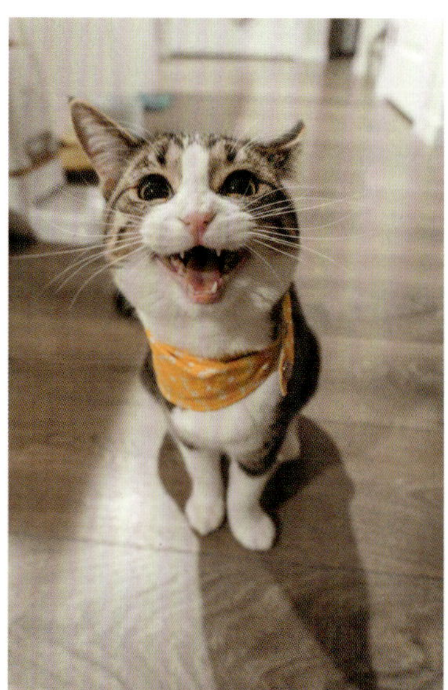

FIGURE 1.36

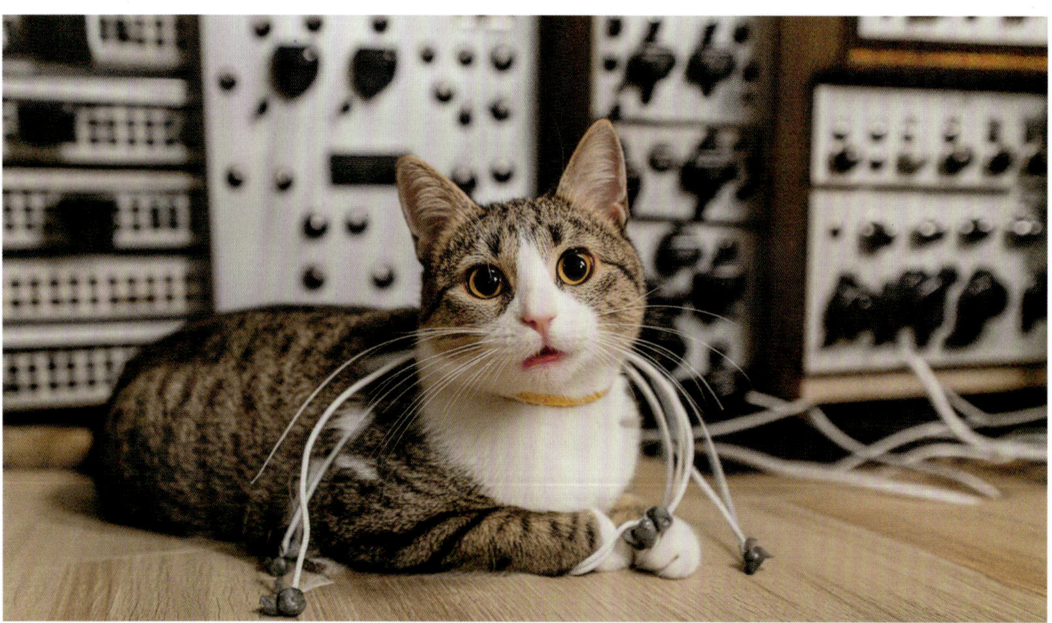

FIGURE 1.37

Generative Workspace

The Generative Workspace is a useful tool if you need to batch-generate images. This works much like Generate Image, but you can do a few extra things. Let's take a quick look. I'll try to keep it concise—we don't want to spend too much time on generating images from scratch, as that's not the emphasis of this book.

1. In Photoshop, choose Edit > Generative Workspace to open the tool. Let's do something simple—maybe we want a series of images with a woman wearing a blue shirt.

2. In the field at the bottom of the workspace, enter a prompt and click Generate (**FIGURE 1.38**). I chose "A woman wearing a blue tshirt at the beach." Four variations will be generated.

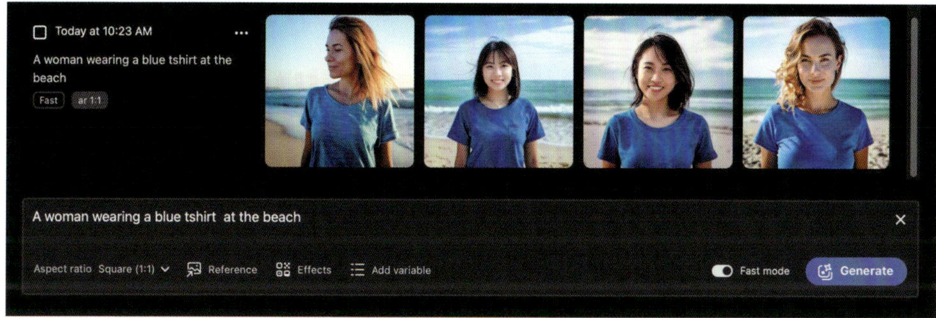

FIGURE 1.38

3. Let's change the location to the mall (**FIGURE 1.39**). You don't have to wait for the results from the first prompt to appear before you add a new prompt; you can keep adding prompts and clicking Generate, and they will cue up.

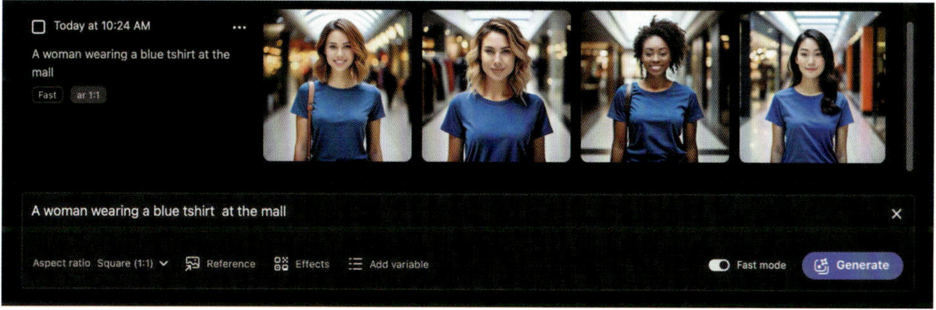

FIGURE 1.39

Variables

What if we want to generate a series of images? Let's say we want a woman in a white shirt at three locations: the beach, a mall, and a park. While we're at it, why don't we also do a set with a woman wearing a red shirt? Imagine how long this could take. But not if we use variables!

When we use a variable, it enables us to reuse a prompt automatically for several options without having to interact with the prompt again.

1. Highlight the color blue in our original prompt and click Add variable (**FIGURE 1.40**). This will add square brackets around the highlighted word.

FIGURE 1.40

2. The square brackets around a word or series of words separated by a comma sets a variable. Change "blue" to "white, red" (**FIGURE 1.41**). Now, eight variations will be generated: four with white and four with red.

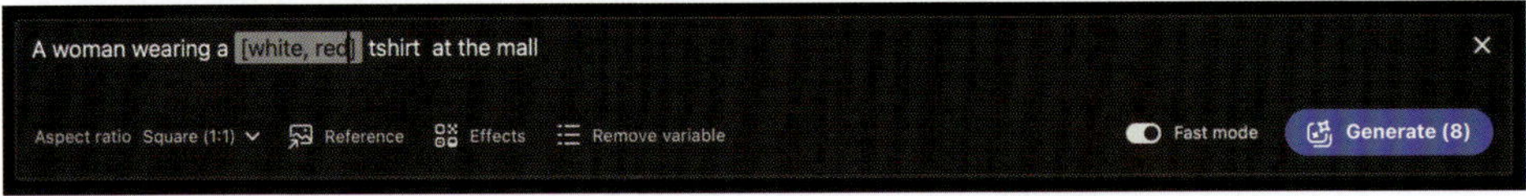

FIGURE 1.41

3. We can add more than one variable to a prompt. Let's also add one for location and use three variables: mall, beach, and park (**FIGURE 1.42**).

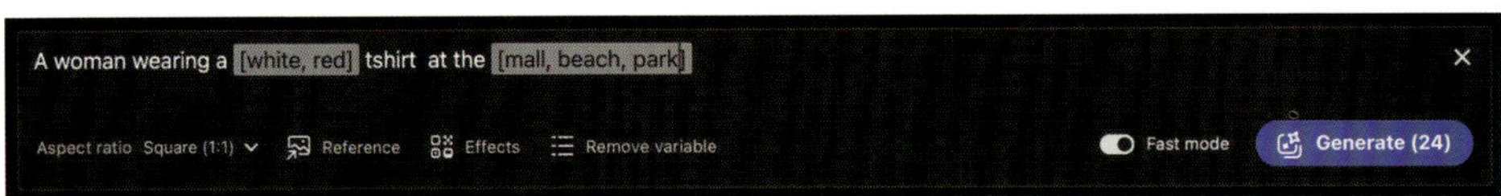

FIGURE 1.42

4. Choose Generate, and the prompt will run six times—once for each possible combination—generating four variations each, which means we now have twenty-four variations (**FIGURE 1.43**).

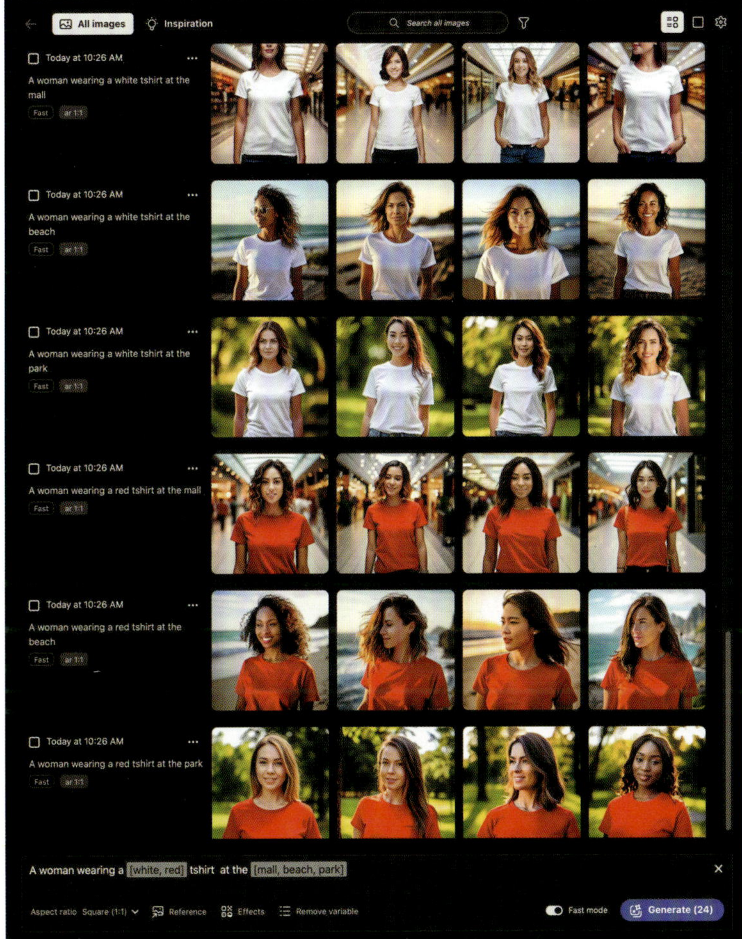

FIGURE 1.43

To view any variation at full size, click on the image. This also provides additional information about the image in the Info panel (**FIGURE 1.44**). Click All Images to return to the grid view.

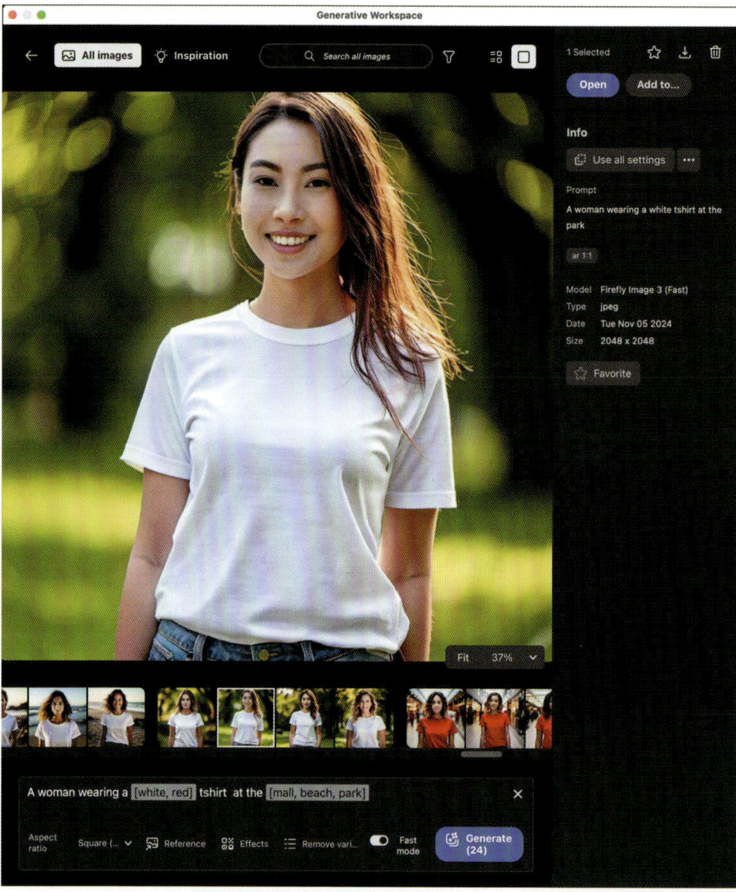

FIGURE 1.44

All the images in the grid are saved and will show up in the future when you return to the Generative Workspace.

You can also change the shape of the generated variations by choosing the Aspect ratio drop-down menu at the bottom of the workspace (**FIGURE 1.45**).

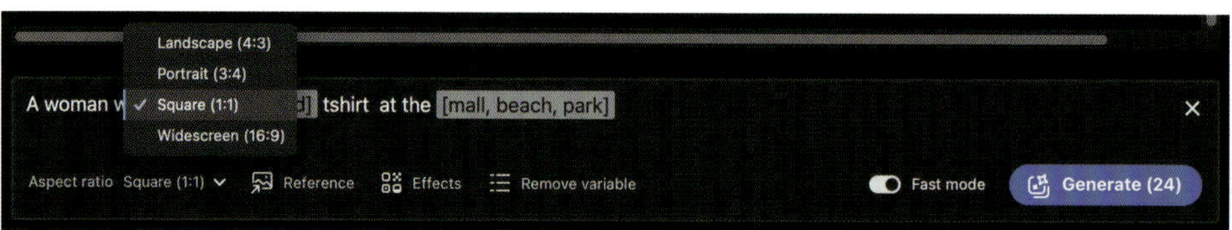

FIGURE 1.45

Using References

If you click on the Reference button at the bottom of the workspace, a pop-up will appear that allows you to use two types of reference images to help guide the generation (**FIGURE 1.46**):

- Composition reference: This will use the structure of your reference image, such as the shape or a pose, as well as depth to guide the generation.

- Style reference: This is the style of the image, such as a photo, illustration, painting style, or color scheme.

1. For Composition, let's use one of my photos of Callen (**FIGURE 1.47**). Click Upload image to select an image from your files. This photo will guide the pose used in the variations. The higher the Strength, the more closely Firefly will try to match the composition of the reference image.

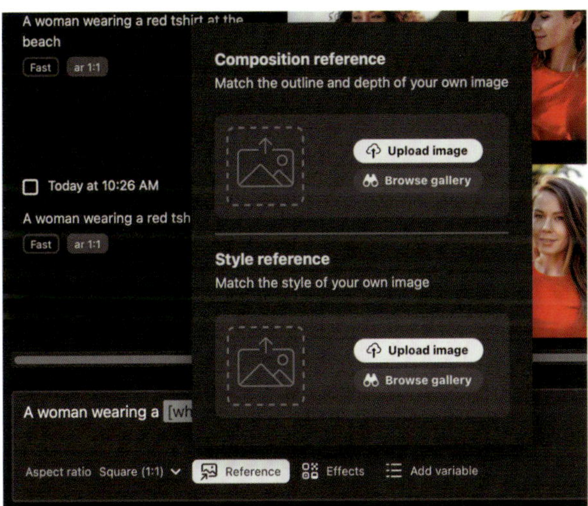

FIGURE 1.46

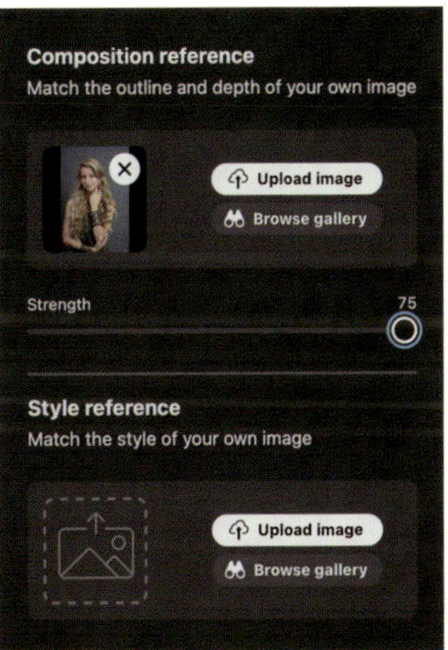

FIGURE 1.47

2. Let's also choose a Style reference. We could upload another photo, but let's use one from the built-in gallery so you can see how that works as well. Under Style reference, select Browse gallery.

3. Let's choose the wispy looking photo under Photo manipulation (**FIGURE 1.48**)

4. Now that we have both references loaded in (**FIGURE 1.49**), let's run the same prompt variables again, this time with the references. Click Generate (**FIGURE 1.50**).

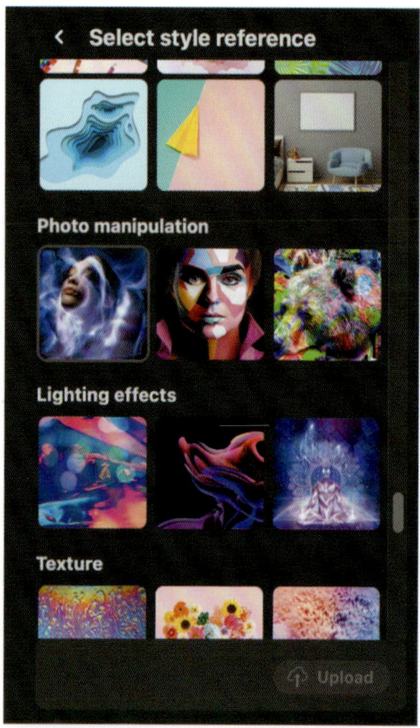

FIGURE 1.48

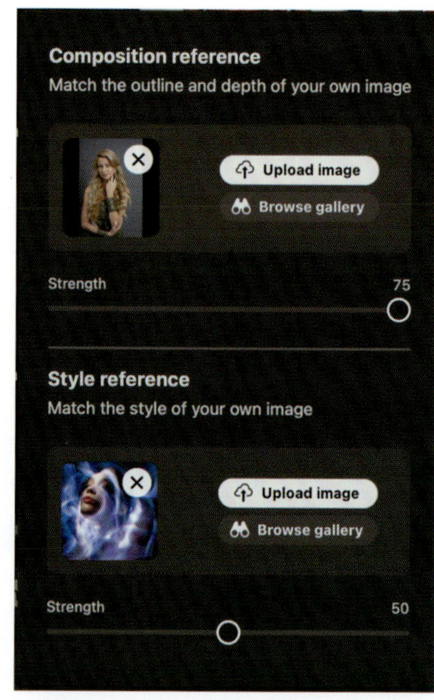

FIGURE 1.49

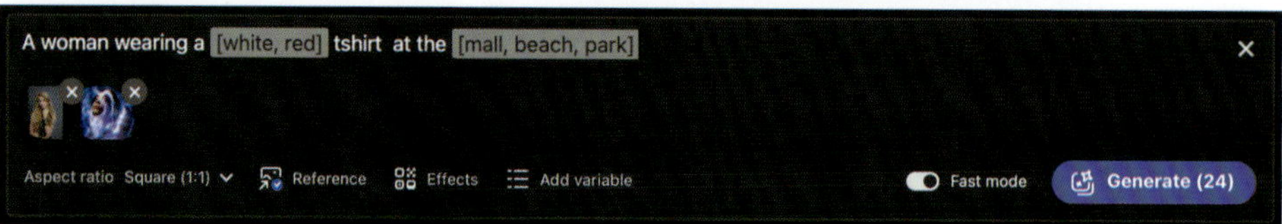

FIGURE 1.50

As you can see, the pose is set by the Composition reference and the artistic style and color comes from the Style reference (**FIGURE 1.51**).

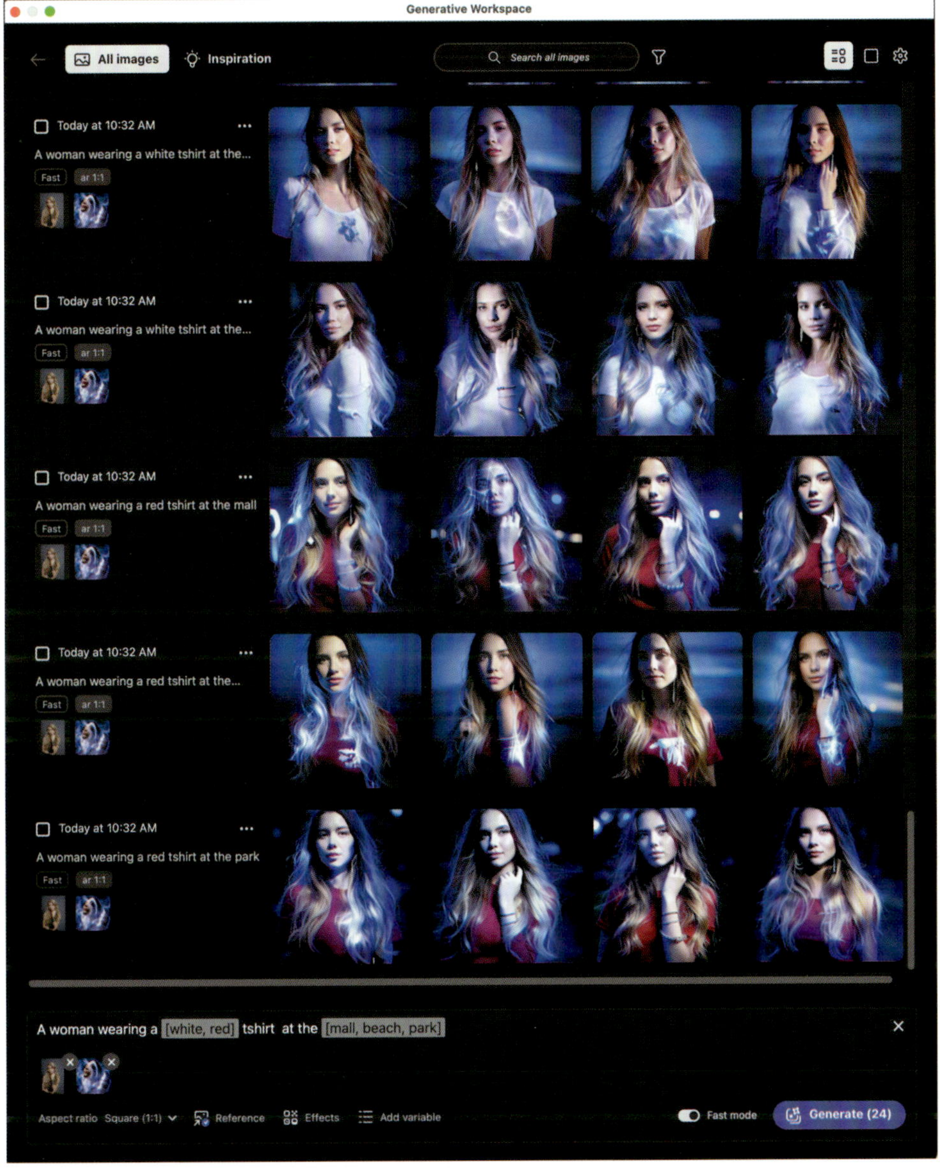

FIGURE 1.51

Opening and Downloading the Images

To open a generated image in Photoshop, click on the thumbnail to view it at full size, and then click Open near the top-right corner of the workspace (**FIGURE 1.52**).

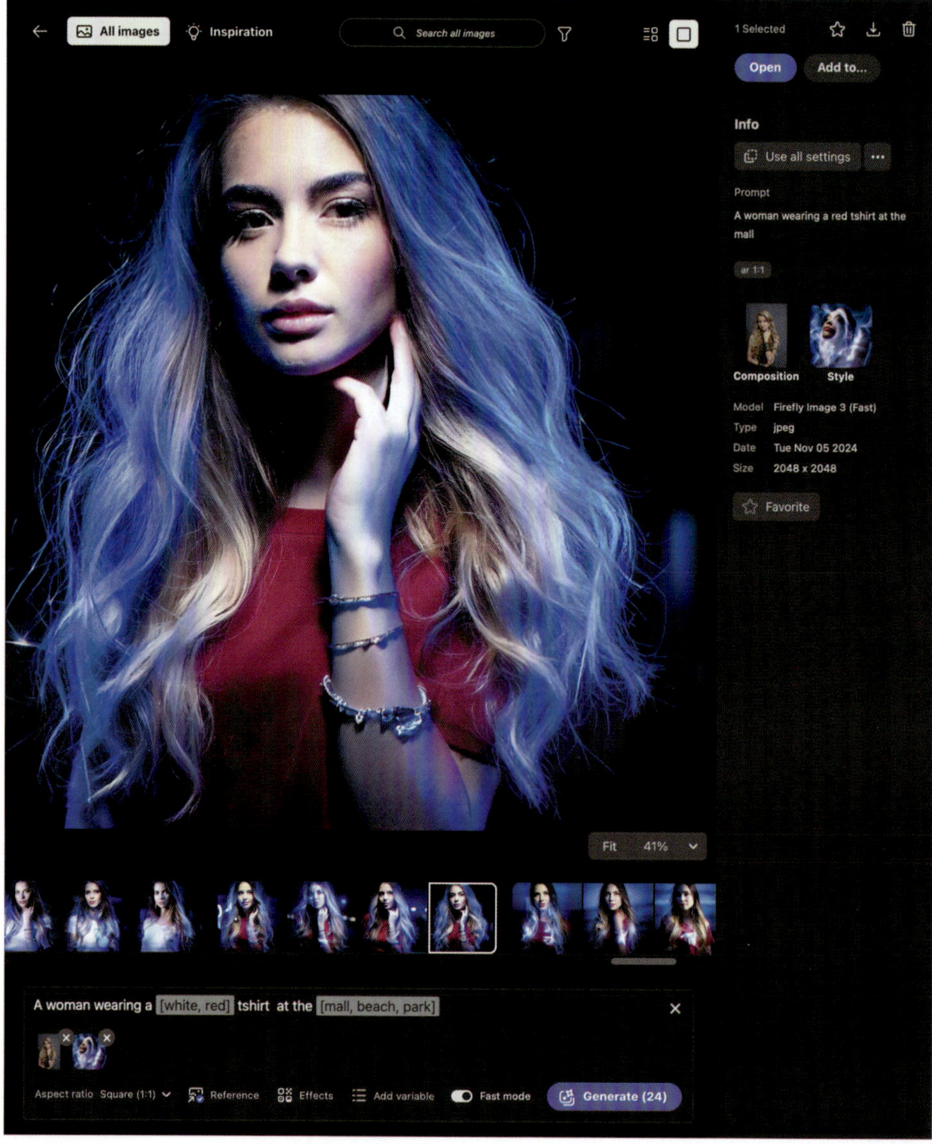

FIGURE 1.52

If you want to open multiple images, hover over the top-left corner of each thumbnail you'd like to select and click the checkbox, then click Open (**FIGURE 1.53**).

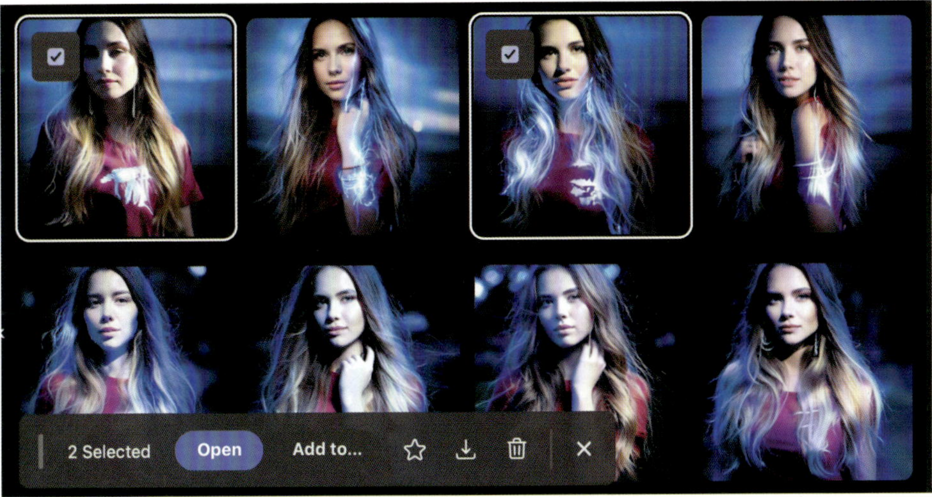

FIGURE 1.53

To download the images, click the three-dot menu next to the variations and choose Download (**FIGURE 1.54**). This is also where you could rerun a prompt. If you choose Use prompt from this menu, it will be added to the prompt box at the bottom where you can modify it and make more variations.

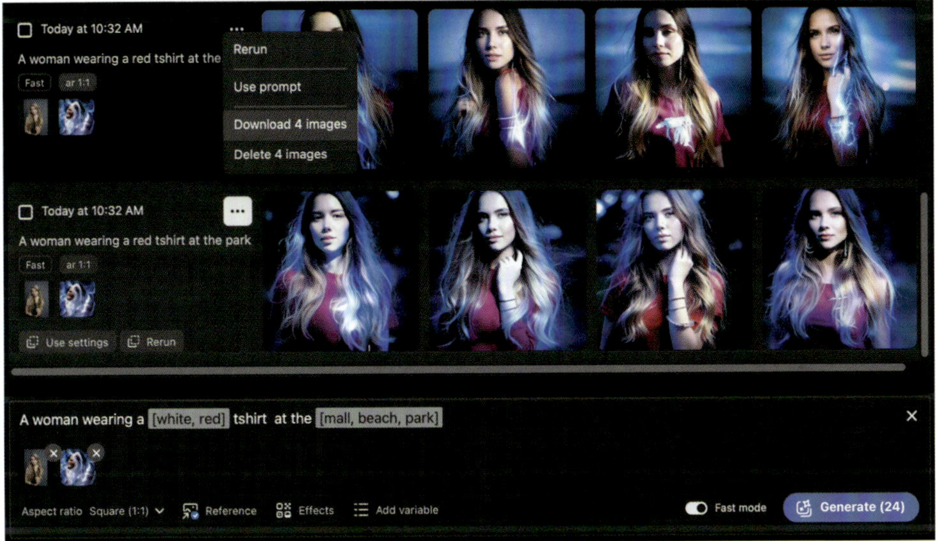

FIGURE 1.54

Using Generative Fill with Existing Images

It's one thing to generate images from scratch. When we are generating with selections on existing images, the same logic applies. When we are using Generative Fill, most of the time we are modifying existing images.

Generative Fill examines the existing image and considers the style, color, lighting, atmosphere, angle, weather, depth of field, type of lens used, and even more factors. It attempts to find as many clues as it can in the image and then match them. If it doesn't see these clues, you can add appropriate words to the prompt.

You will not need to add as much to the prompt to describe the image because it's already being described. Extreme examples include object removal or image extension, where you will often leave the prompt field blank because the description needed is already in the image.

Generative Fill Matches Color and Lighting

If you have a scene like the sunset image shown in **FIGURE 1.55**, you don't have to use "sunset," time of day, or lighting direction in the prompt. When a seagull is generated, all these things are picked up from the base photo. Notice the lighting—even the rim light matches the scene.

In the second example, I photographed the model in the studio using colored gels to create the blue and pink cyberpunk colors. These colors are influenced by neon lights and are not generally found in nature. When I generated the pane of glass, it picked up the colors from the image. You don't have add "blue and pink color" in the prompt; it already knows this.

Generative Fill Matches Depth of Field

Depth of field is controlled by the size of the aperture in the camera (the larger the opening, the shallower the depth of field) and the distance of the objects from the lens. The focal plane is the distance between the closest and furthest objects that can simultaneously be in focus.

A shallow focal plane means objects cannot vary much in distance from the lens to remain in focus. This is known as a shallow depth of field or shallow focus. A deep depth of field is a large focal plane, meaning objects can be different distances from the camera and still remain in focus. This effect decreases over

COLOR AND LIGHTING

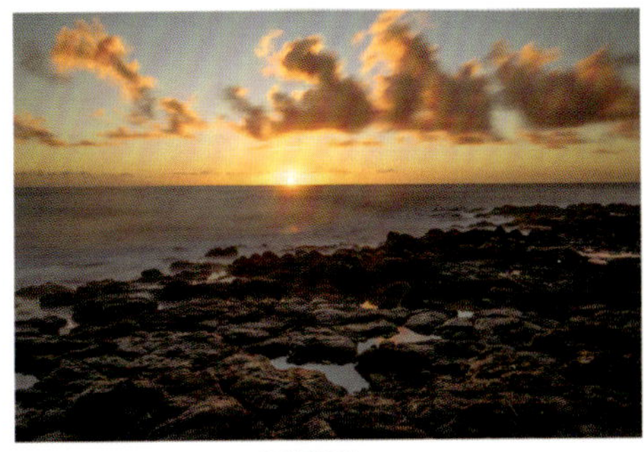

ORIGINAL

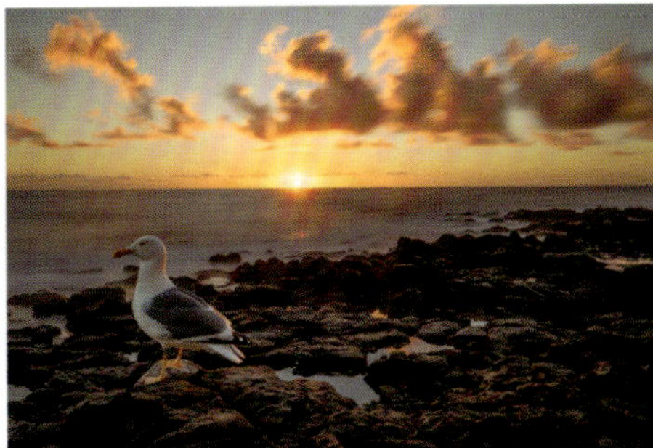

GENERATED (NOTICE RIM LIGHT)

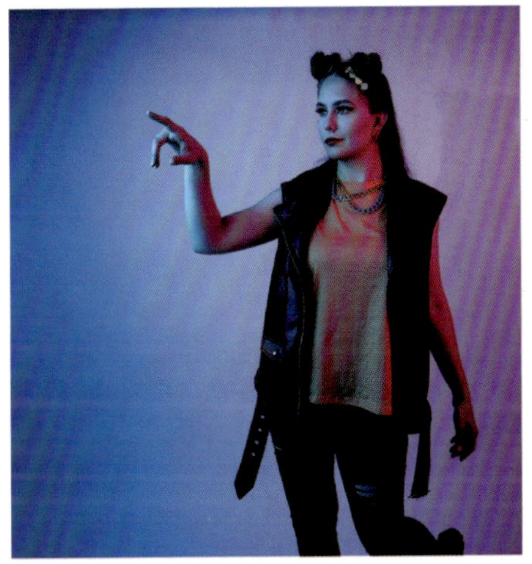

ORIGINAL

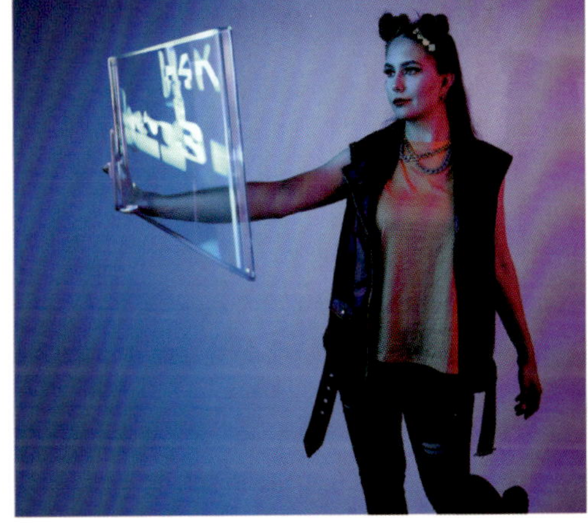

GENERATED (PICKS UP THE COLORS)

FIGURE 1.55 © Colin Smith

distance, which is why faraway objects tend to be on the same focal plane as one another, whereas an object very close to the camera will more likely have a blurred background than an object far away.

Certain artifacts and distortions can happen in the area outside the focal plane, such as specular highlights taking the shape of the aperture. This is called bokeh and is highly prized in certain types of photography.

Generative Fill also takes depth of field into account. If it notices a shallow depth of field, it will generate objects with the focal plane taken into account.

Look at the original image of the chess board (**FIGURE 1.56**). The two knights are in focus, but objects in front of and behind them are not because of their relative closeness to the camera and the large aperture setting of f/1.4. If you generate an object on the same focal plane, such as the queen in the second image, it will be in focus. If you generate an object farther away, such as the pawn in the third image, it will be blurry and out of focus.

DEPTH OF FIELD

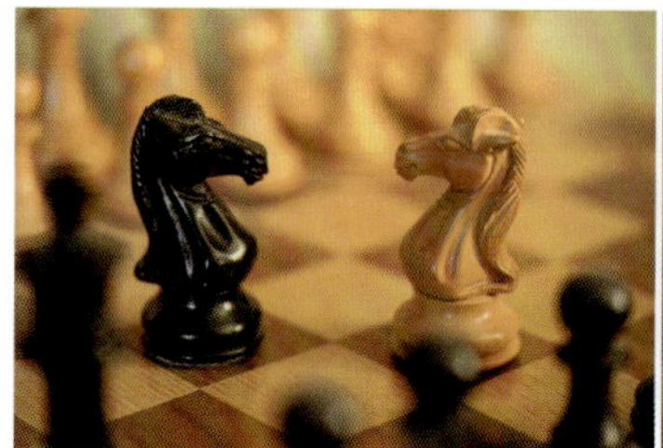
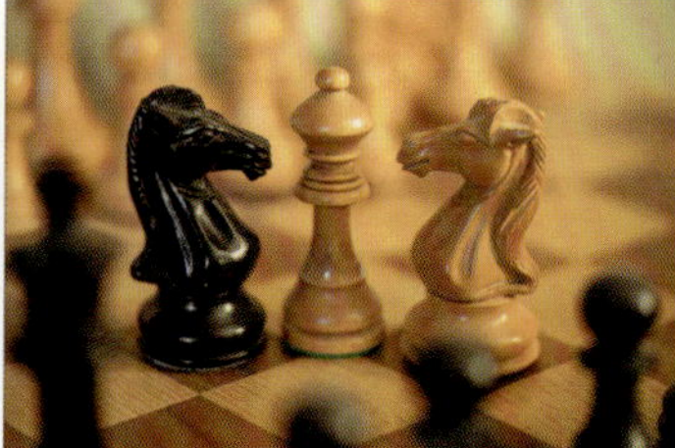
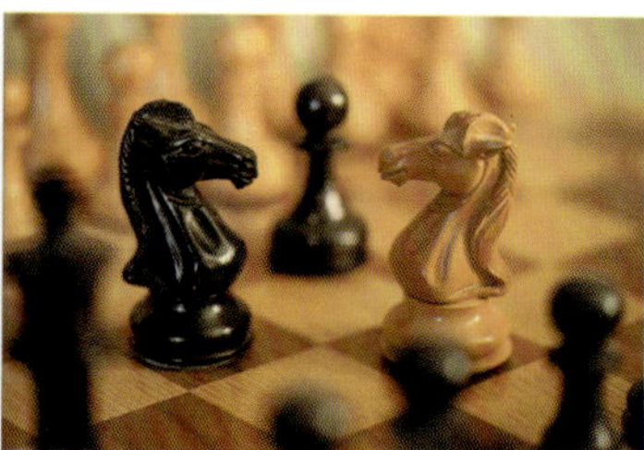

ORIGINAL   **GENERATED CLOSE TO FOCAL PLANE**   **FURTHER FROM FOCAL PLANE**

FIGURE 1.56 © Colin Smith

Reflections

Reflections are very interesting. In nature, "the angle of incidence is equal to the angle of reflection when a beam of light strikes the reflecting surface." In other words, you have the object, the reflector (surface that reflects the light), and the viewer. If a car (object) is parked over a puddle of water (reflector) and you (viewer) look down at the car, you will see all the top faces of the car. If you look into the puddle, however, you will see that the reflection reveals what you can't see directly, the underside of the car. This is how mirrors work.

Very often in compositing, the artist merely flips the image, moves it under the object, and maybe adds a bit of a blur to imply a reflection. While this may be enough to fool a novice or casual viewer, on close examination, it will be obvious the reflection is positioned at the wrong angle. In the past, this was a very difficult problem to address without using additional photos of the object from different angles. Now with Generative AI, we can easily generate reflections that show the correct angles.

Take this photo of musician Taylor Davis in a field of wild Californian poppies (**FIGURE 1.57**). Add a body of water and notice that the reflections are accurate. While Generative Fill will do a good job of producing reflections on its own, this is a good place to help it with a text prompt. Use prompts like "reflective surface," "reflective puddle," "reflective water," "reflective glass," etc., to help increase this effect.

REFLECTIONS

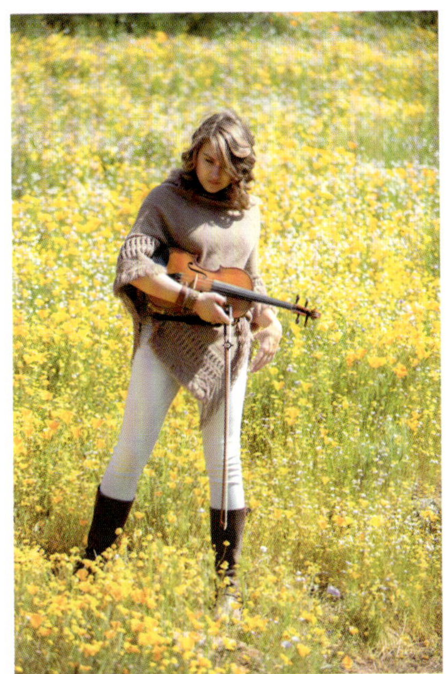

ORIGINAL   **GENERATED (WITH REFLECTION)**

FIGURE 1.57 © Colin Smith

Atmosphere

Generative Fill knows if there is atmosphere—such as smog, fog, or haze—in the image and generates accordingly.

In **FIGURE 1.58**, I've made a selection around a foggy scene.

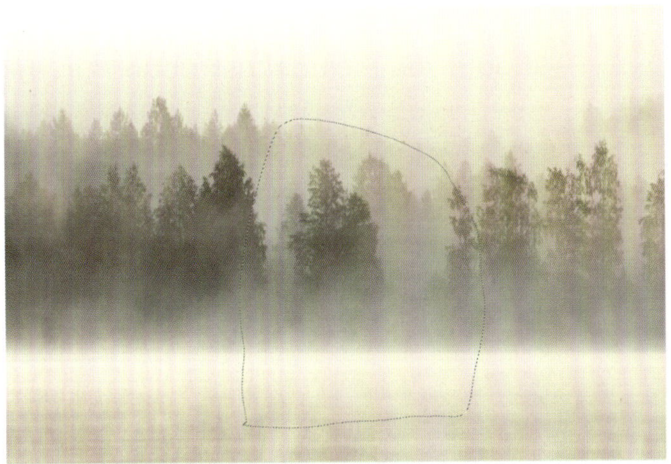

FIGURE 1.58 © Adobe Stock

Then I added the prompt:

```
tall masted wooden ship coming toward us
```

Notice how nicely it blends into the image (**FIGURE 1.59**).

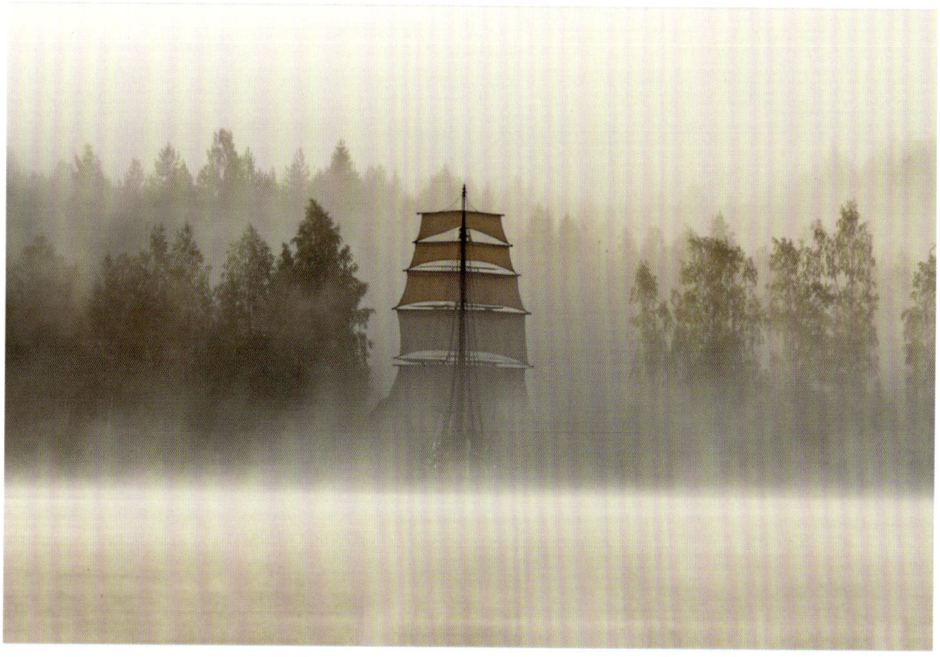

FIGURE 1.59

Should You Include Instructions in the Prompt?

When removing objects, Adobe previously told us, "There is no need to add instructions to the prompt." For example, words like "remove the person" or "replace the car" did absolutely nothing with the Firefly model. Simply making a selection and leaving the prompt blank to remove something was sufficient. While you can still use a blank prompt to remove objects, in Firefly Model 3, this has changed. Adobe is now encouraging us to use words like remove or replace. If the removal is simple and obvious, I would suggest leaving the prompt blank. However, if there are multiple overlapping objects and you want to remove something specific, use a prompt. If your removal isn't working well, try using a removal or replacement prompt.

Content Warning

Because of the commercial nature of the program, there are strict guidelines on what can be generated. You will see a content warning appear if you violate the rules, and the image won't display. This includes strict guidelines on things like sexuality, gore, violence, and depicting known people. On the plus side, Adobe is doing its best to limit misinformation and abuse of AI imagery. The downside is it can be difficult to generate things like battle scenes and weapons. You can see the full set of guidelines on the Adobe website.

What If You Get a False Error with Content Warning?

When you try to generate something that falls outside the guidelines, Photoshop will give you an error message (**FIGURE 1.60**). You can click the View Guidelines button to see how you can modify your prompt to fall within them.

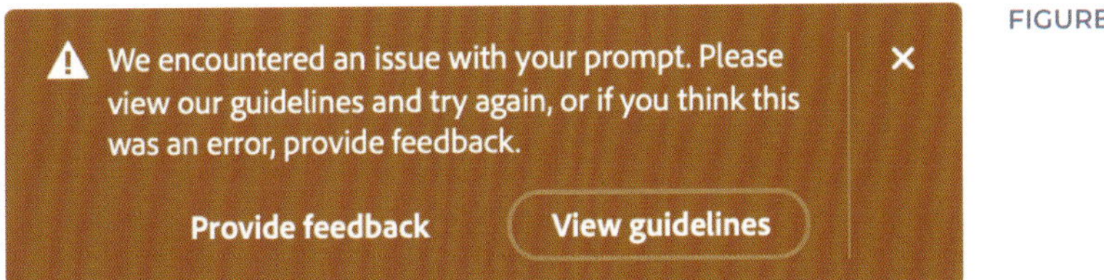

FIGURE 1.60

If you are trying to generate without a prompt, to remove something, sometimes you will get a false positive. I find this happens mostly when working on isolated areas of skin, but it can happen anywhere. If this box pops up and won't let you generate with your selections, first try adding anything into the text field. An Adobe engineer I know, suggests typing a period into the box. If that still doesn't work, try making your selection again.

Alright, now that we have discussed the basics, it's time to roll up our sleeves and go to work. The rest of this book will be practical step-by-step examples of many of the things we can do with Generative AI in Photoshop.

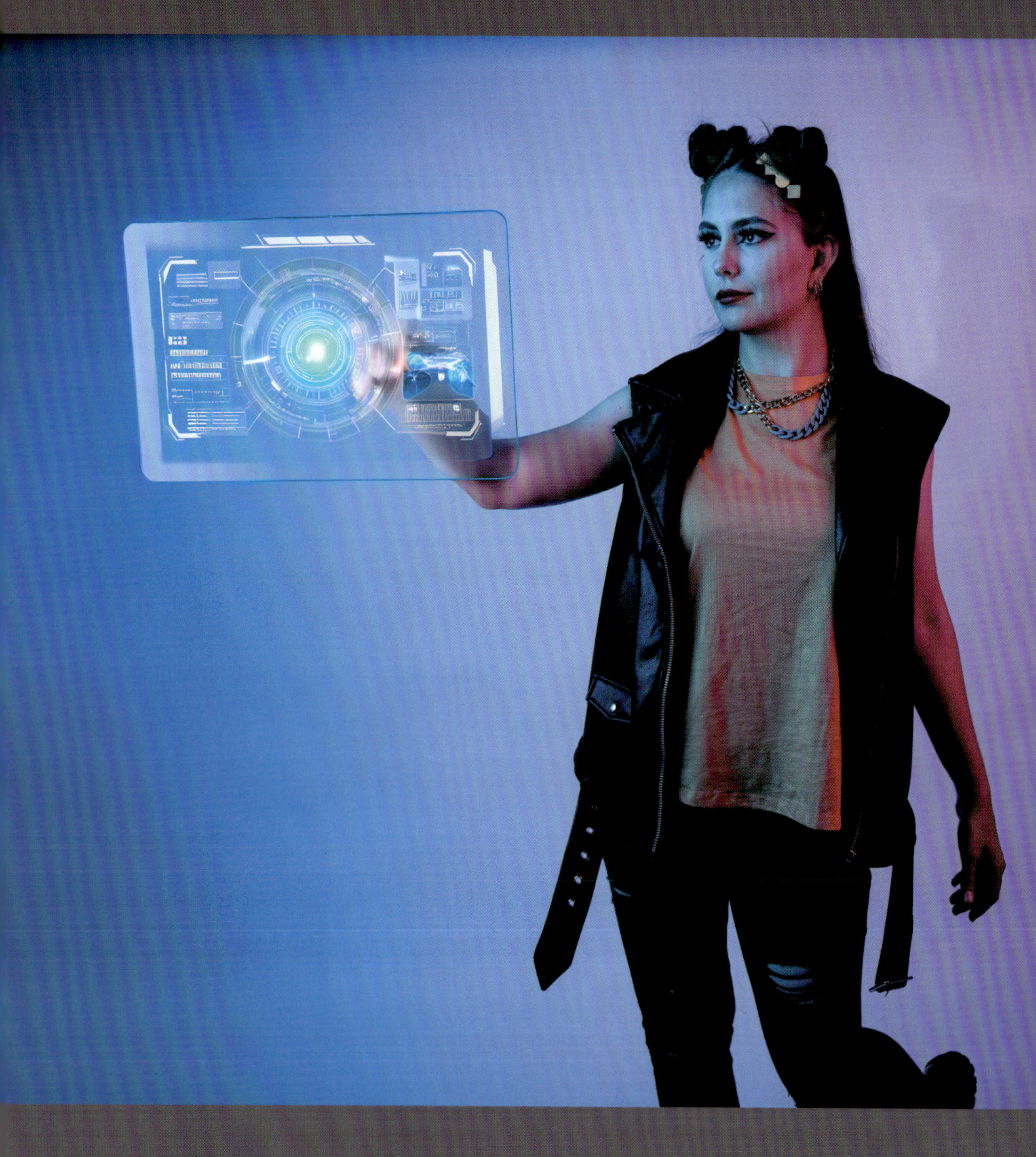

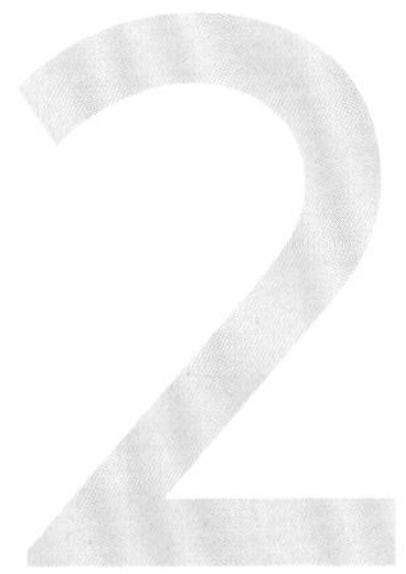

GENERATE

In this chapter, we jump right into the heart of the book with Generative
Fill (Gen Fill, for short), which is powered by Adobe Firefly. Here, we will
be generating realistic objects that interact with existing photographs.
This is similar to what we used to do with stock imagery and, before that,
clip art. Generative Fill will speed up your workflow significantly, as you
no longer need to spend hours searching for the right stock photo that
matches the lighting and angle of your image. It also takes care of the
blending and creates shadows for you.

When we are generating with selections over photographs, the prompts can be simpler than when we are generating from scratch. We will prompt Gen Fill and it will generate an entirely new image that has never existed before.

We still need to describe our desired objects well with the prompts, making the text prompts clear and specific. When we are interacting with existing images, Generative Fill will get a lot of cues visually from the base images. It will attempt to figure out the context of the image, what it is, where it is, and when it is. It will recognize the lighting direction, brightness, and quality of light from the photo. It will know if it should add shadows, a color cast, atmospheric fog, and match the depth of field.

Assume if you see something in the photo, Gen Fill sees it too. You don't need to clutter your text prompts with visual cues that are already present in the image. Let Gen Fill build the image and add additional words to the prompt only if it isn't getting it right.

Basics of Generating Images with Photoshop Generative Fill

Let's start with a simple example so you can understand how everything works. Here is a photo I captured of a rock by the ocean in Hawaii (**FIGURE 2.1**). Wouldn't it be exciting of there was a lizard on top of the rock? Let's add one with Generative Fill.

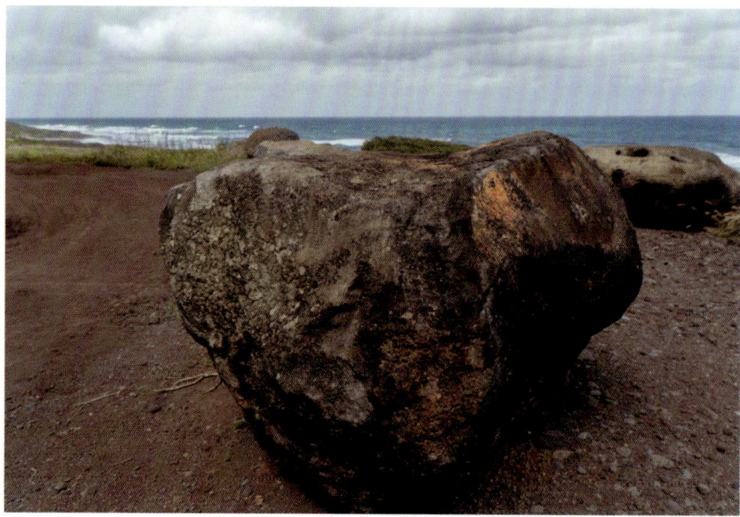

FIGURE 2.1
© Colin Smith

Here's how it's done:

1. You can usc any of the selection tools to make a selection. We will use the Lasso Tool here (**FIGURE 2.2**).

2. Make a selection around the area of the photo where you want the lizard to be generated (**FIGURE 2.3**). When you make the selection, make sure you leave enough room for Generative Fill to wrap the legs and tail around the rock, and also enough space for shadows. You don't need to create a new layer; Gen Fill will create a new layer on its own.

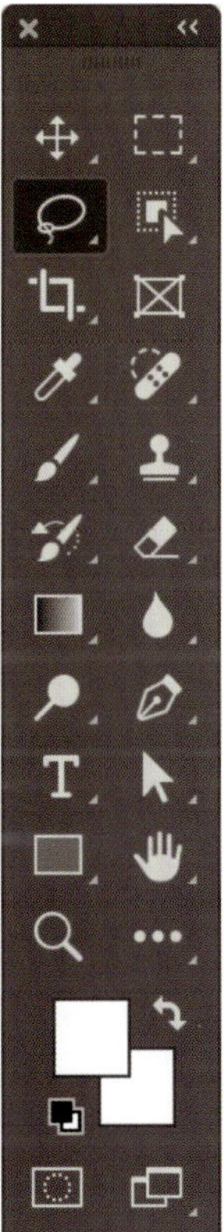

FIGURE 2.2

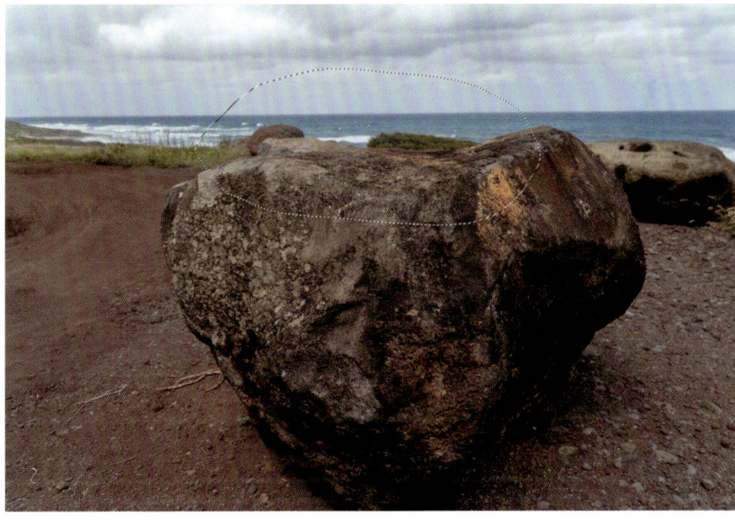

FIGURE 2.3

3. Click on Generative Fill in the Contextual Task Bar (**FIGURE 2.4**). If you don't see it, choose Window > Contextual Task Bar.

> **TIP** If you want to pin the Contextual Task Bar so that is stays in the same place and does not move around, click on the three-dot (meatball) menu and choose Pin Bar Position.

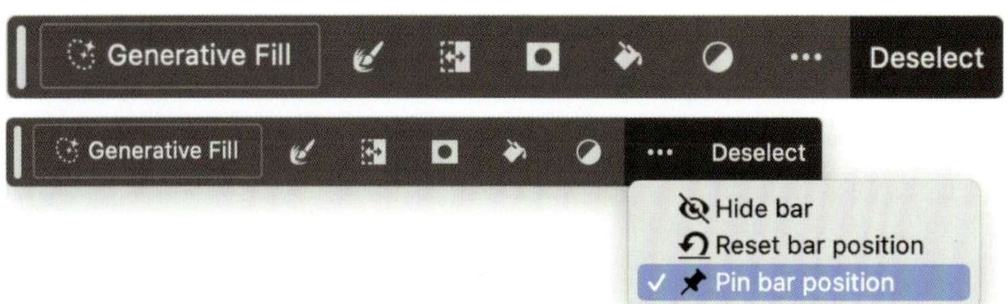

FIGURE 2.4

4. You will now see a box where you can type in your text prompt. Let's keep it simple for this example—just type in "Lizard" and click generate (**FIGURE 2.5**).

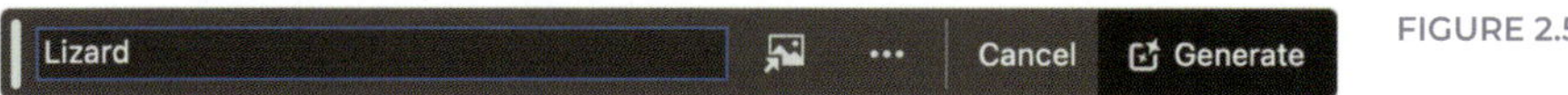

FIGURE 2.5

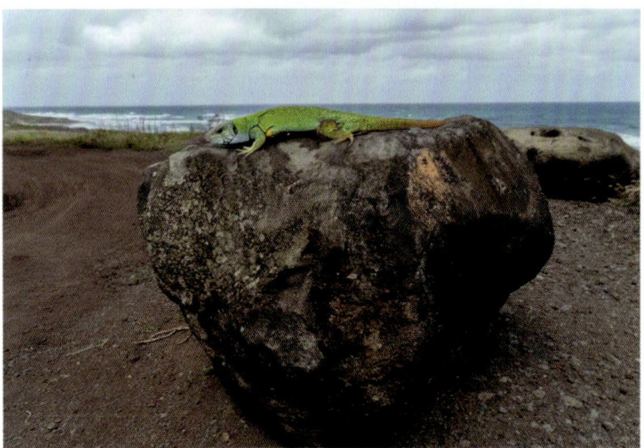

FIGURE 2.6

Photoshop now sends the image and text prompt up into the cloud, utilizing the power of the massive server farm that Adobe uses to run their AI, dubbed *Firefly*, to generate the new pixels. These servers are much more powerful than your computer. You will need an active internet connection to use Generative Fill.

Firefly sends the info back and you will see a lizard sitting on the rock (**FIGURE 2.6**). The lighting should match that of your original image, and shadows are also generated. Gen Fill does its best to estimate scale, but that will largely be governed by the size of your selection.

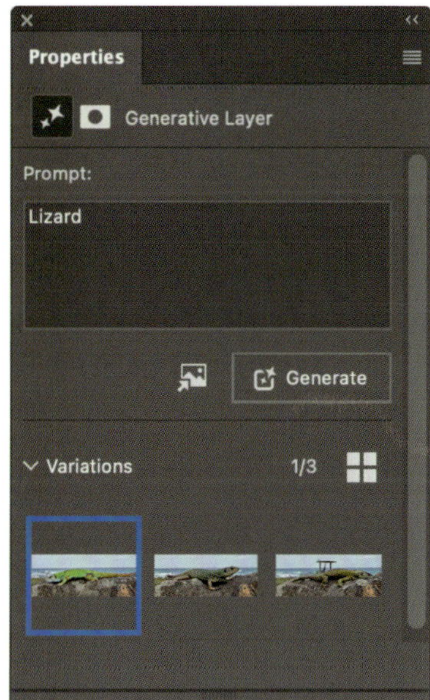

FIGURE 2.7

What if you want a different lizard? No problem. Each time Generative Fill generates, it gives you three different options.

5. Open the Properties panel and you will see a Variations section with image thumbnails. Click a different variation to see what else has been generated (**FIGURE 2.7**).

Alternatively, you can try out different variations directly from the Contextual Task Bar. See "1/3" with arrows on each side (**FIGURE 2.8**)? Click these arrows to cycle through the same variations that are in the Properties panel (**FIGURES 2.9 AND 2.10**).

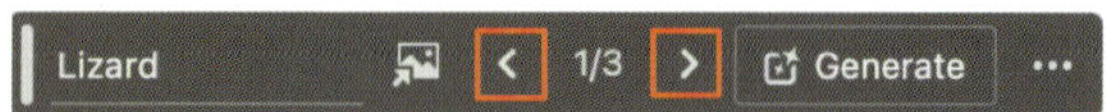

FIGURE 2.8

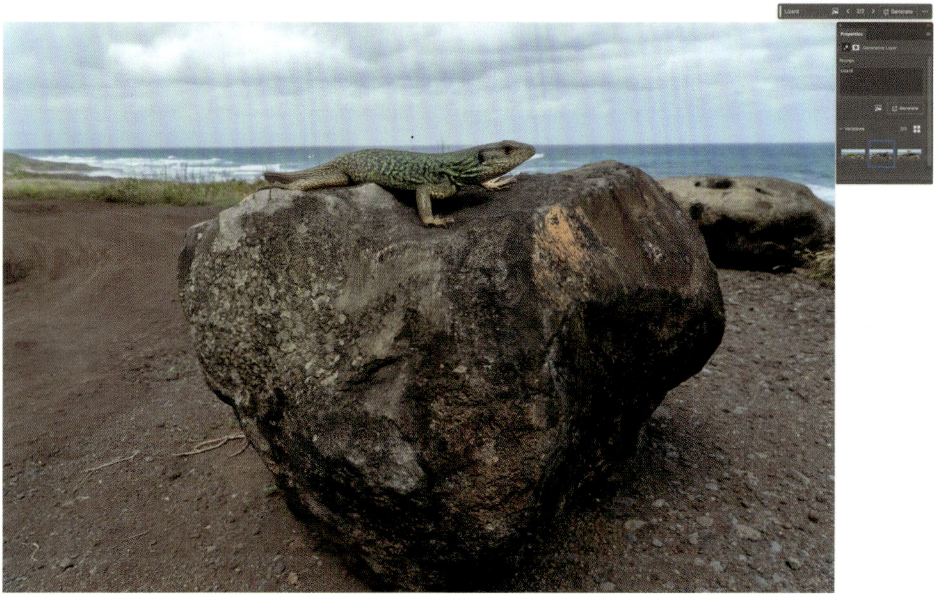

FIGURE 2.9

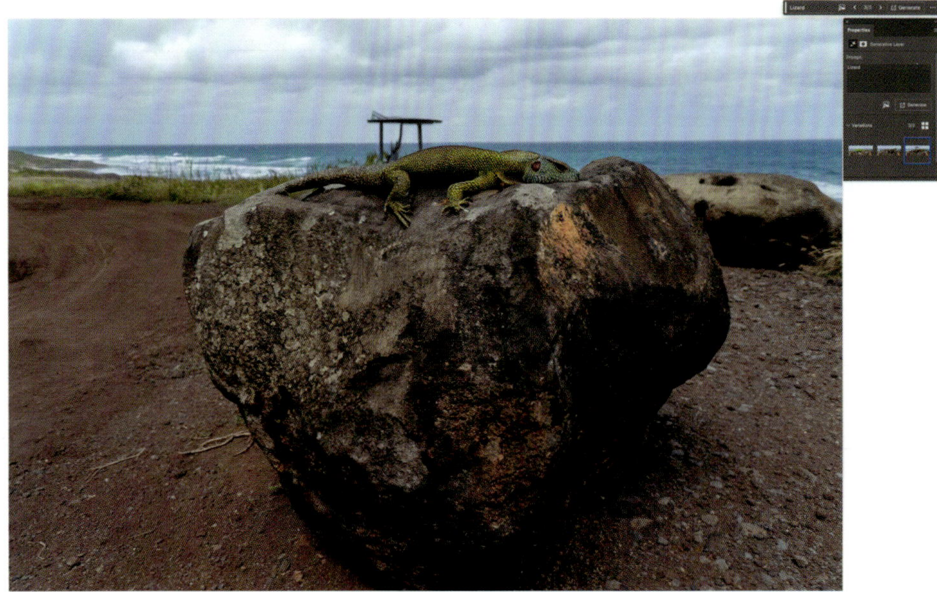

FIGURE 2.10

I think I like the second option best, so we will use that.

Generative Layer

When you use Generative Fill, Photoshop will create a new layer and generate onto that layer. This new Layer is called a *Generative Layer*. You will see a badge that contains two stars in the lower corner of the layer thumbnail to indicate that it's a Generative Layer (**FIGURE 2.11**). The text prompt and image variations will travel with this layer. The variations are part of the layer and will be available even after you reopen the document, duplicate the layer, or copy it to another image.

When you generate a layer, it generates pixels within the area of your selection, ensuring that only the selected area is replaced. Gen Fill cannot generate pixels outside the selection. It will attempt to blend the generated pixels into

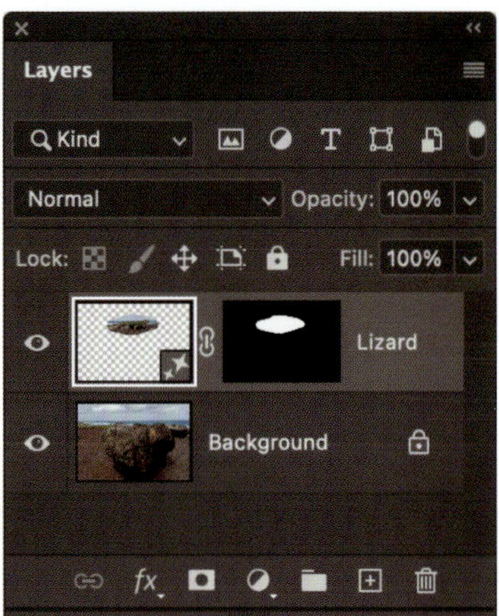

FIGURE 2.11

the surrounding pixels in your image. You will notice that a mask is created to accomplish this (**FIGURE 2.12**). Without the mask, the generated area has hard edges, making blending difficult (**FIGURE 2.13**).

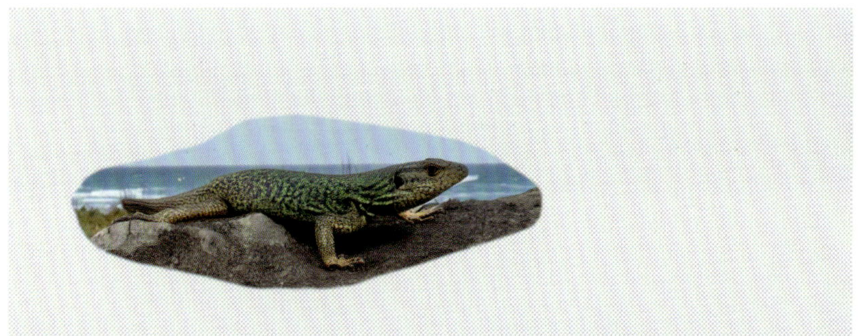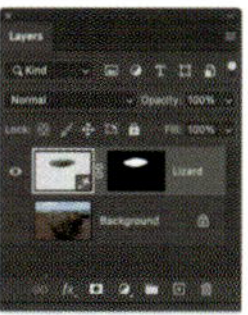

FIGURE 2.12

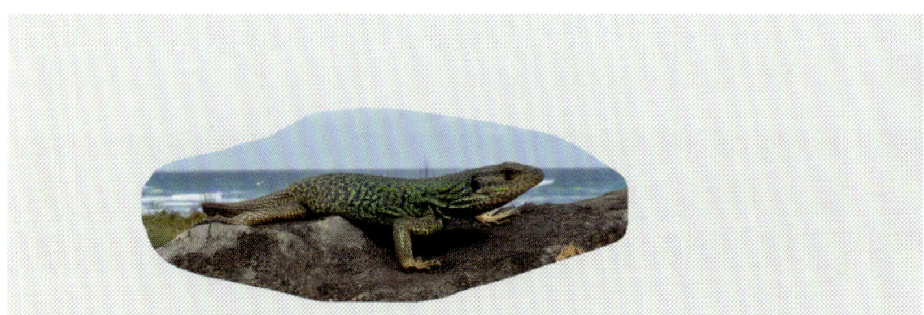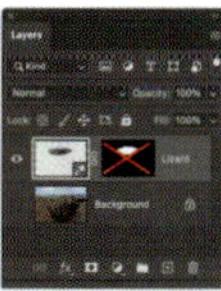

FIGURE 2.13

Gen Fill does not isolate the object, but blends it in like a jigsaw puzzle. This is why as you move the generated layer, it will no longer blend into the surroundings, as shown in **FIGURE 2.14**. We will look at a solution to this issue near the end of this chapter.

FIGURE 2.14

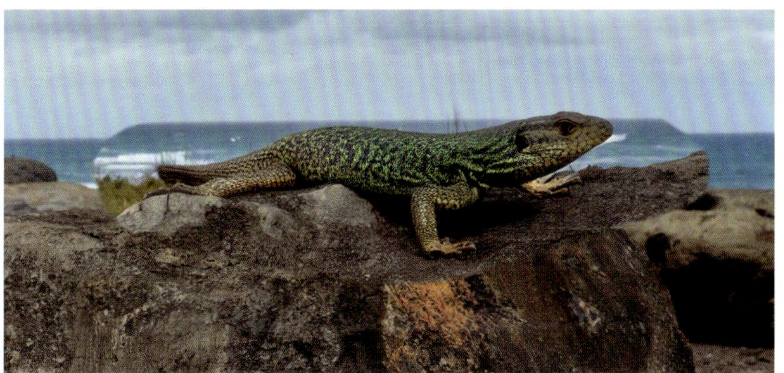

Generating More

What if you aren't satisfied with any of the three variations? You can always generate more.

1. Either go to the Contextual Task Bar and once again click Generate, or head to the Properties panel, where you should see your prompt and image variations. (If you don't see them, make sure you have selected the Generative Layer and the image thumbnail, not the mask.) Click Generate.

Three additional variations will be generated and added to the available variations (**FIGURE 2.15**). I like the one that looks like a bearded dragon (**FIGURE 2.16**).

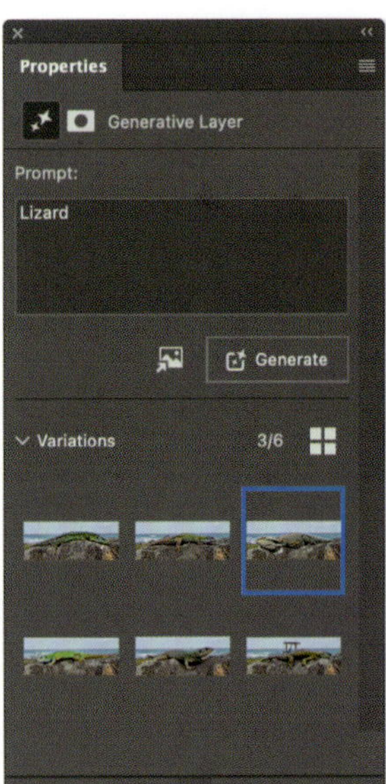

FIGURE 2.15

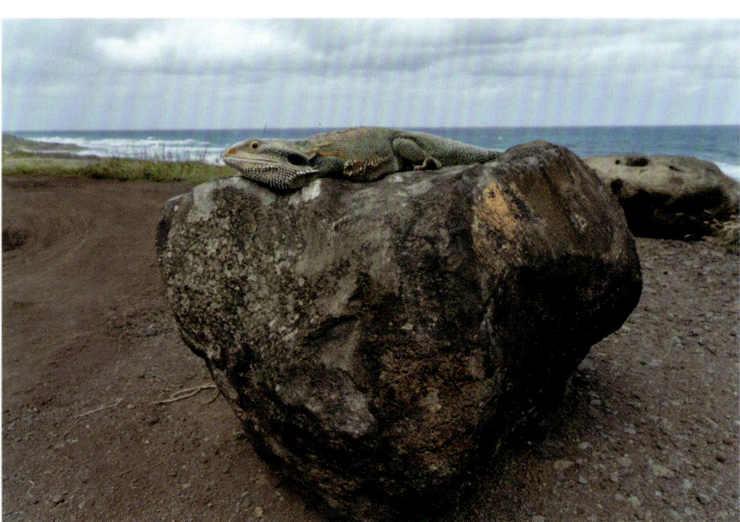

FIGURE 2.16

Generate Similar

Sometimes you will get a variation that is almost but not quite there. In this case, we can generate similar variations. These will be influenced by the selected variation.

1. Choose your preferred variation in the Properties panel and right-click on the thumbnail, or click the three dots that appear at the top right of the variation as you roll over it, then select Generate Similar (**FIGURE 2.17**).

Now we have a very similar lizard (**FIGURE 2.18**). In fact, we will get three more.

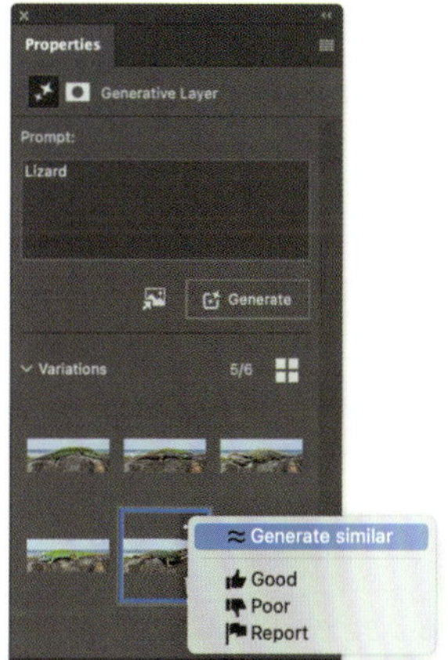

FIGURE 2.17

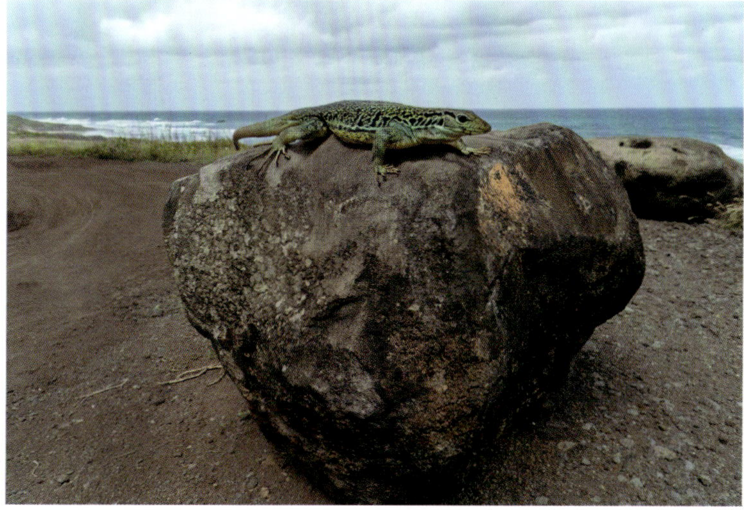

FIGURE 2.18

Managing Variations

All these variations will add to your file size. If you have generated a number of variations and you know there are some that you will never use, you can delete them. This also reduces the chances of confusion if you have a large number of variations.

1. Simply select the variations you don't need in the Properties panel, and then click the trash can icon in the lower-right corner of the thumbnail (**FIGURE 2.19**).

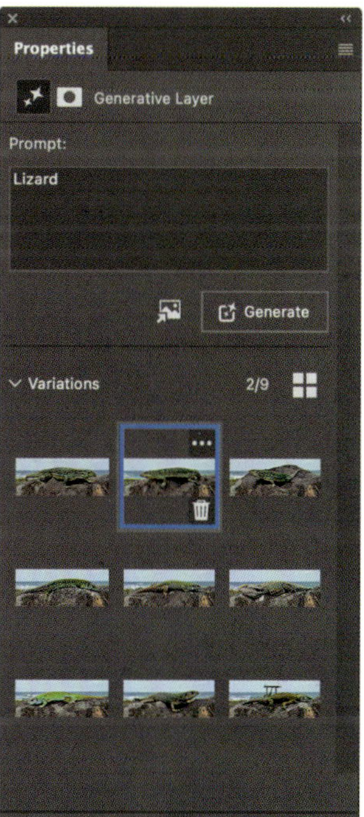

FIGURE 2.19

Mind the Shape of Your Selection

The shape of your selection greatly influences what is generated—maybe more than anything else, in some cases. If you want to generate an animal, the shape can influence the direction the animal is facing and if it's standing or lying down.

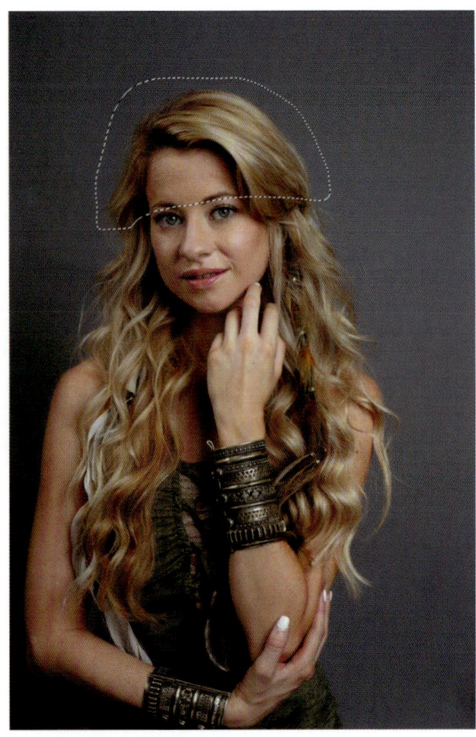

FIGURE 2.20 © Colin Smith

To demonstrate the power of selection shape, let's make different selections on this woman's head and use a single word in the prompt: "hat." Based on the selection shape, we can predict (and influence) what kind of hat is generated.

1. Using the Lasso Tool, make a selection that allows room for the hat to extend beyond the top of the head (**FIGURE 2.20**). Bring it down low enough to sit in a natural way.

2. Click Generate in the Contextual Task Bar.

3. Enter "hat" as the prompt (**FIGURE 2.21**).

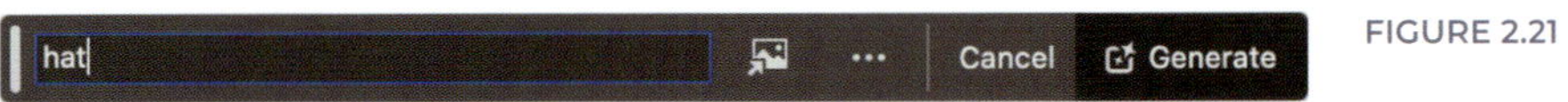

FIGURE 2.21

4. Click Generate again.

This gives us something like a baseball cap (**FIGURE 2.22**). We could type in "baseball cap" if we specifically want that, but that would defeat the purpose of this lesson, where we are using only the shape of the selection to determine what type of hat we get.

Notice that new eyebrows have been generated because we selected over the original ones. Anything that is included in the selection is game to be changed.

Okay, what if we want something like a top hat or a party hat?

5. Make a larger selection in the shape of a tall hat (**FIGURE 2.23**).

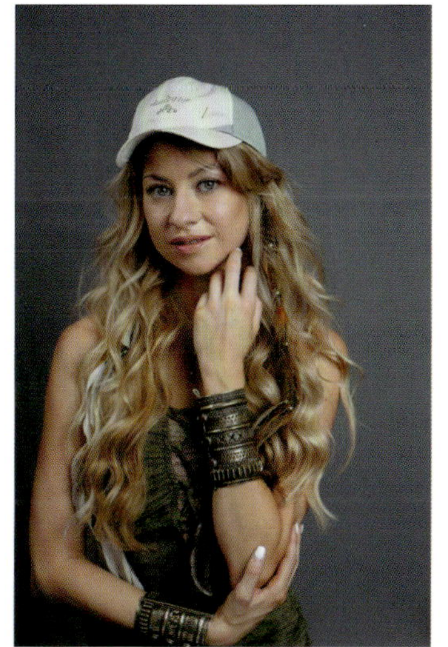

FIGURE 2.22

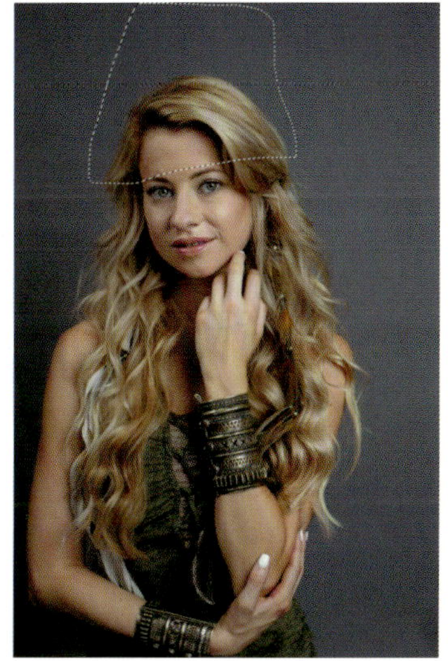

FIGURE 2.23

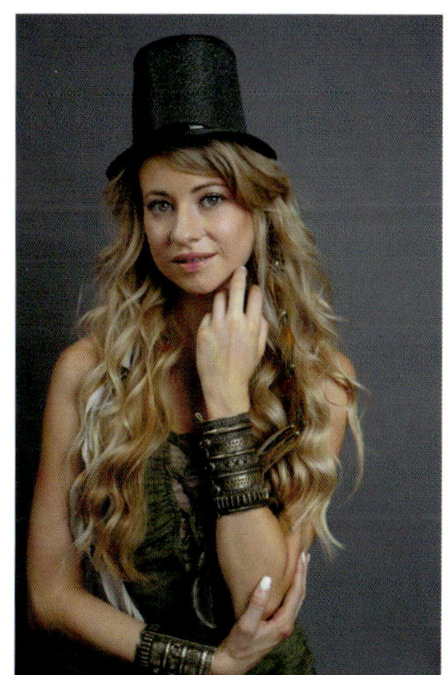

FIGURE 2.24

As predicted by the shape of the selection, we now have a tall party hat
(**FIGURE 2.24**). Notice we didn't get new eyebrows this time because we didn't select
over them.

Selection Warning

Let's look at what not to do for a second. We'll go for a beanie, but keep the selection very close to the top of the head (**FIGURE 2.25**). See how it makes a hat, but it's
sitting too low and makes the woman's head seem out of proportion (**FIGURE 2.26**)?
We also didn't get a beanie.

Let's make a new selection and give it a bit more space (**FIGURE 2.27**). Now we get a
better fitting hat (**FIGURE 2.28**).

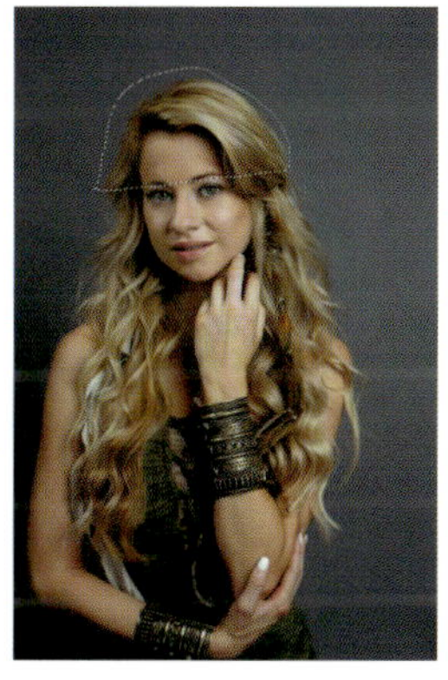

FIGURE 2.25

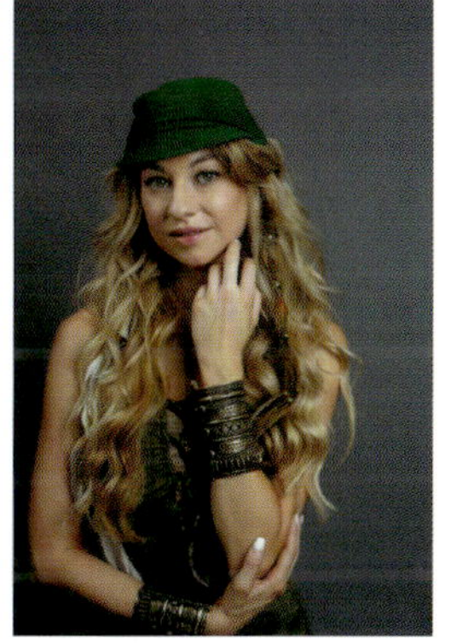

FIGURE 2.26

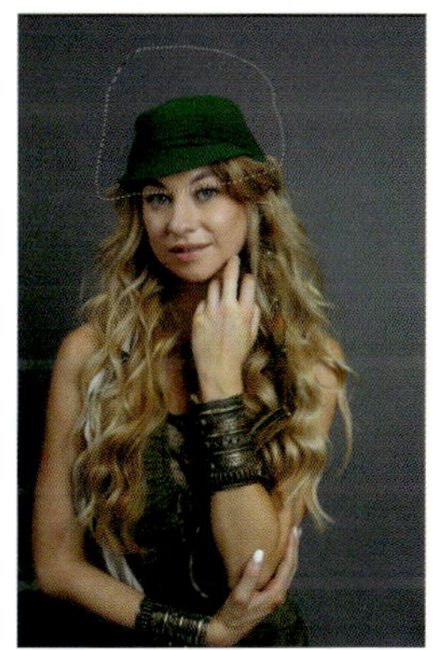

FIGURE 2.27

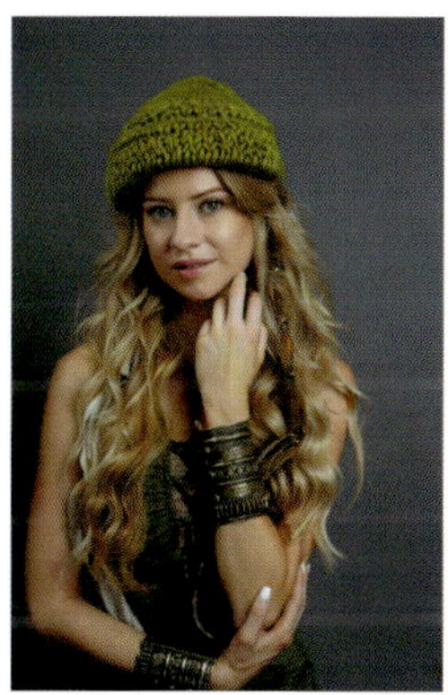

FIGURE 2.28

Fixing Details

Notice that, once again, we got new eyebrows because we selected over the originals. Because Generative Fill is applied on a mask, we can paint into the mask to reveal the original eyebrows.

1. Choose the Brush Tool and a soft-edged brush.

2. Set the foreground color to black.

3. Click on the black mask on the hat layer to select (**FIGURE 2.29**).

4. Carefully paint over the generated eyebrows on the image to reveal the original eyebrows from the layer underneath.

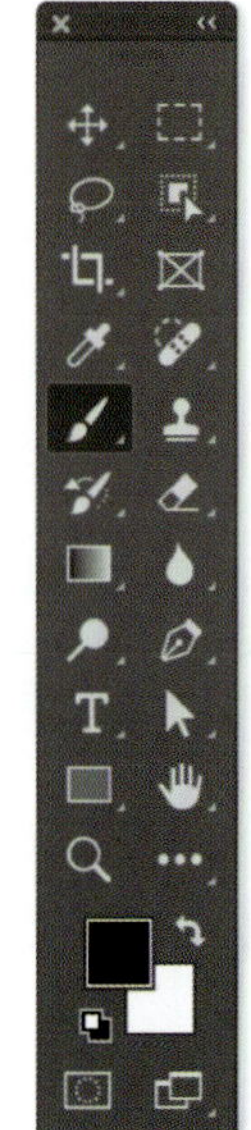
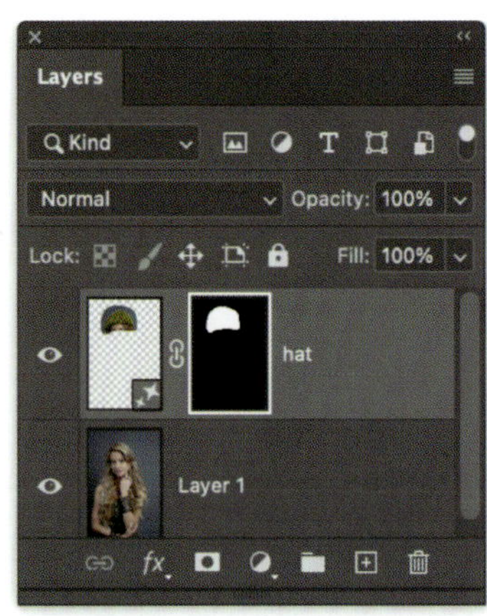

FIGURE 2.29

Even with Generative AI, we can still use it in a subtle way and utilize our existing Photoshop skills to craft the perfect image (**FIGURE 2.30**).

In the real world, we might specify a color, type, and material of the hat to get something closer to our desires. But this illustrates the power of changing only the selection shape.

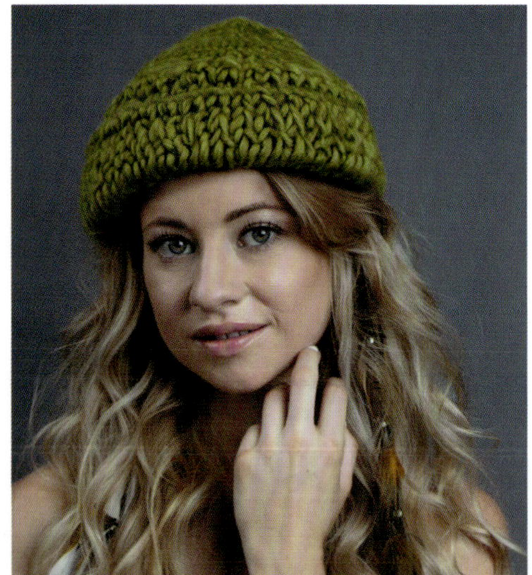

FIGURE 2.30

Using a Reference Image to Generate

If you really want to generate something specific, use a reference image to guide Generative Fill.

Here, our model Lina will get a hat. But we want it to match the style of clothing she is wearing (**FIGURE 2.31**).

I think something like this beige hat will work nicely (**FIGURE 2.32**). Ideally, you would already have a photo of the object you want to use—maybe take a snapshot with your phone.

Wait? You don't have a good reference image to use? I'll let you in on a secret. The woman in the hat isn't real. I generated her in Photoshop using Generate Image (covered in chapter 1). Yes, you can generate your own reference images—why not?

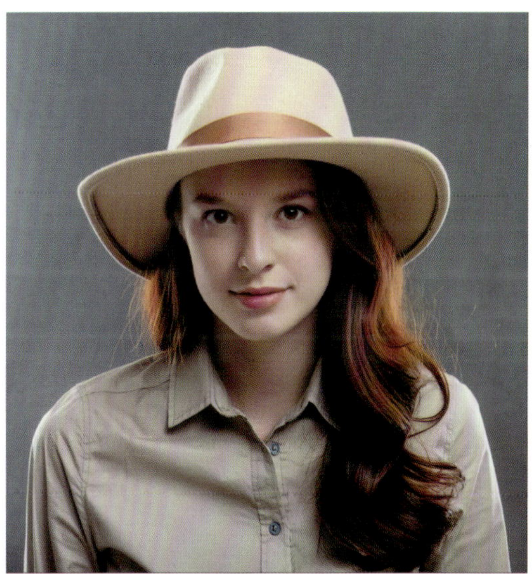

FIGURE 2.32

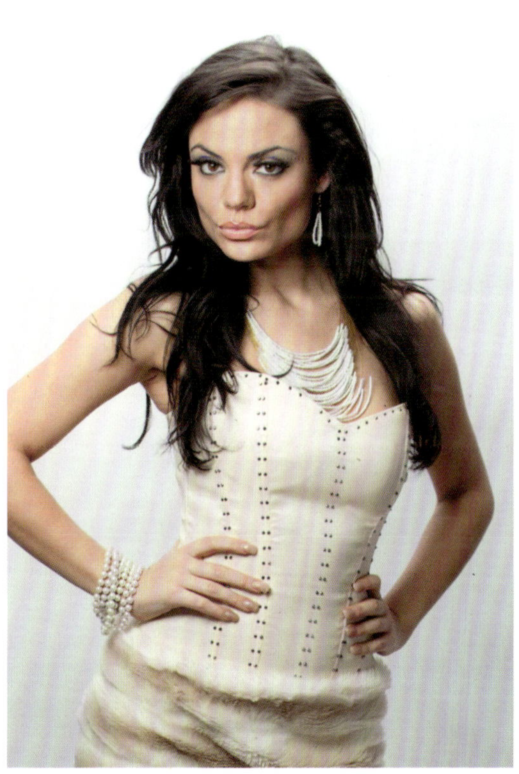

FIGURE 2.31 © Colin Smith

This is the prompt I used to generate the image (**FIGURE 2.33**):

"beige fedora hat, isolated background"

I just got the person wearing it as a free bonus.

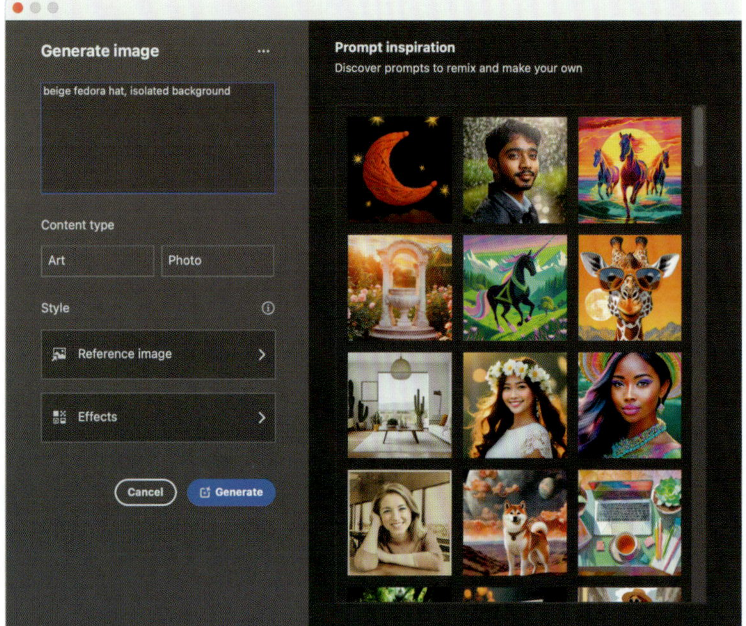

FIGURE 2.33

You can generate a whole bunch of hats quickly and choose the one you like. Here, I added three hats in a row to the prompt in Generate Image (**FIGURE 2.34**).

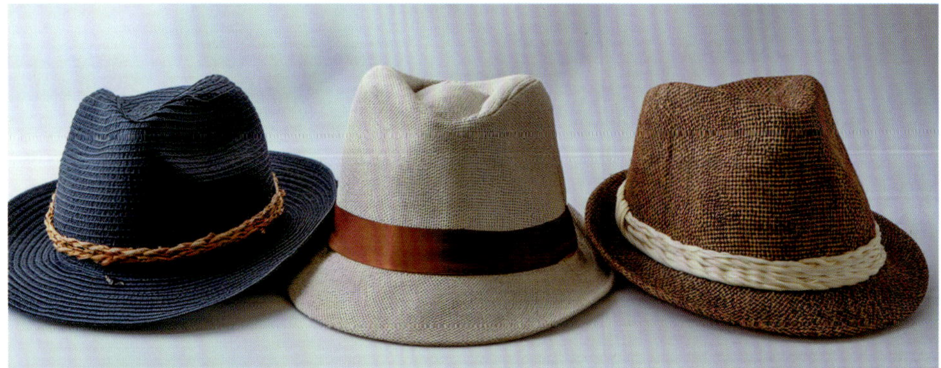

FIGURE 2.34

To get the best result, you want to isolate your reference image on a plain background. To do this, you can use Remove Background in the Reference Image menu, which we will look at in a moment. For now, lets do it manually. To isolate the hat:

1. Choose the Quick Selection Tool from the Tools panel.

2. Select the hat. Use Alt/Option (Windows/Mac) to subtract from the selection if you select too much.

3. Press Ctrl/Command + J (Windows/Mac) to copy the selection to a new layer.

4. In the Layers panel, click the eyeball next to the background to hide it. You should see just the hat and the checkerboard pattern (**FIGURE 2.35**).

5. Choose File > Save to Web, select jpg, and save the image.

   You don't have to do a great job of isolating the object, just enough to guide Generative Fill to copy the style (**FIGURE 2.36**). It's not actually using the reference image per se.

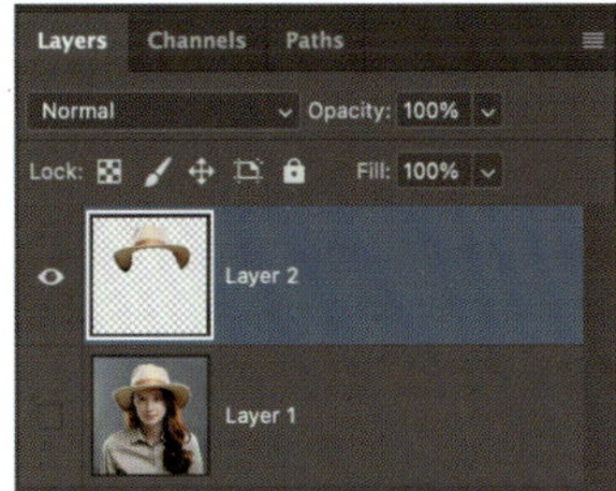

FIGURE 2.35

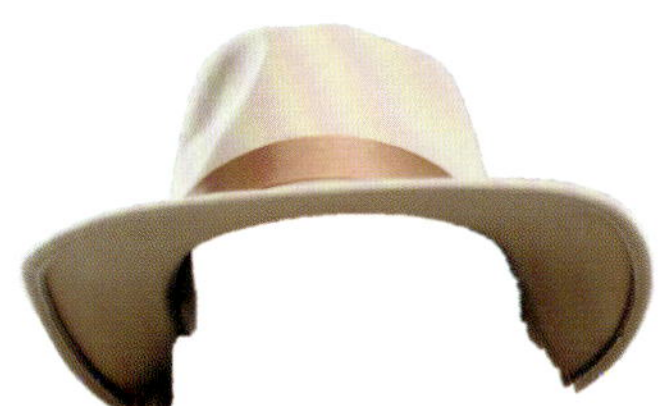

FIGURE 2.36

Generating a Hat with a Reference Image

Now let's put this hat on our model's head.

1. Make the selection around the subject's head. Make sure you leave room for the hat to sit on the head as well as protrude above the head (**FIGURE 2.37**).

2. Choose Generative Fill from the Contextual Task Bar.

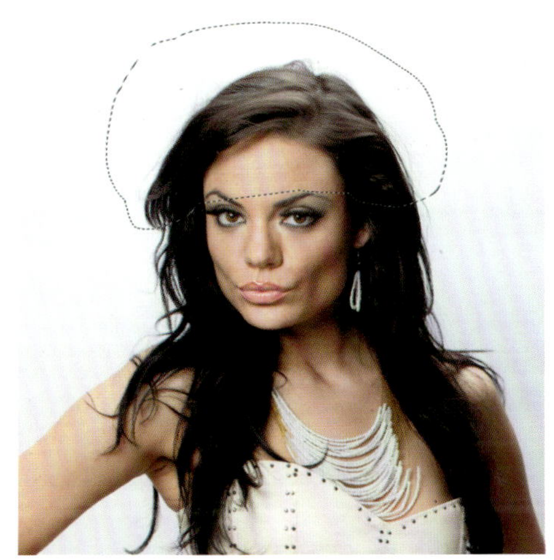

FIGURE 2.37

3. In the Contextual Task Bar, type in "hat."

4. Let's load the reference image. Click the image icon next to the "hat" prompt you just typed in.

5. Click the Choose Image button (**FIGURE 2.38**).

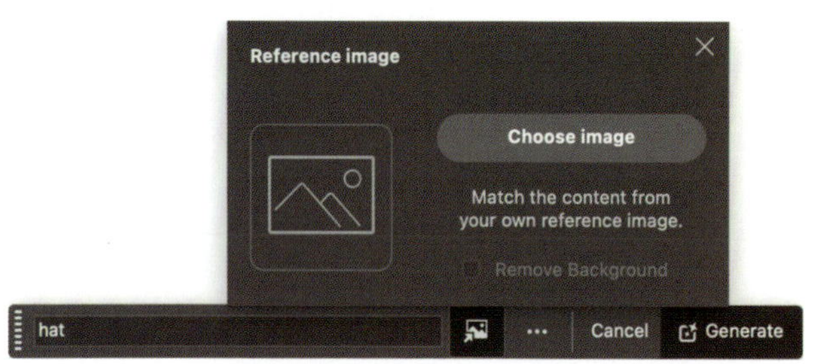

FIGURE 2.38

6. Navigate to your reference image and select it.

7. **Optional:** You can choose the image with the background and click the Remove Background button to automatically remove the background, as shown in **FIGURE 2.39**. This will work, but not as well as the isolated hat in **FIGURE 2.40** because the Remove Background function also kept the woman and didn't isolate the hat. But it's worth remembering that the auto-remove option is available.

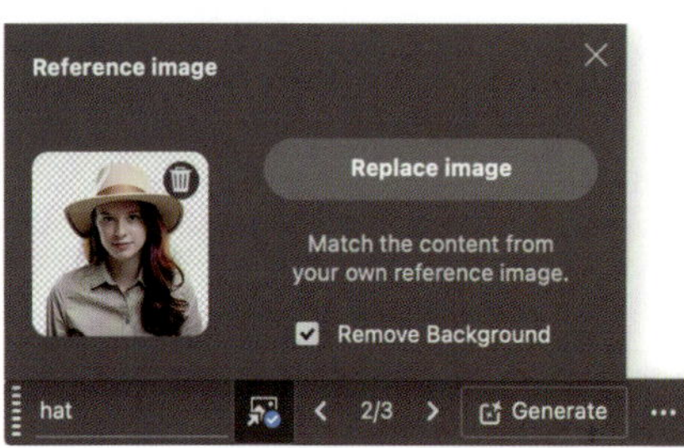

FIGURE 2.39

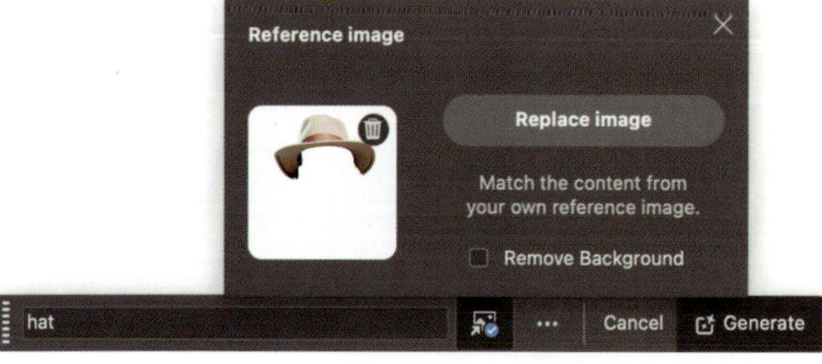

FIGURE 2.40

You will now see a blue check mark on the image icon in the Contextual Task Bar to tell you Generative Fill is using a reference image (**FIGURE 2.41**). The reference image will take priority over anything else. A picture is worth a thousand words? Maybe a few less are needed, but a picture is still better.

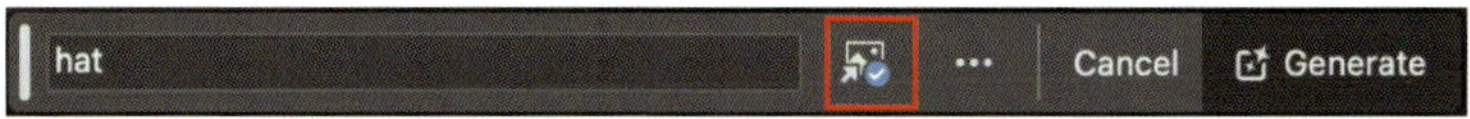

FIGURE 2.41

8. Click Generate.

And now you get the perfect hat you are looking for (**FIGURE 2.42**).

FIGURE 2.42

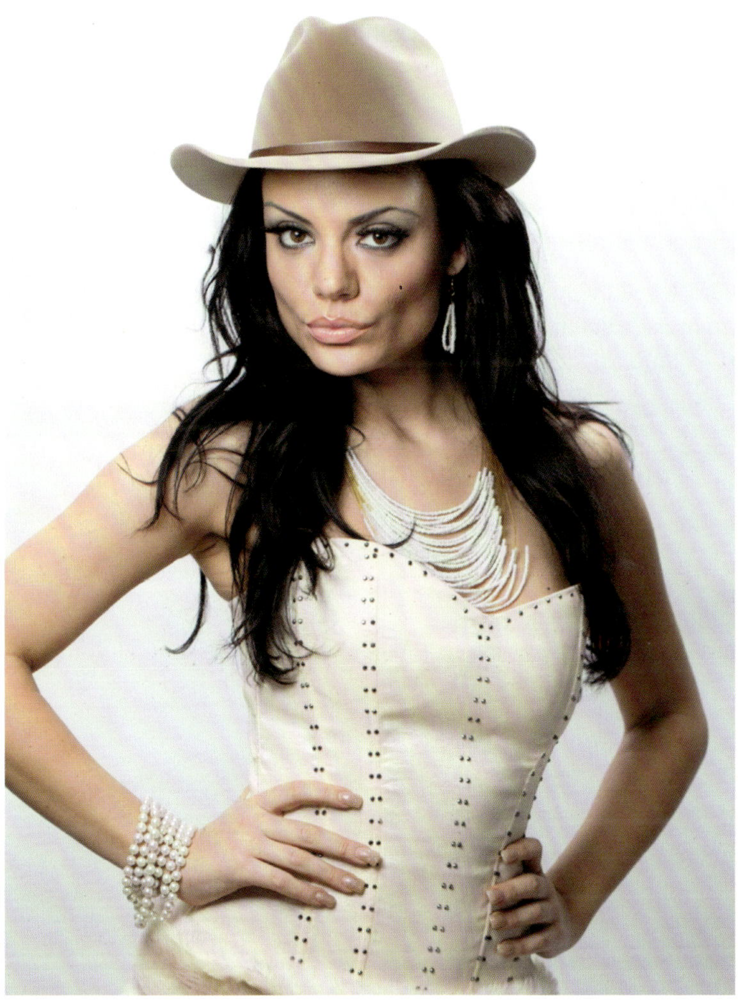

Generating Incrementally

It's funny how we often have an all-or-nothing mentality. We try do to do everything in a single sitting. In the case of Generative Fill, we try to generate our result with a single selection and a mega-prompt. It's like trying to eat a giant-sized piece of sushi in a single mouthful.

Sometimes, it's better to approach a task piecemeal, perfecting the foundation before building on top of it. Let's take this studio photograph I shot of our model Meghan (**FIGURE 2.43**). I'm going for a futuristic/cyberpunk feel with blue and pink gels over the lights. I want her to be interacting with a screen.

Of course, the floating glass screen I imagine doesn't exist yet. I'm hoping to get the right style of glass screen as well as some kind of interface for her to interact with.

I already used Generative Fill to expand the canvas to our left to make a square image. (We'll cover how to expand an image in chapter 3.)

The smart approach is to get the screen right first, and then we will add the content on the screen.

1. Choose the Rectangular Marquee Tool.

2. Drag on your image to make a selection in the position and size we want for our screen.

3. Choose Generative Fill from the Contextual Task Bar.

4. I typed "floating semi transparent glass touch screen" into the prompt (**FIGURE 2.44**).

5. Click Generate.

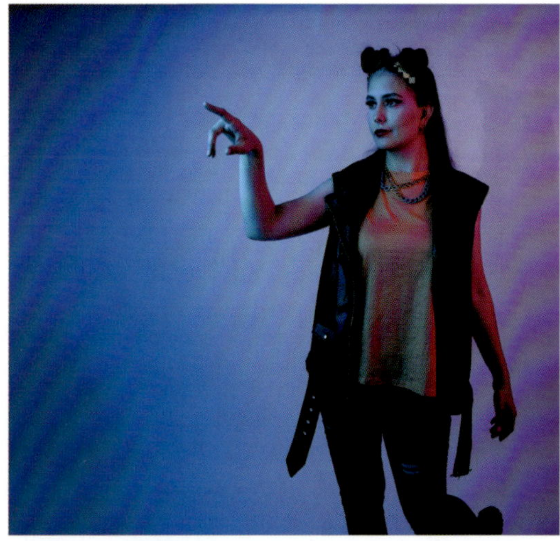

FIGURE 2.43 © Colin Smith

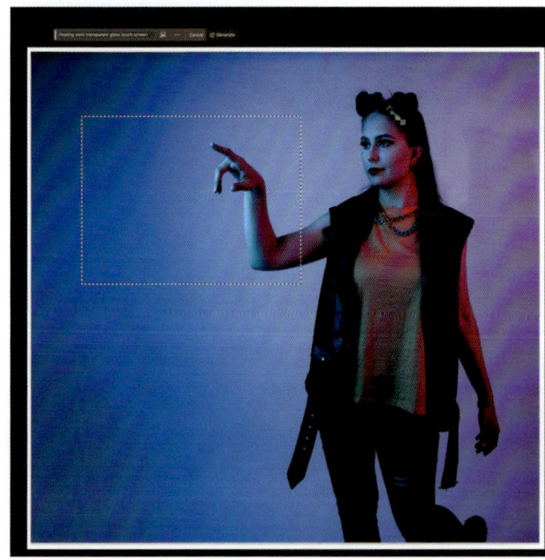

FIGURE 2.44

You may have to modify your prompt by adding or removing words to get the result you are looking for. After several attempts and variations, I got the screen you see in **FIGURE 2.45**.

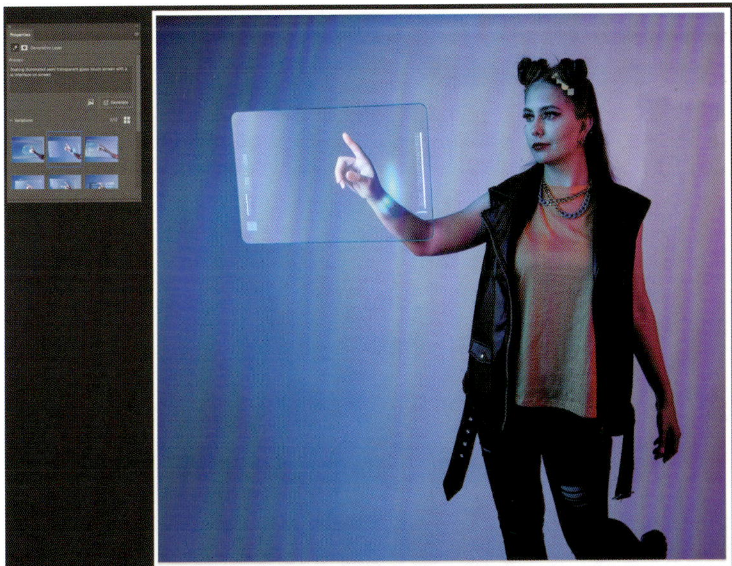

FIGURE 2.45

This screen is exactly what I want. Don't worry about the hand because it will be replaced. Now it's time to add some content to it.

1. With the Polygonal Lasso Tool, make a selection around the inside of the screen (**FIGURE 2.46**).

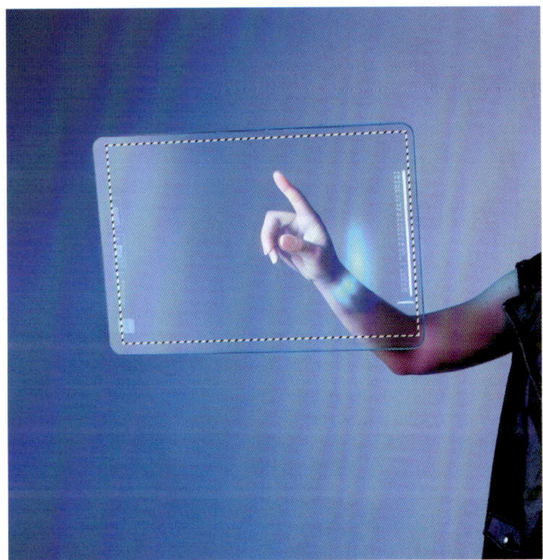

FIGURE 2.46

2.   Choose Generative Fill from the Contextual Task Bar.

3.   Add the prompt "Futuristic, interactive, user interface, sci fi style" (**FIGURE 2.47**).

4.   Click Generate.

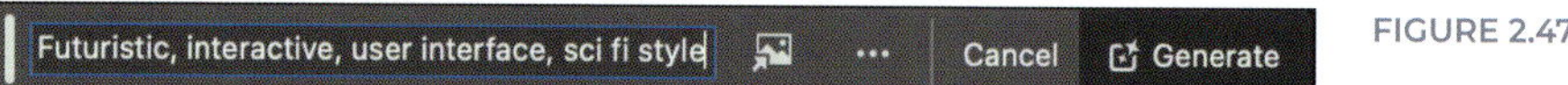

FIGURE 2.47

Now we get the content for the screen (**FIGURE 2.48**). This is exactly what we needed to complete this image.

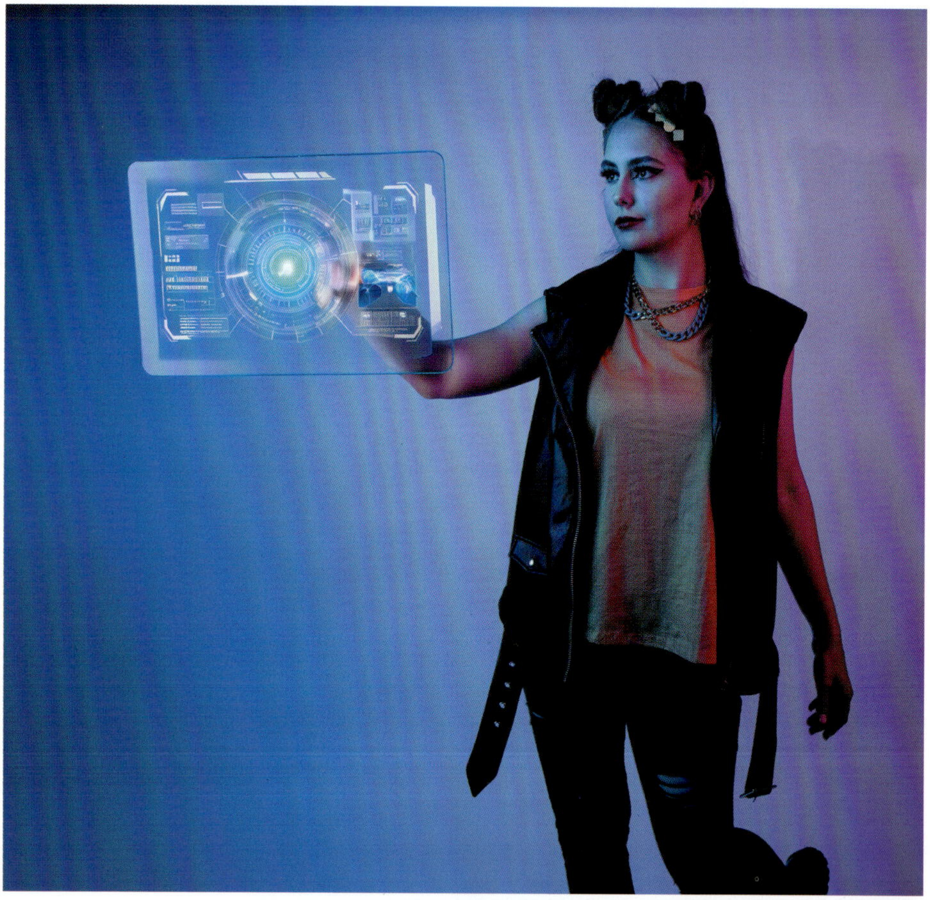

FIGURE 2.48

Generating Reflections

Generative Fill is capable of generating all kinds of things, including reflections.
Let's explore this now. We'll start with this photo of an Aston Martin DBS on dry
ground (**FIGURE 2.49**).

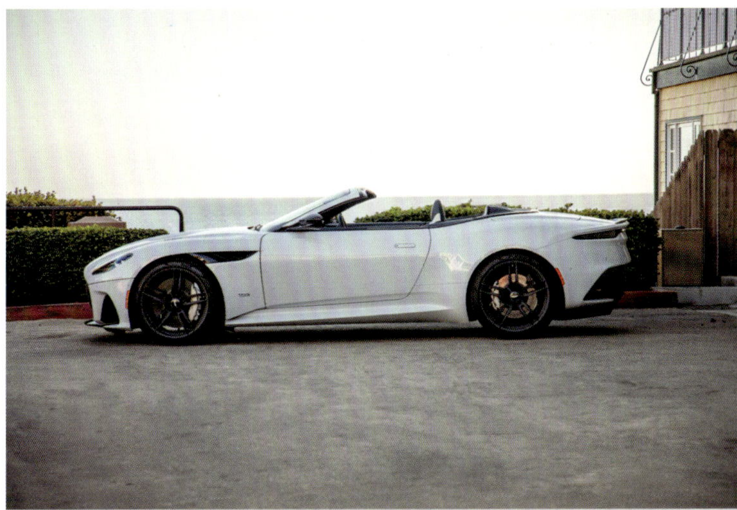

FIGURE 2.49
© Colin Smith

1. Using the Lasso Tool, make a selection where you want to add a puddle
    (**FIGURE 2.50**).

2. Click Generative Fill in the Contextual Task Bar.

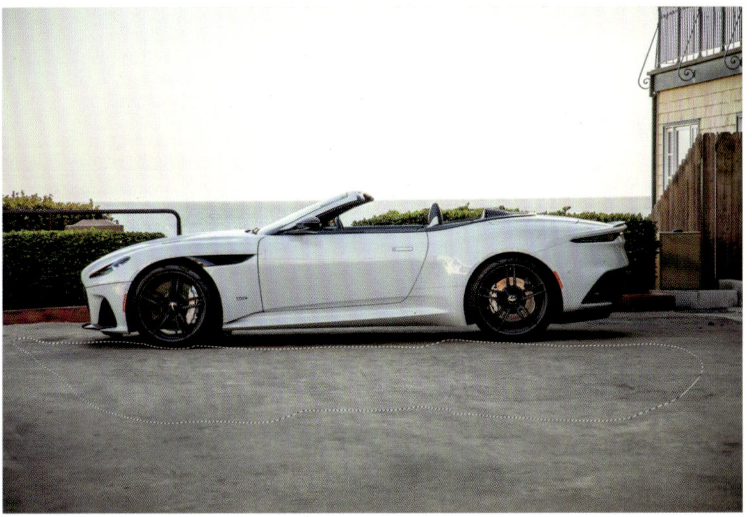

FIGURE 2.50

3. Type "reflective puddle of water" into the text prompt (**FIGURE 2.51**).

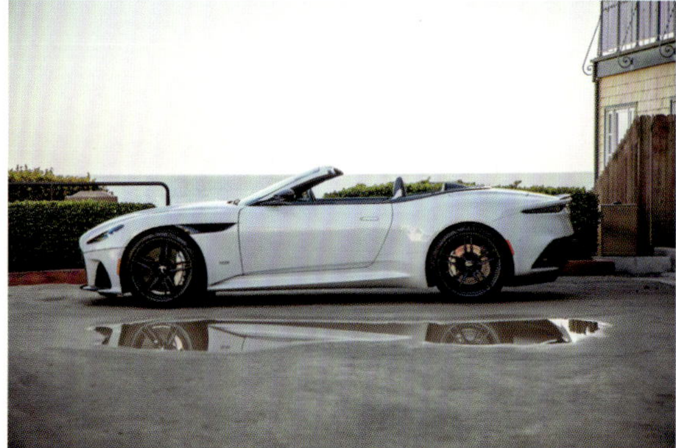

FIGURE 2.51

4. Click generate.

And now we have a puddle with realistic looking reflections (**FIGURE 2.52**).

5. Let's modify the prompt a bit. You can modify prompts in the Contextual Task Bar or in the Properties panel. Add the word "highly" to the beginning of the prompt, so that it now reads "highly reflective puddle of water."

6. Click Generate.

Notice this really increases the reflection (**FIGURE 2.53**).

FIGURE 2.52

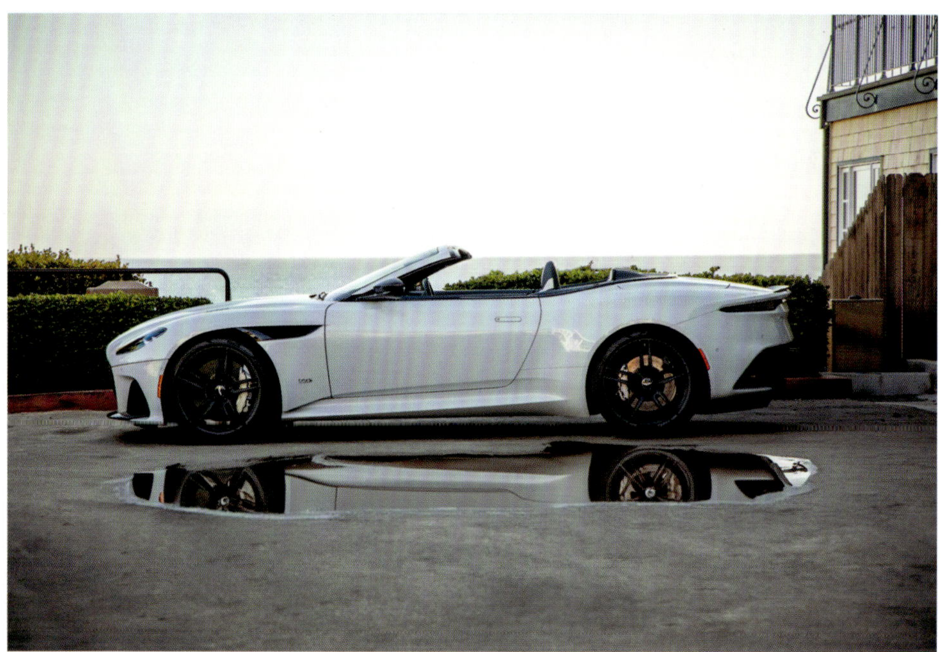

FIGURE 2.53

Add Reflections to Glass

Let's add a reflection into some glass. This can add a nice touch of realism when you are making composites.

The glass on this car already has some reflection (**FIGURE 2.54**), but we will add more.

1. Choose the Quick Selection Tool (**FIGURE 2.55**).

2. Make a selection around the windshield of the car (**FIGURE 2.56**).

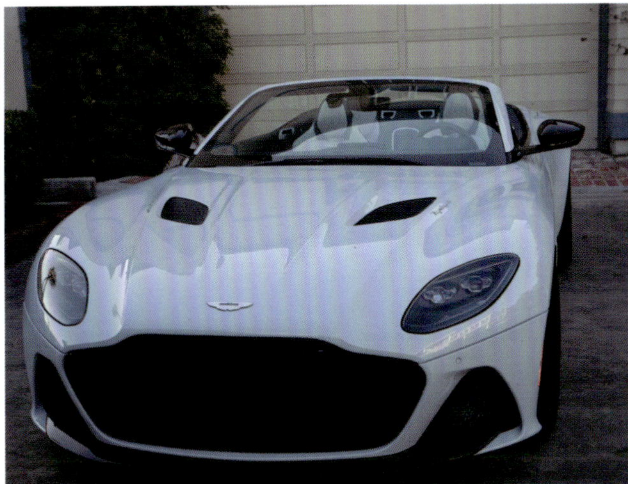

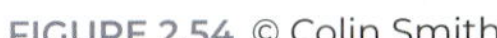

FIGURE 2.55

FIGURE 2.54 © Colin Smith

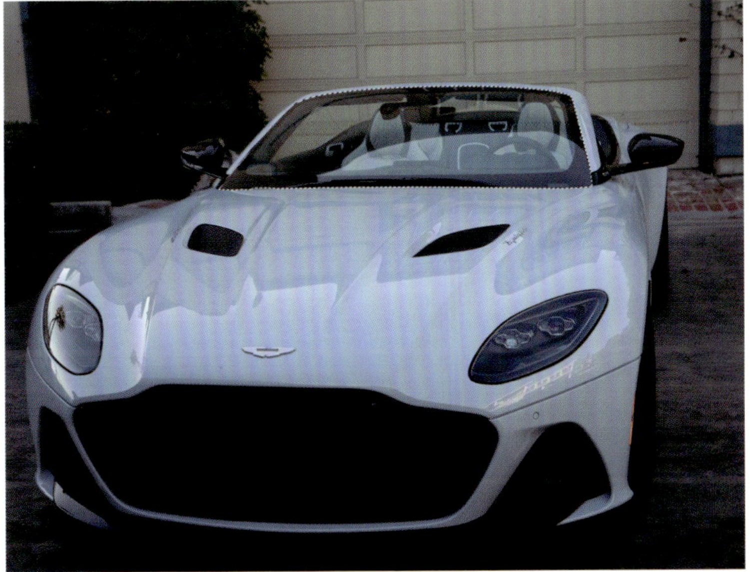

FIGURE 2.56

3. Choose Generative Fill from the Contextual Task Bar and enter "reflection of city street" into the text prompt (**FIGURE 2.57**).

4. Click Generate.

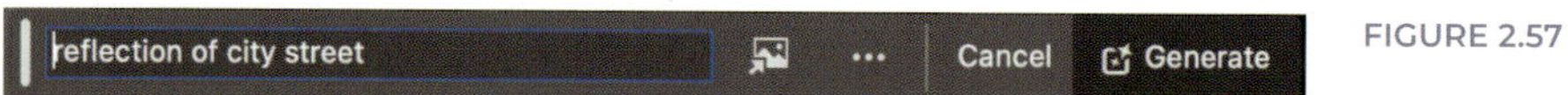

FIGURE 2.57

Now we have a reflection, but it's way too strong (**FIGURE 2.58**).

5. In the Layers panel, make sure the Generative Layer is selected, and change the blending mode to Lighten (**FIGURE 2.59**). This will hide black and allow only the brighter pixels to show—much more realistic. Also lower the Opacity to suit your needs. I used 38% here.

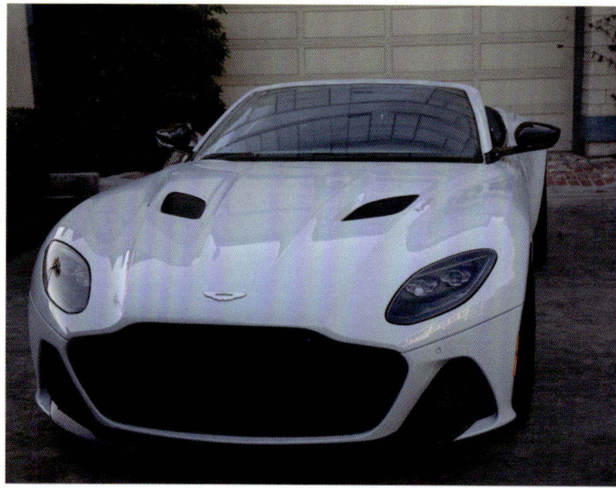

FIGURE 2.58

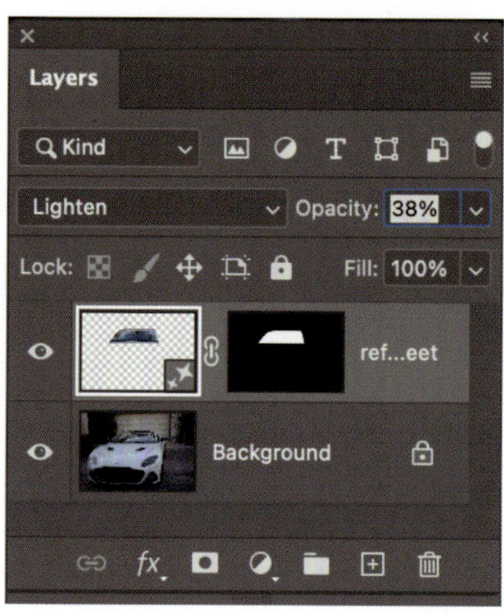

FIGURE 2.59

Now we have added reflections to the glass (**FIGURE 2.60**).

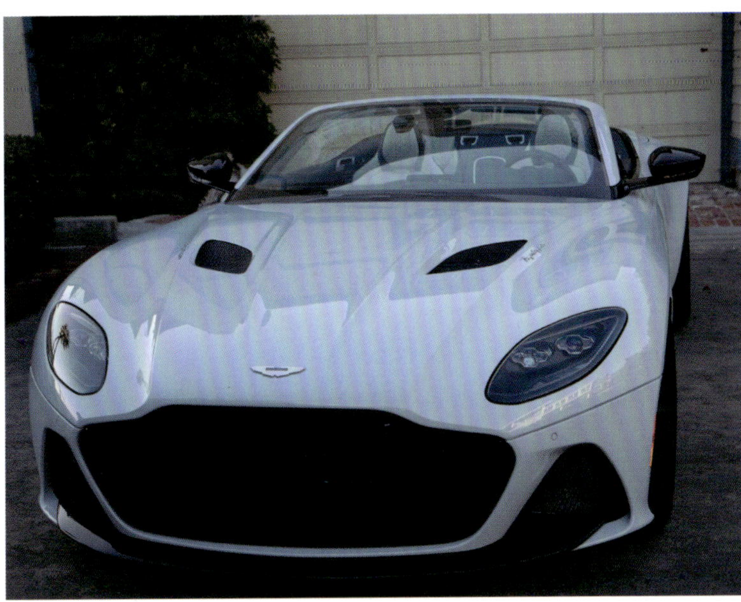

Generating Density

When we are generating, we can change the density of the generated image. Density is not quite the same as transparency. A Generative Layer is always produced at 100% opacity. If we were to reduce the transparency of the layer, objects under the subject would appear. Rocks under fish or the stars shining through the moon would be visible, making the fish or moon appear see-through. Instead, when something is generated with a lower density, it makes it look like the object is solid but obscured—underwater, in the mist, etc.

Changing Density

We'll start with some surfers at Waikiki Beach, Hawaii. Let's add a shark to the water.

1. Using the Lasso Tool, make a selection on the image where you want the shark to appear (**FIGURE 2.61**).

2. Click on Generative Fill.

3. Enter "shark" into the prompt, then choose Generate.

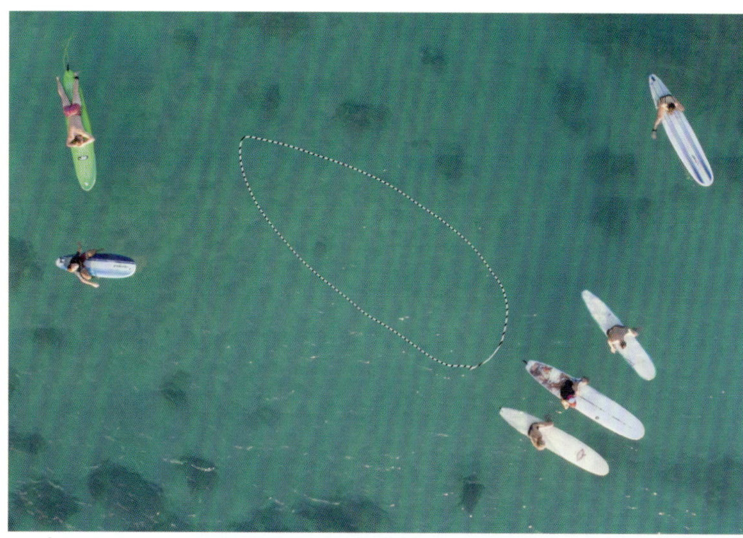

FIGURE 2.61
© Colin Smith

Chances are the shark that appears in your image will look like it's on top of the water and not really *in* the water (**FIGURE 2.62**).

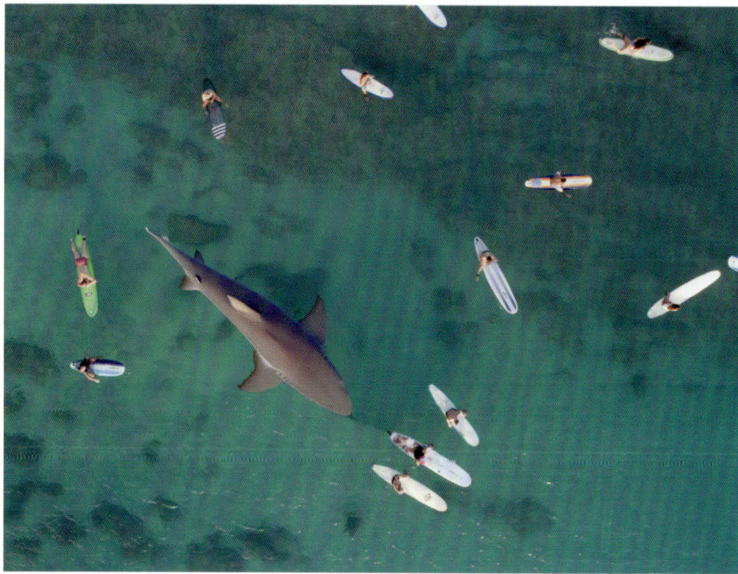

FIGURE 2.62

However, we can use density to make the shark look like it's under the surface of the water.

To make this happen, we will start over with the original image and use the Selection Brush Tool.

The Selection Brush Tool, the newest addition to the selection tools in Photoshop, is ideal for making selections for Generative AI. The Opacity slider enables us to create a selection that isn't fully opaque. We will walk through it step-by-step—let's get the settings right first.

Setting Selection Brush Tool Options

1. Choose the Selection Brush Tool from the Tools panel (**FIGURE 2.63**).

2. Go to the Options Bar at the top of the interface, open the drop-down menu where it says the size of the brush, and set the Hardness to zero (**FIGURE 2.64**).

3. Click OK.

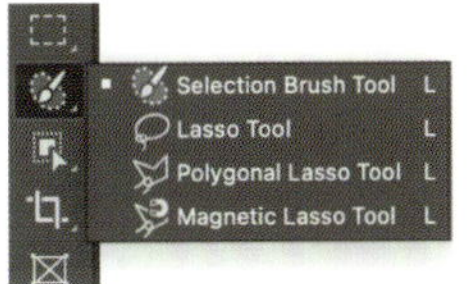

FIGURE 2.63

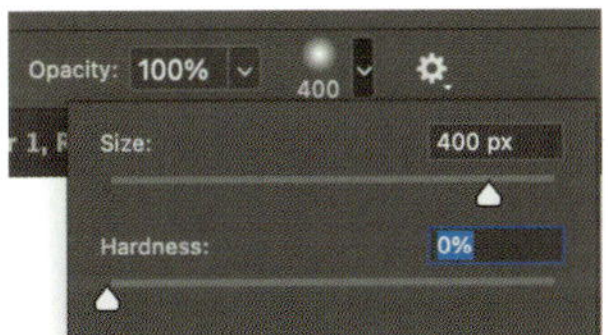

FIGURE 2.64

Let's Generate with a Lower Density Selection

1. In the Options Bar, change the Selection Brush Opacity to 20% (**FIGURE 2.65**).

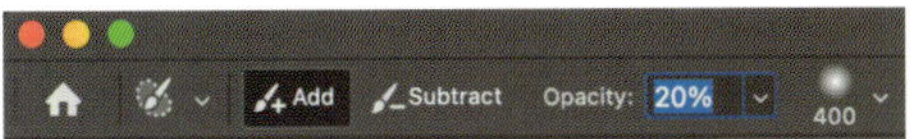

FIGURE 2.65

2. Paint over the entire area where you want the shark to appear (**FIGURE 2.66**). You will see a light reddish color where you paint. This is the rubylith mask color.

3. Click on Generative Fill in the Contextual Task Bar.

4. Type "Large shark swimming" into the text prompt in the Task Bar, then click Generate.

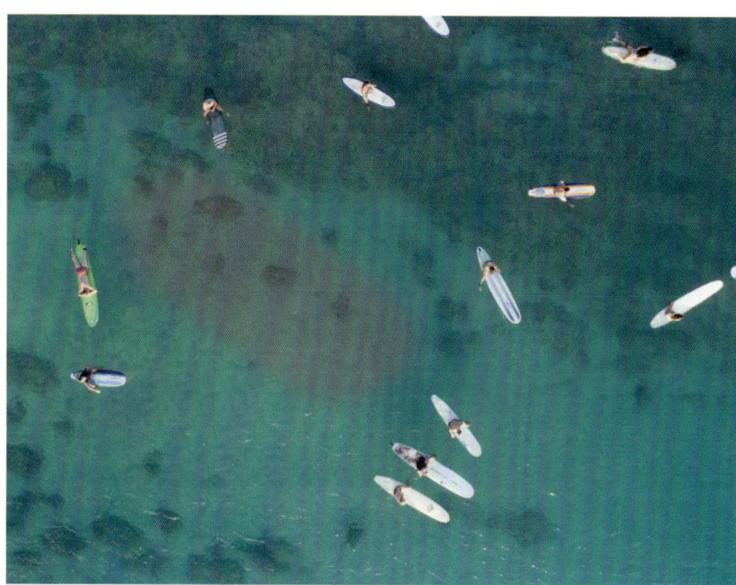

FIGURE 2.66

Now your shark will be created with less density and appear underwater (**FIGURE 2.67**). Again, density isn't the same as transparency. If we adjusted transparency, you would see the rocks under the shark. Instead, it looks like the shark is submerged in the water.

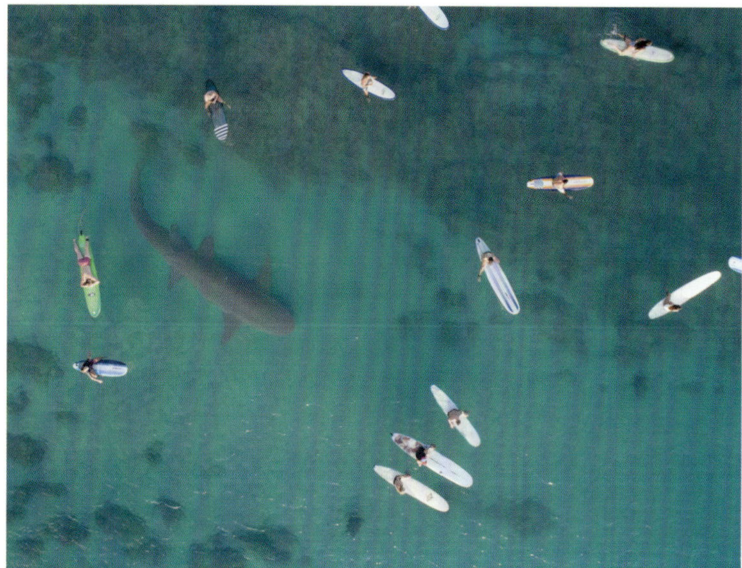

FIGURE 2.67

Just to demonstrate how density works, let's do the opposite.

1. Choose the Selection Brush Tool from the Tools panel.

2. In the Options Bar, change the Opacity to 80% (**FIGURE 2.68**).

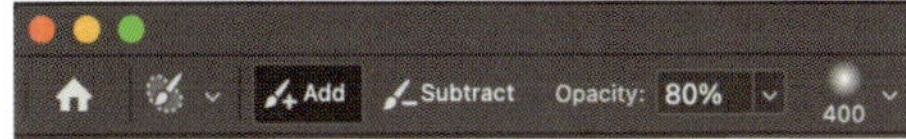

FIGURE 2.68

3. Paint with the brush where you want to generate the shark—notice it's a darker red this time (**FIGURE 2.69**).

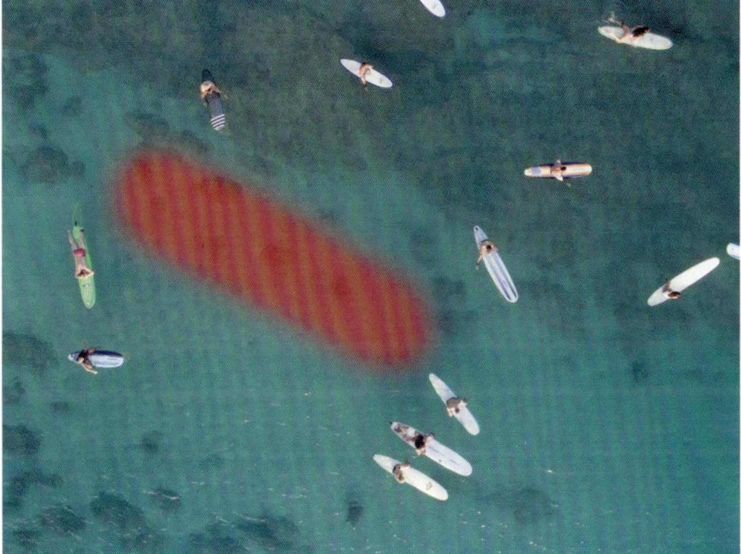

FIGURE 2.69

4. Generate the shark as before and use the same prompt: "Large shark swimming."

Notice this time the shark is denser than before (**FIGURE 2.70**). Changing the Opacity of the Selection Brush Tool varies the density of the generated image and is useful for water, fog, and other situations.

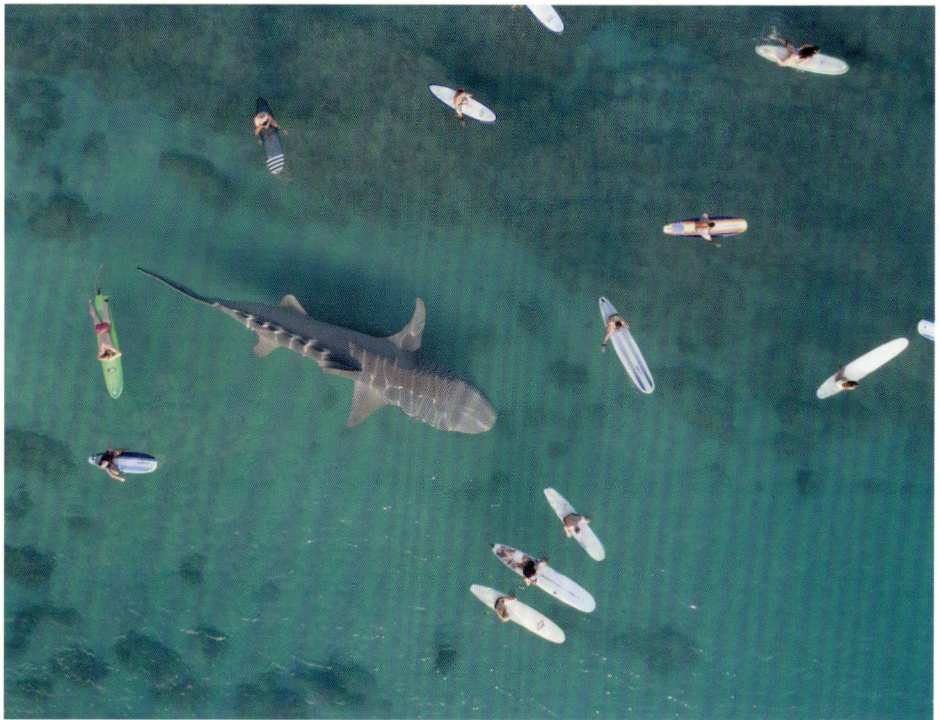

FIGURE 2.70

Generate Similar

When you don't see a variation that you want to use, you can always choose Generate once again to produce three more variations. These can vary wildly in appearance. Sometimes, it's almost what you want, but not quite. In that case, we can use Generate Similar.

Let's go back to the shark we generated in **FIGURE 2.67**.

1. Look at the Properties panel and see which variation is selected (**FIGURE 2.71**).

2. Roll over the thumbnail of the selected variation and click on the three-dot menu in the top-right corner to open an options menu (**FIGURE 2.72**).

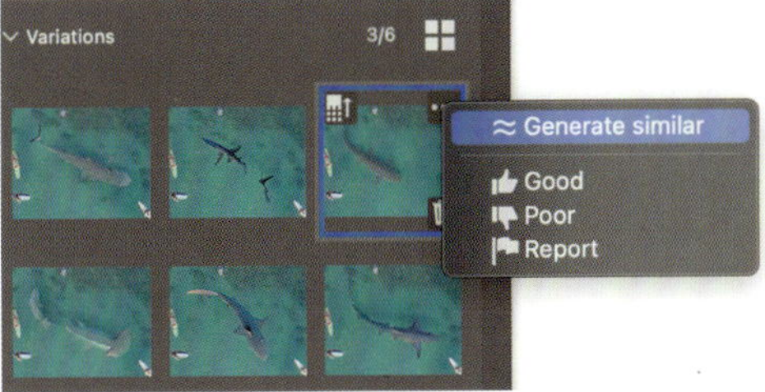

FIGURE 2.72

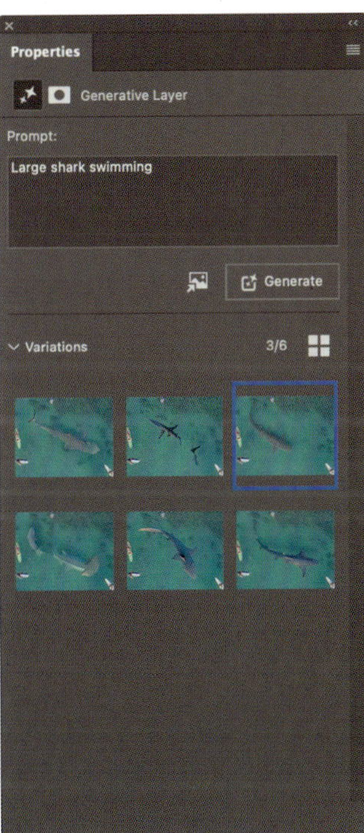

FIGURE 2.71

3. Select Generate Similar from the menu, and three more variations will be generated (**FIGURE 2.73**).

The generated results will look similar to the original variation. This is basically the same shark, but it's swimming differently (**FIGURE 2.74**).

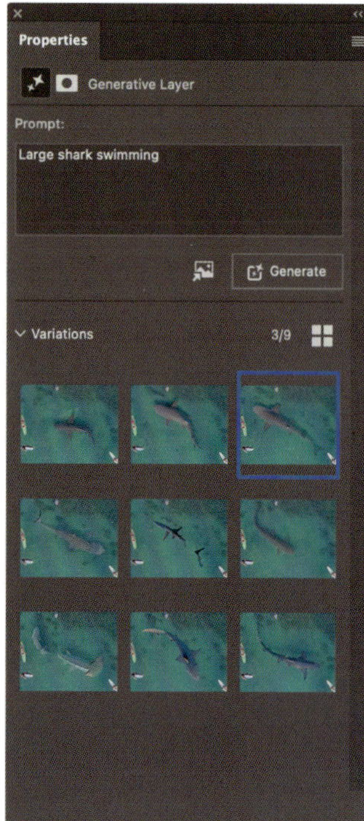

FIGURE 2.73

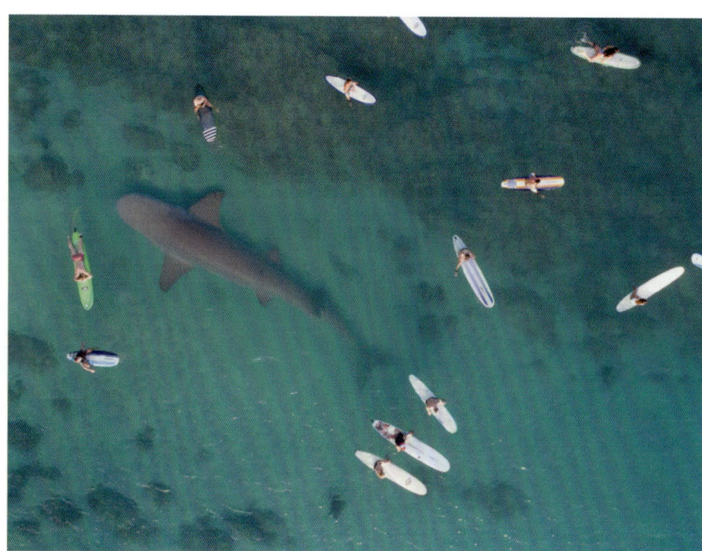

FIGURE 2.74

Moving a Generated Object

Sometimes you need to move a generated image. Maybe you really like the image and don't want to generate it again and end up with a different object. You can easily move and scale things using the tools in Photoshop. Here is what I call the donut selection trick.

Let's generate a car. We'll start with this photo of a city street (**FIGURE 2.75**).

1. Make a selection and choose Generative Fill from the Contextual Task Bar.

2. Enter a prompt to generate a car. I used "black sedan frontal view."

3. Click Generate.

Okay, we've have made a car, but why does it look so small (**FIGURE 2.76**)? The perspective isn't quite right.

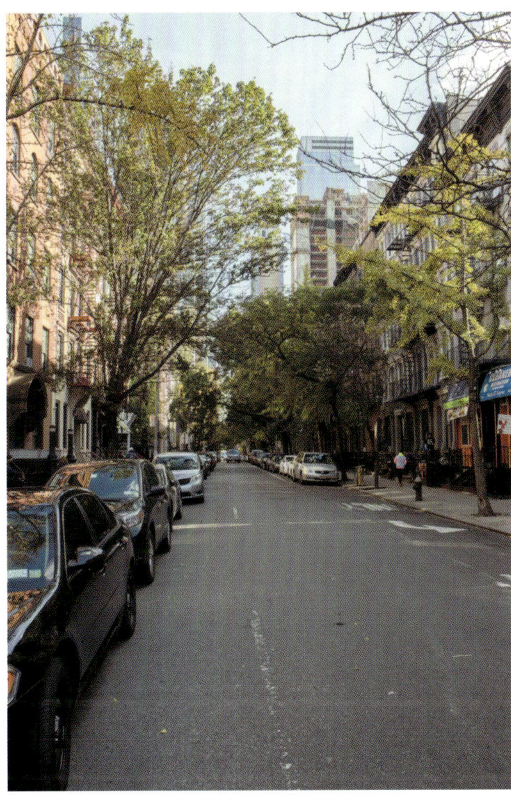

FIGURE 2.75 © Colin Smith

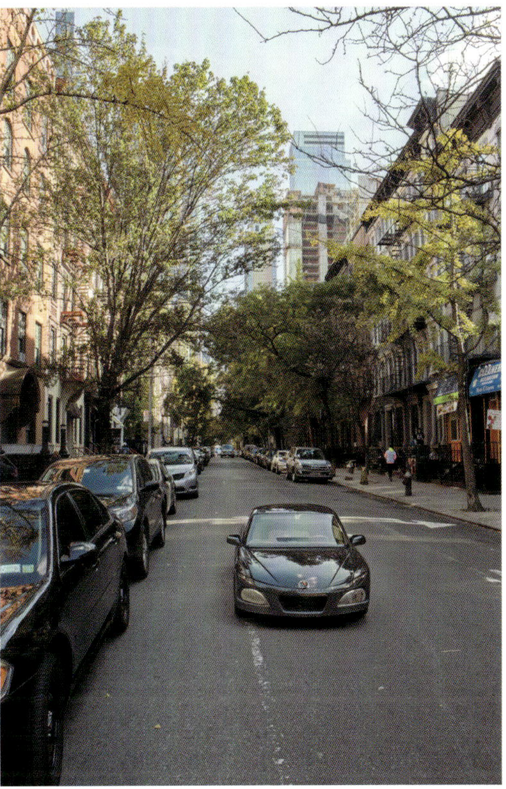

FIGURE 2.76

If we move the car down the frame so that it appears closer, it looks even smaller because of its size relative to its position and the scale of everything else in the image (**FIGURE 2.77**).

If we raise it in the frame, it appears as if it's further away, and now it looks larger (**FIGURE 2.78**).

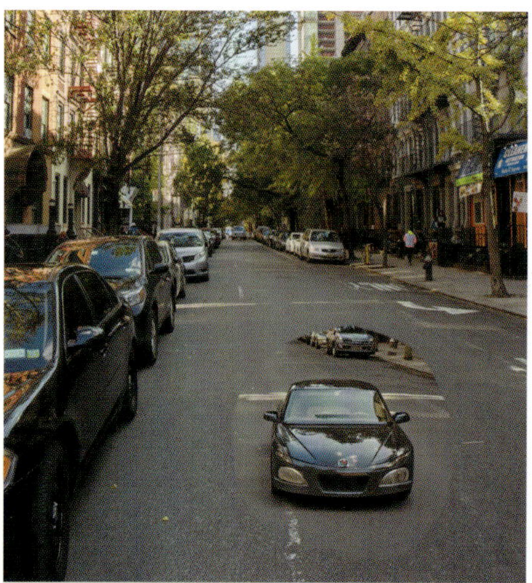

FIGURE 2.77

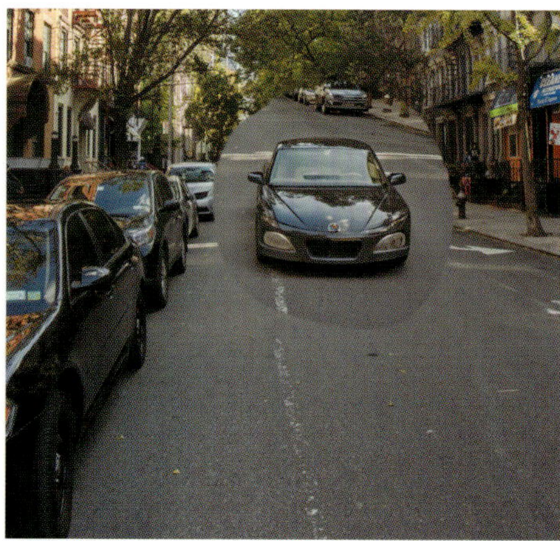

FIGURE 2.78

1. With the Move Tool, drag the car layer to a position in the frame where it looks like it's the correct size.

Now we want to blend the car into the image in the new position (because the edges don't match anymore) and have Photoshop make the shadows.

We want to select what I'm going to call the donut, which is the area between the car and the background (**FIGURE 2.79**).

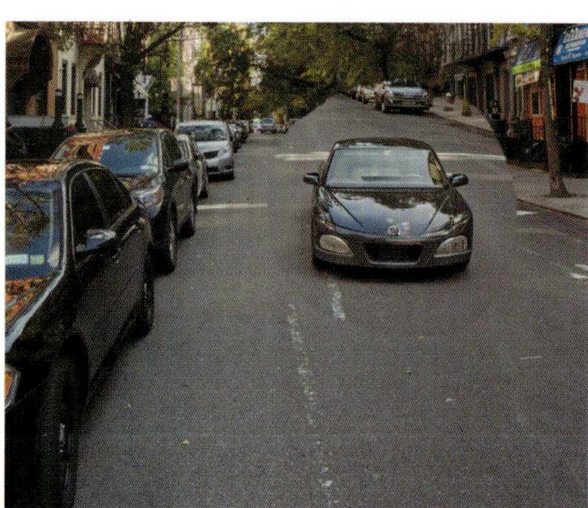

FIGURE 2.79

2. Choose the Quick Selection Tool from the Tools panel (**FIGURE 2.80**).

3. Make a selection of the car (**FIGURE 2.81**).

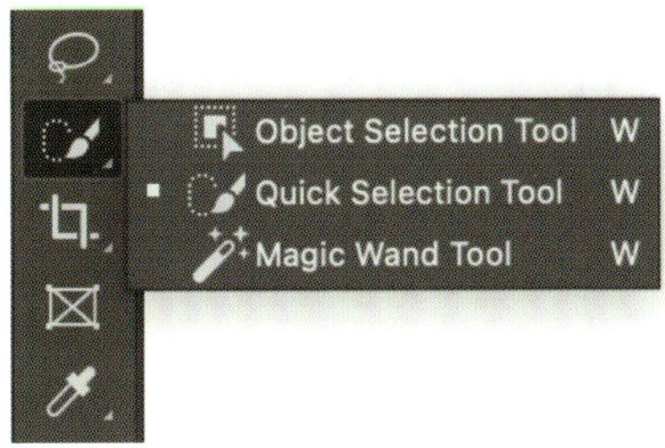

FIGURE 2.80

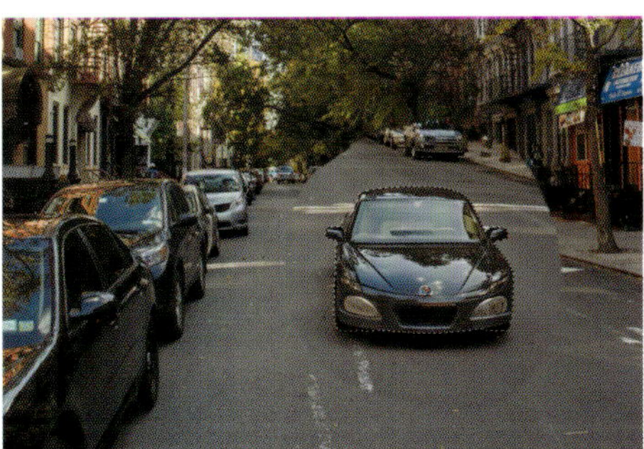

FIGURE 2.81

4. Choose Select > Save Selection and name it "car."

Just so you can easily see what's happening, I've hidden the background for now.

5. Hold the Ctrl/Command key (Windows/Mac) and click on the layer mask of the car to load the mask as a selection.

Notice how the entire generated patch is selected (**FIGURE 2.82**). We want to remove the car from the selection.

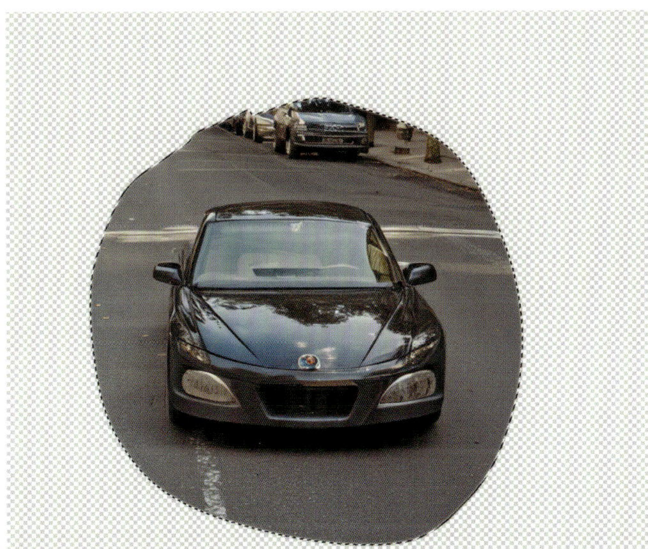

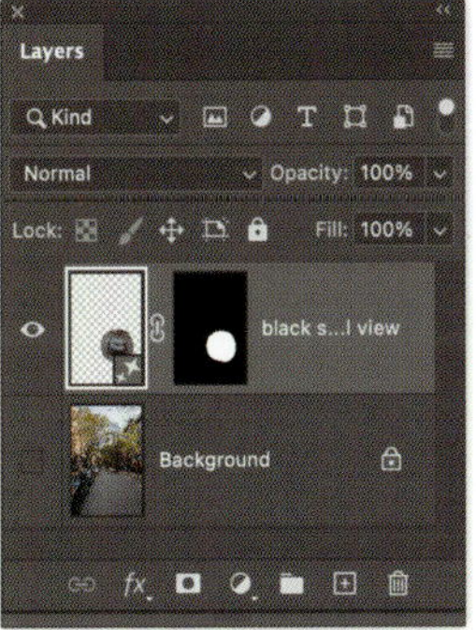

FIGURE 2.82

6.   Choose Select > Load Selection.

7.   Under Channel, click on the car selection we just saved (**FIGURE 2.83**).

8.   Under Operation, select Subtract from Selection. Click OK.

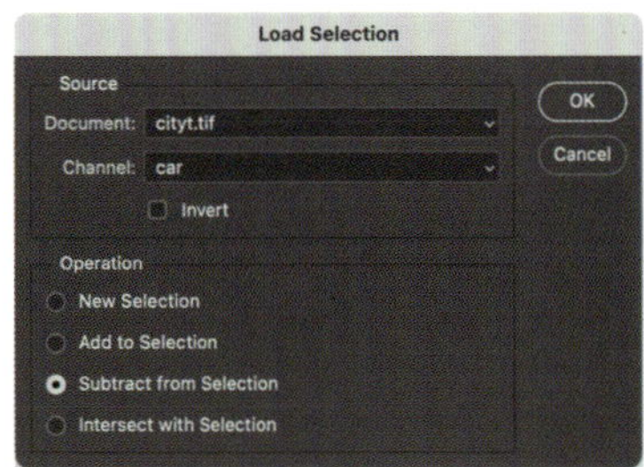

FIGURE 2.83

Now have the donut selected (**FIGURE 2.84**). The car isn't selected, so it won't change when we generate.

Let's turn the background layer visibility back on (**FIGURE 2.85**).

9.   Click on Generative Fill in the Task Bar, leave the prompt blank, and click Generate.

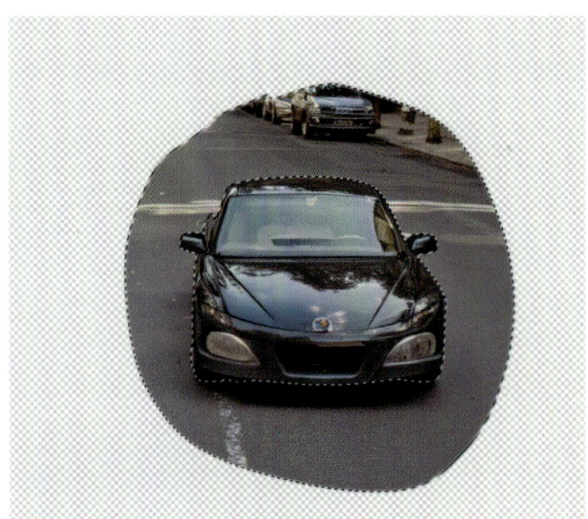

FIGURE 2.84

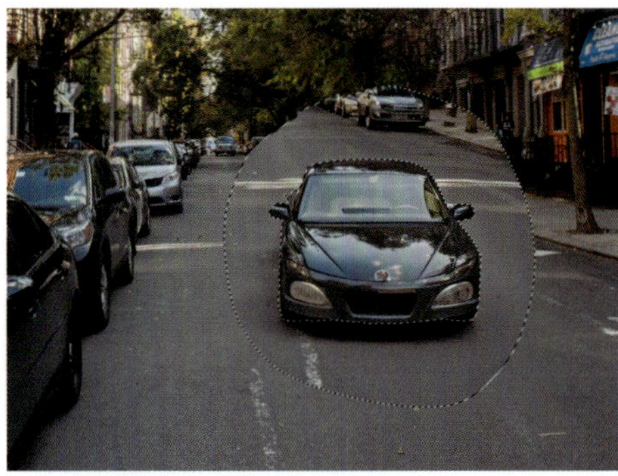

FIGURE 2.85

The donut is generated again and will seamlessly fit into the scene and a new shadow is generated (**FIGURE 2.86**). Now our car looks about the right size. That's how you can move almost any generated object.

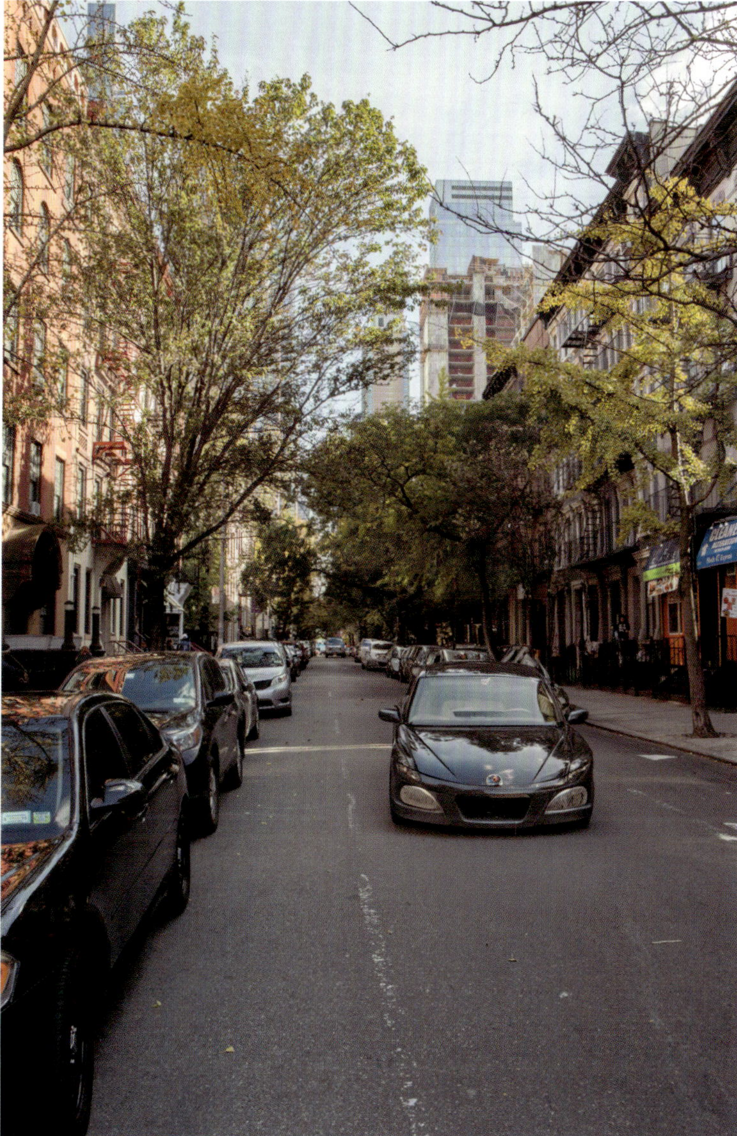

FIGURE 2.86

We have just learned about generating images with Generative Fill. I hope you are finding this useful and practical.

In the next chapter we are going to look at extending and expanding images with Generative Fill and Generative Expand.

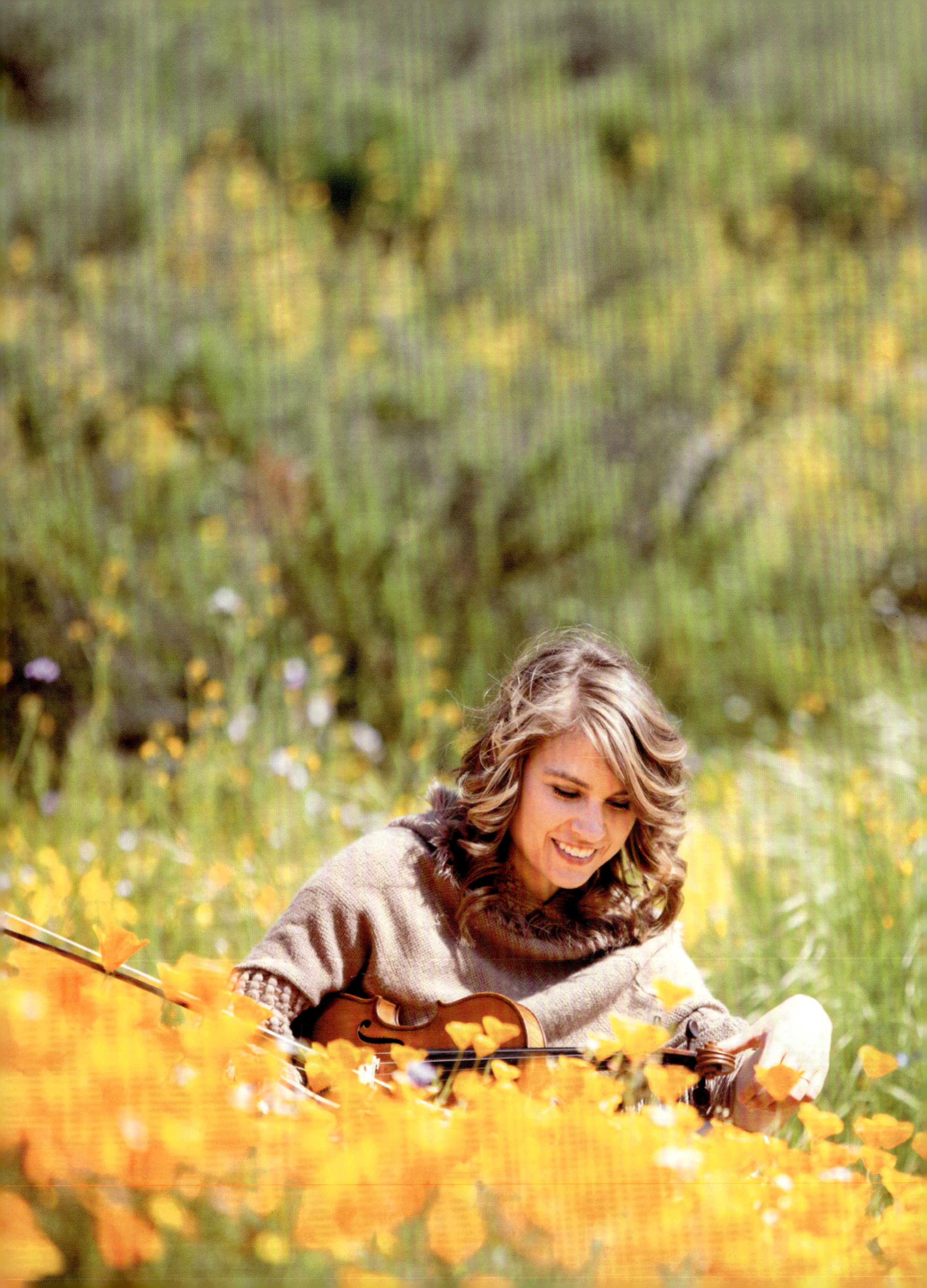

3

EXPAND

Sometimes you need to make an image wider or taller than the original. Or perhaps you need to change a horizontal photo to a vertical one. Maybe part of the subject didn't fit into the frame, or you framed the shot in such a way that you lost part of an interesting object. Maybe you are losing part of your image when cropping panoramas or straightening photos. Perhaps you need to perform a set extension. In the past, we would hope that Content-Aware Fill could help us, or patching and cloning could.

Now, however, one of the things Generative Fill does really well is expand an image. Because of this, Generative Expand was added. Generative Expand is nothing more than outcropping. This is when you crop an image larger than its original size.

Without Generative Expand, this is a three-step process:

1. The image is enlarged with the Crop Tool or Image > Canvas Size, and the new borders will be the same as the background color (Transparency if you are working on a layer).

2. You select the borders with the Rectangular Marquee Tool.

3. Choose Generative Fill, leave the prompt empty, and click Generate. The borders will be filled to match the image.

With Generative Expand, this is all done in one step. The selection and fill will be applied automatically when you complete the crop. You get the same result with two fewer steps. We will use both methods in this chapter.

Outcropping Missing Parts of a Photo with Generative Expand

Sometimes important parts of an image didn't make it into the frame, like in this image of a fountain in New York City's Central Park (**FIGURE 3.1**).

In this case, we can expand the canvas. The best way to do this is to outcrop. Outcropping is where we crop outward and make the image larger, as opposed to traditional cropping in, where we reduce the image size. When we outcrop, Generative Fill adds to the picture to fill the new frame.

Let's try it now, shall we?

1. Choose the Crop Tool (**FIGURE 3.2**).

2. You will see a Fill drop-down menu on the Options Bar at the top of the interface when the Crop Tool is selected (**FIGURE 3.3**).

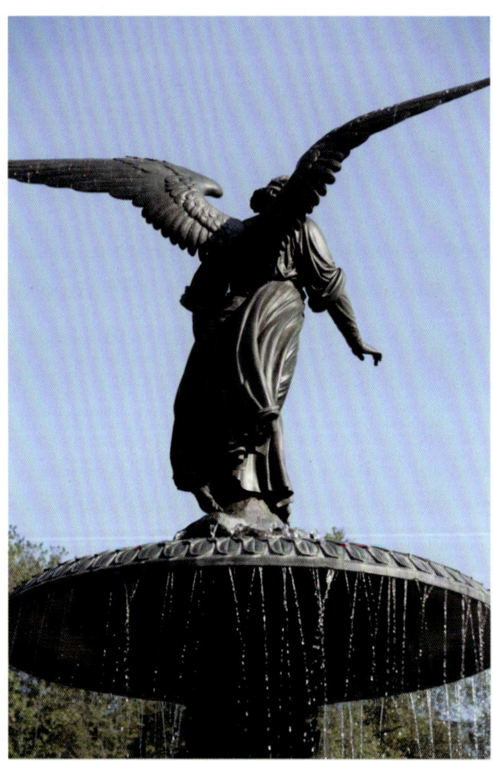

FIGURE 3.1 © Colin Smith

You can choose from the following options:

- Background or Transparent: This works like it always did, filling with the background color. If Delete Cropped Pixels is off, it will say Transparent.

- Generative Expand: Fills with Generative Fill.

- Content-Aware Fill: Uses Content-Aware Fill, a non-AI function that samples surrounding pixels.

3. We will be using Generative Expand, so choose that option. The Contextual Task Bar will say Generative Expand, rather than Generative Fill like in the previous chapter; it works the same, but Generative Expand will fill new pixels as the canvas size is increased.

4. Drag the edges of the canvas outward to expand it to your desired size (**FIGURE 3.4**).

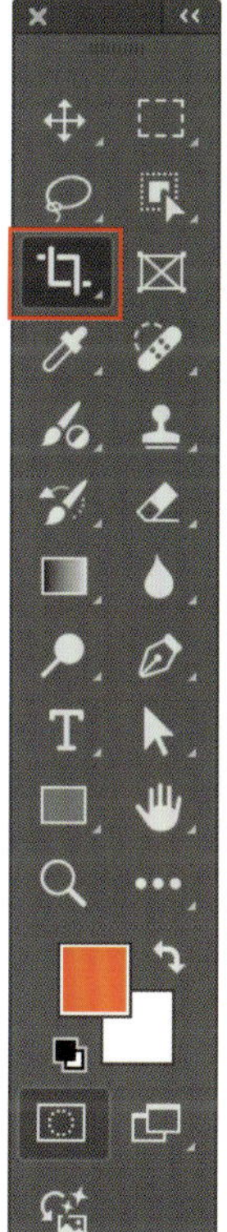

FIGURE 3.2

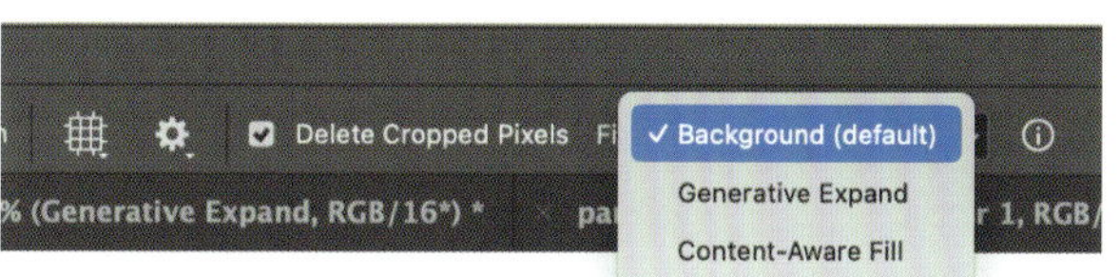

FIGURE 3.3

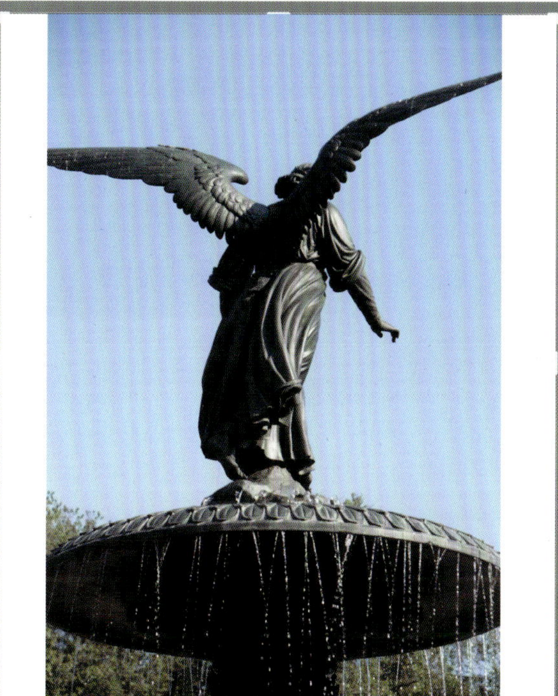

FIGURE 3.4

5. You will see the text prompt field appear in the Contextual Task Bar (**FIGURE 3.5**). If you'd like to fill the new area with something specific, enter a prompt; otherwise, leave it blank and click Generate, or simply press the enter key. We're going to leave the field blank in this example.

FIGURE 3.5

The pixels will be generated around the edges to match the rest of the image (**FIGURE 3.6**). Just like with Generative Fill, there will be three variations to choose from.

If you look at the Layers panel, you'll see a new Generative Layer with the new pixels at the top (**FIGURE 3.7**).

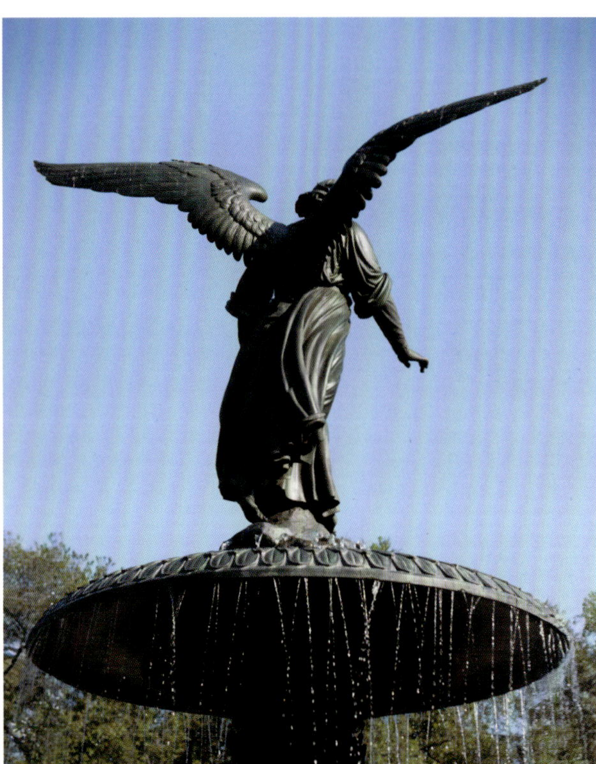

FIGURE 3.6

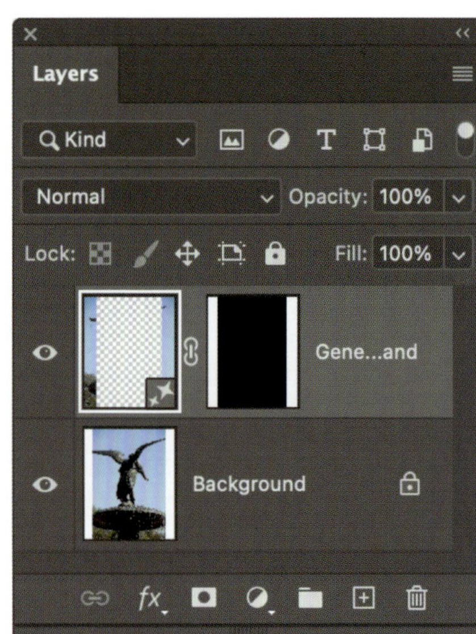

FIGURE 3.7

Extending an Image

Sometimes we can get more extreme and expand an image far beyond its frame. Generative Expand fills with whatever it thinks should be there. This is not the technique you would use for a famous landmark because the results are purely fictional. In fact, a lot of people are having fun with this feature, expanding famous posters and album covers for some very entertaining results.

Let's expand this shot from the platform at the San Juan Capistrano train station (**FIGURE 3.8**).

1. Choose the Crop Tool and make sure the Fill menu in the Options Bar is set to Generative Expand.

2. Drag outward from the left edge of the image with the Crop Tool (**FIGURE 3.9**). If you can't freely move the Crop Tool, click Clear in the Options Bar.

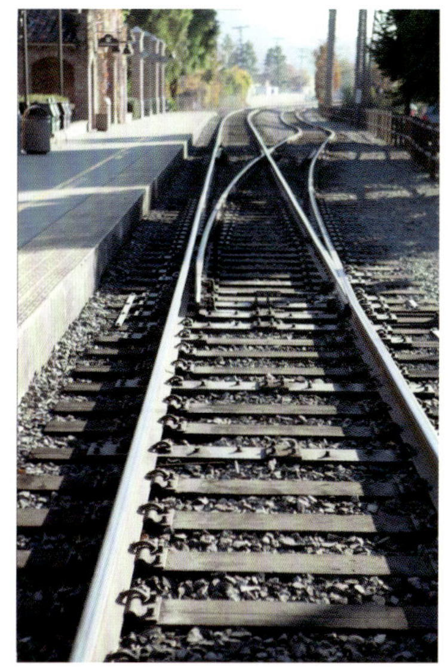

FIGURE 3.8 © Colin Smith

3. Press the enter key or select the check mark in the Options Bar at the top to apply the crop.

Generative Expand (really, Generative Fill) will be applied, and you can look at the three variations in the Properties panel or by clicking the arrows in the Contextual Task Bar.

As you can see, a whole new world has been created (**FIGURE 3.10**).

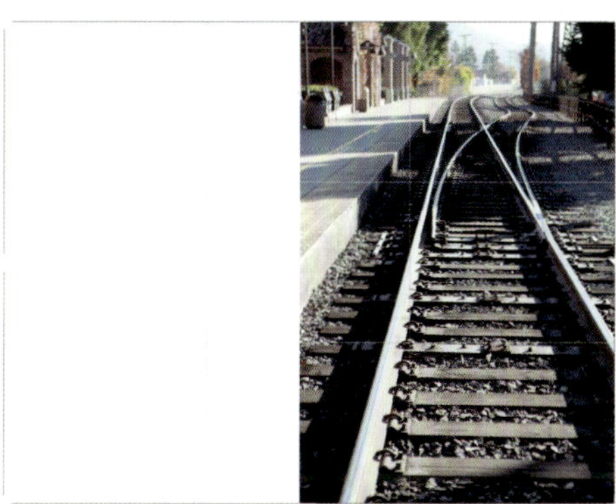

FIGURE 3.9

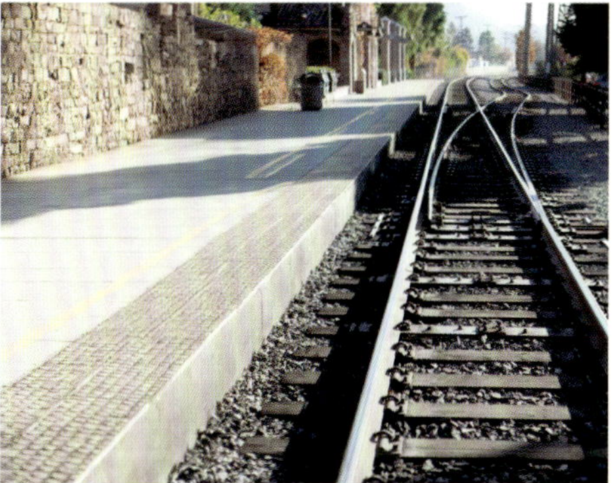

FIGURE 3.10

Depending on when you read this, Generative Fill results could be available in higher resolutions. At the time of writing, the resolution of the fill content is often not as high as that of the original image. For web-based sharing and social media, you wouldn't really notice the resolution mismatch.

Let's look at a closeup (**FIGURE 3.11**).

Here, I have added a red line on the closeup so you can see the generated pixels on the left versus the original image on the right. Zoomed out, most people won't notice, but you can see the difference on close examination.

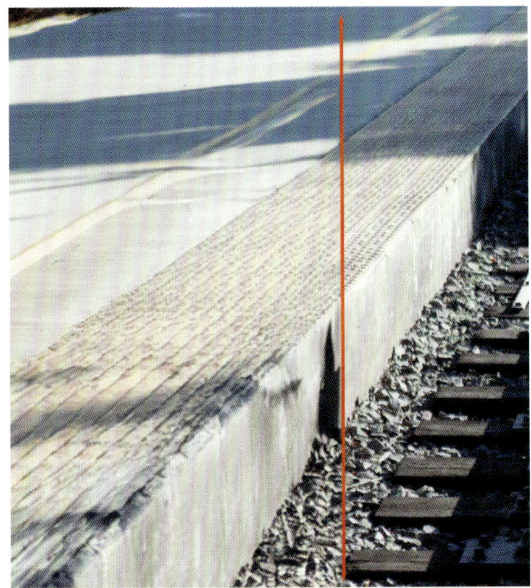

FIGURE 3.11

Enhance Detail

Let's see what we can do to improve this a bit.

1. Roll over the variation thumbnail in the Properties panel. You will see the Enhance Detail button (**FIGURE 3.12**).

For variations smaller than 1024px X 1024px, the Enhance Detail button won't be available because the image is already at full resolution. This only applies to larger selections (see "A Resolution Problem" below).

2. Click this button to apply super-resolution and enhance the details. This doesn't download a higher-resolution version of the variation; it just enhances the quality of the existing variation.

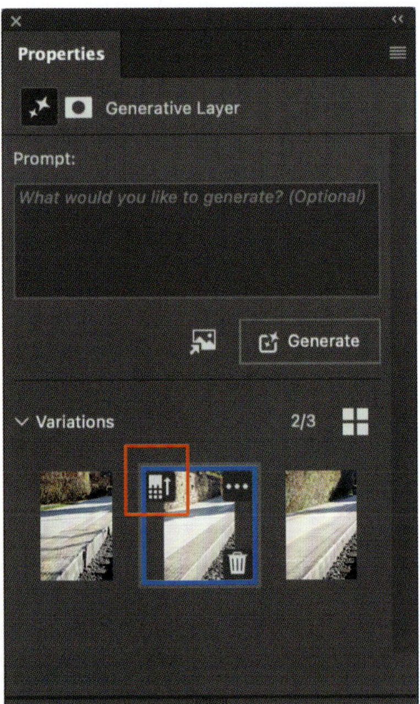

FIGURE 3.12

If you look closely again, you can see that Enhance Detail does help the image a lot (**FIGURE 3.13**).

It doesn't always perfectly match, but it's an improvement on what we had. Like all the features in Generative Fill, they will continue to improve and get better over time. It's possible by the time you are reading this, the feature will be working perfectly.

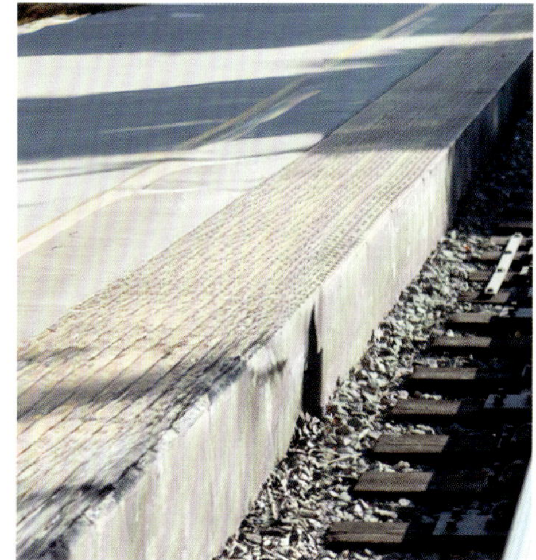

FIGURE 3.13

A Resolution Problem

This resolution limitation will change over time, and perhaps when you are reading this, it already has (I will certainly announce the change on PhotoshopCAFE.com). The cause of this limitation is the enormous amount of computing power required to generate these images at the data centers.

At the time of this writing, Generative Fill is limited to 1024px X 1024px blocks (2048px X 2048px for Generate Image and Generative Workspace). When you make a selection, Generative Fill generates at a maximum of 1024 pixels wide and 1024 pixels high. If the selection is that size or smaller, the generated image will be full resolution. If the selection is larger, the detail will be stretched to fit the selection and may result in soft or pixelated results, depending on the size.

A Resolution Hack

Bear in mind that with many images, especially for most digital delivery sizes, you won't really notice resolution issues. On images that will be displayed very large, such as at print resolution, it will be noticeable and the image will probably be unusable. I've come up with a little hack for this situation.

Here I have a panorama that is almost 8000px across. It's not a massive image, as far as many panoramas go, but it will work perfectly for our example (**FIGURE 3.14**).

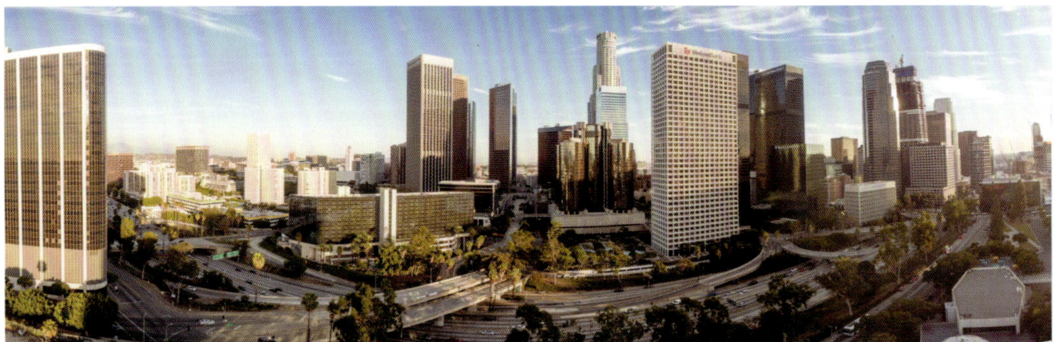

FIGURE 3.14 © Colin Smith

Let's say we want to make this image a bit taller and add to the bottom where there is a lot of detail. Very often, the resolution at the top doesn't matter as much because generally there isn't as much detail in the sky, unless there are very complex cloud structures.

First, let's use Generative Expand to see how it does (**FIGURE 3.15**).

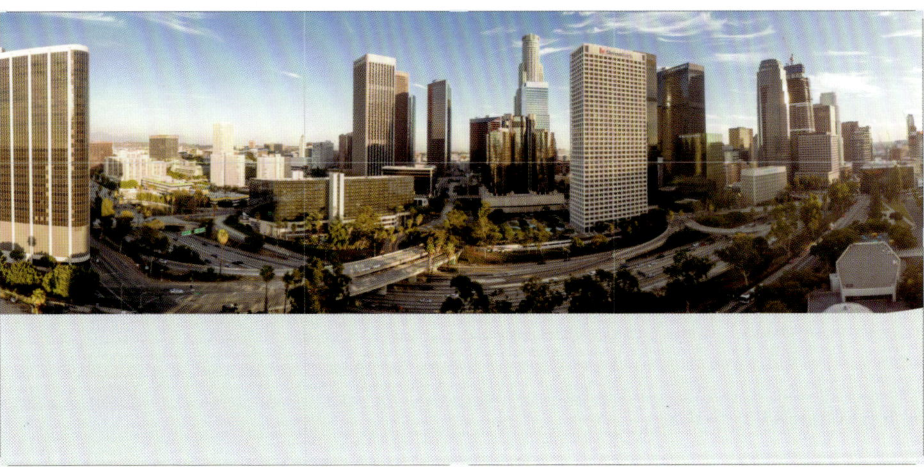

FIGURE 3.15

When we zoom in on the bottom, the resolution mismatch is glaringly obvious and not usable for much other than a small-sized online share (**FIGURE 3.16**).

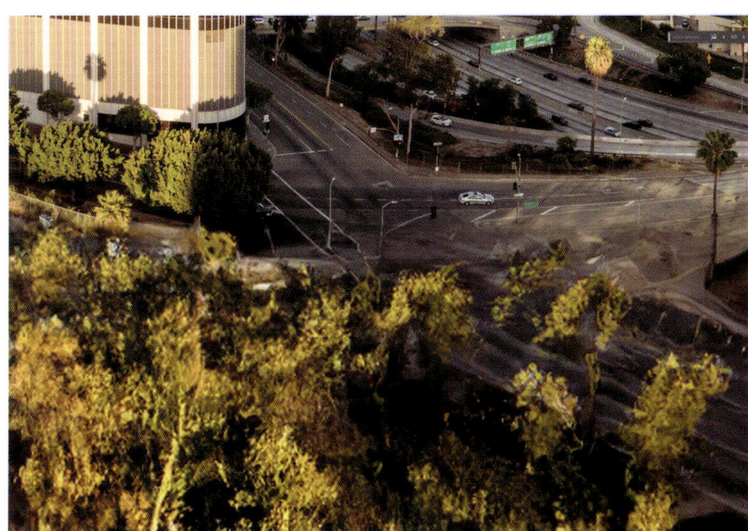

FIGURE 3.16

Okay, here's the trick:

1. With the Crop Tool selected, change the Fill menu in the Options Bar to Background (or Transparent if Delete Cropped Pixels is off).

2. Drag your crop to enlarge the image at the bottom (**FIGURE 3.17**). (Press the Clear button in the Options Bar if the crop is constrained.)

3. Apply the crop by pressing the enter key.

Because we aren't using Generative Expand, the extended border will be blank.

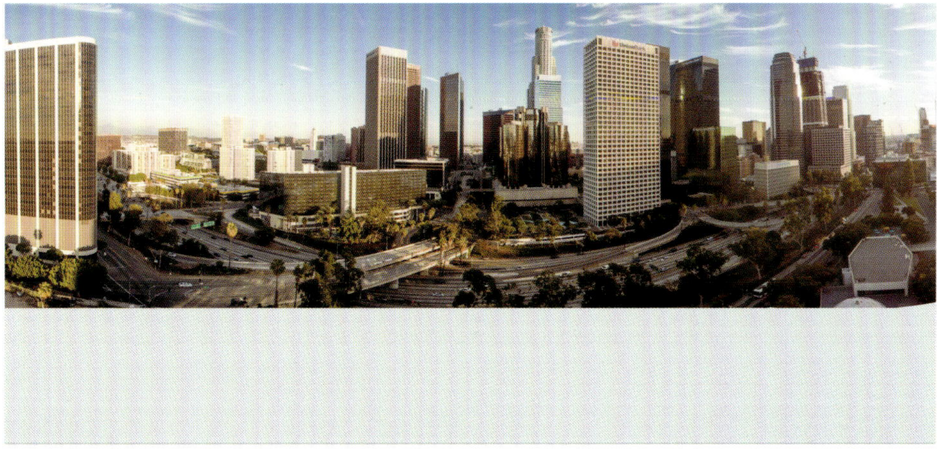

FIGURE 3.17

TIP Don't try to apply Generative Expand first and then patch over the top of it. In this case, Generative Fill will try to match the low-resolution pixels and the result will look soft.

4. Choose the Rectangular Marquee Tool in the Tools panel.

5. In the Options Bar, set the Style to Fixed Size.

6. Set both the Width and Height fields to 1024px (**FIGURE 3.18**). You can make the Height less if it's a shorter crop, but don't exceed 1024px on either side.

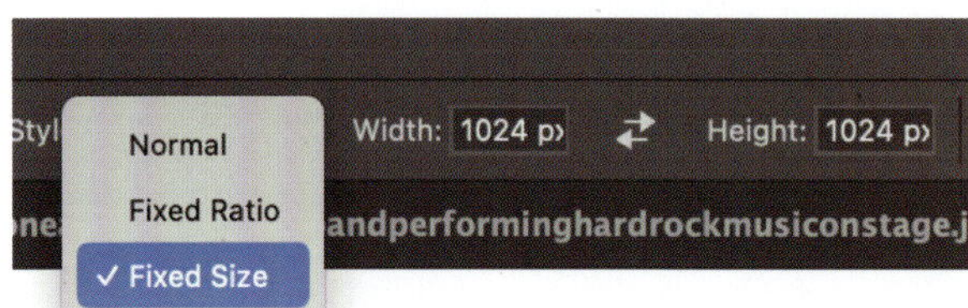

FIGURE 3.18

7. Use the Rectangular Marquee Tool to select the bottom left of the blank border (**FIGURE 3.19**). The selection will be limited to the fixed size.

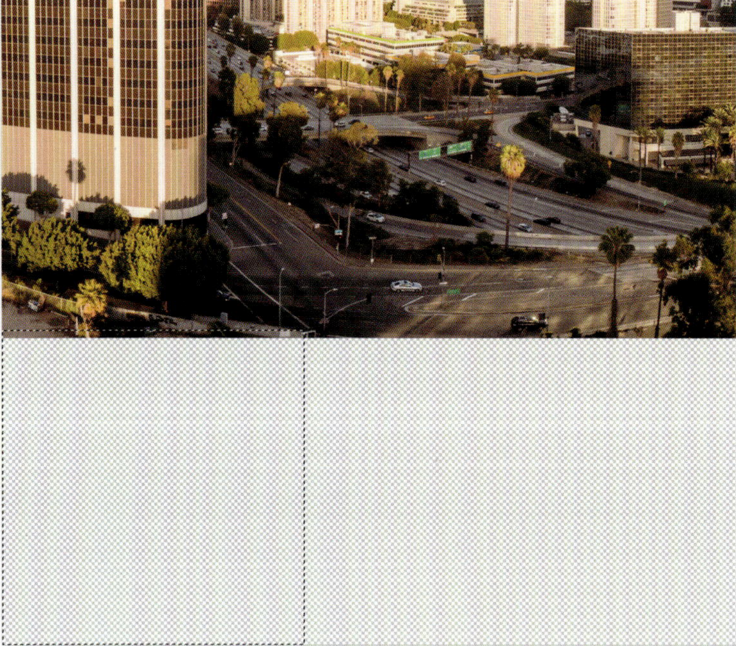

FIGURE 3.19

8. Choose Generative Fill in the Contextual Task Bar, leave the prompt empty, and click Generate to fill.

When you look at this closeup, you can see the resolution now matches perfectly because we aren't exceeding the maximum resolution of Generative Fill (**FIGURE 3.20**). Yes! This what we want.

9. With the Rectangular Marquee Tool, select the area to the right of your previous selection and follow step 8 again.

This new section will match the generated portion to the left and the rest of the image above, like you've inserted the correct jigsaw puzzle piece (**FIGURE 3.21**). The additional advantage of generating in smaller segments is that you get to guide the results by choosing the best variation for each block.

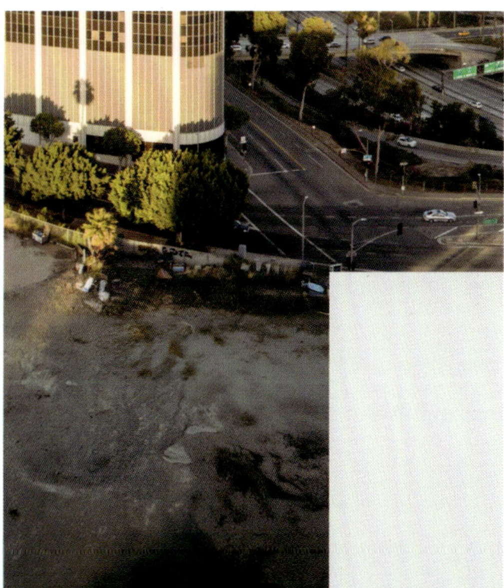

FIGURE 3.20

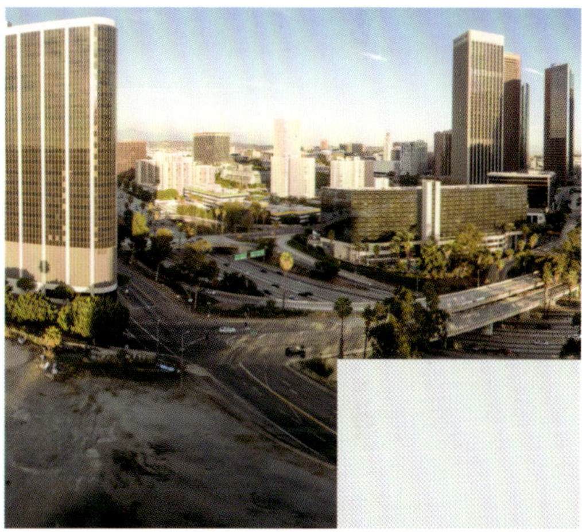

FIGURE 3.21

FIGURE 3.22 shows the final image, with the generated portions at full resolution.

This method takes a little longer, but the quality results are worth it.

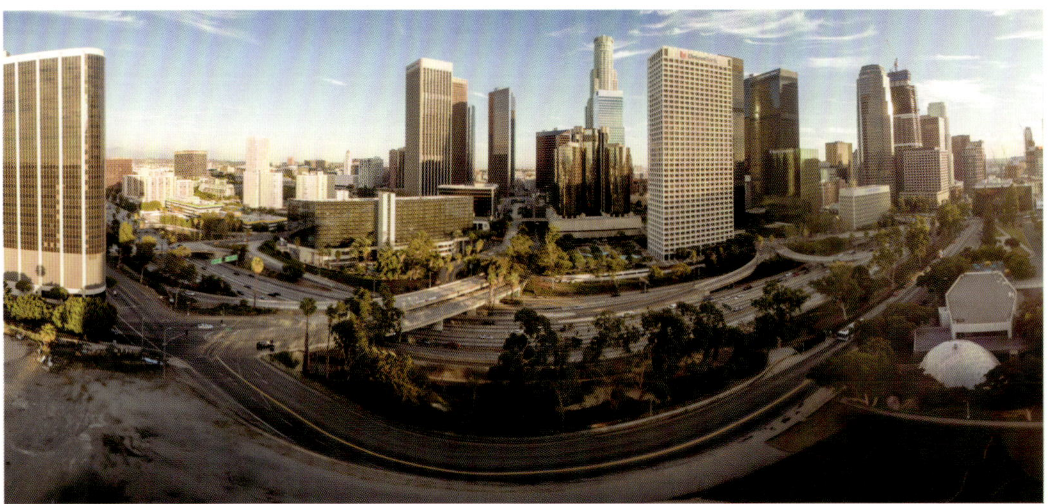

FIGURE 3.22

Using Actions with Generative Fill

You can speed up the proceeding process by using actions. Actions are macros that enable us to automate steps in Photoshop. One small drawback of an action is that you can't choose each variation as you go, unless you insert pauses in your action.

Set to Percentage

If you want your action to work on images of different sizes, you need to change the unit of measurement to percentage.

1. Press Ctrl+ R/Command+R (Windows/Mac) to show rulers around your document.

2. Right-click on a ruler at the top or left side of the interface and choose Percent (**FIGURE 3.23**).

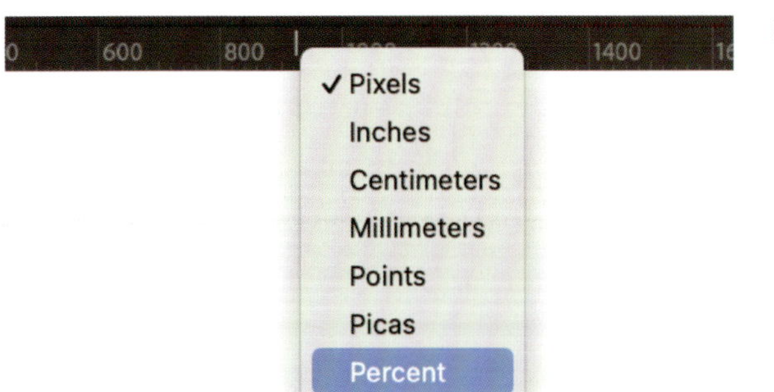

FIGURE 3.23

Creating an Action

1. Open the Actions panel (Window > Actions) and click the folder icon to create a New Set. I named my group "book" (**FIGURE 3.24**).

2. With your new set selected, click the + icon to create a New Action.

3. Name your action and click Record. I named this action "Add resolution +5" (**FIGURE 3.25**).

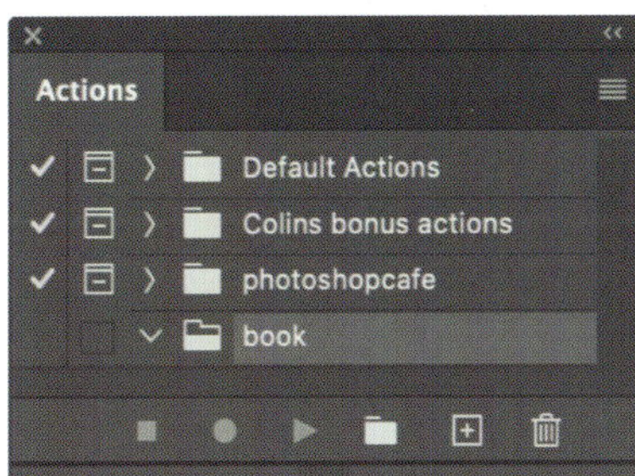

FIGURE 3.24

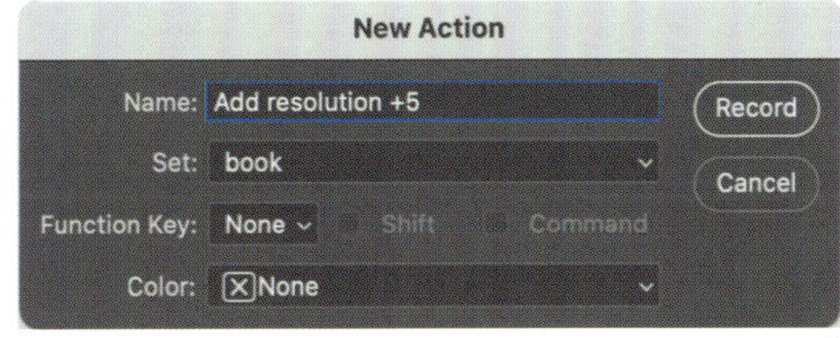

FIGURE 3.25

You will see a red record button at the bottom of the Actions panel. This indicates that each step you take is being recorded in the Actions panel. Note that you do not have to click this, as it was enabled when you pressed Record in the New Action dialog.

4. Follow the steps on pages 78–79 to generate blocks in pieces. Each time you apply a selection, you will see "Set Selection" in the action steps. When you fill, "Generative Fill current document" will be added to the list of steps (**FIGURE 3.26**).

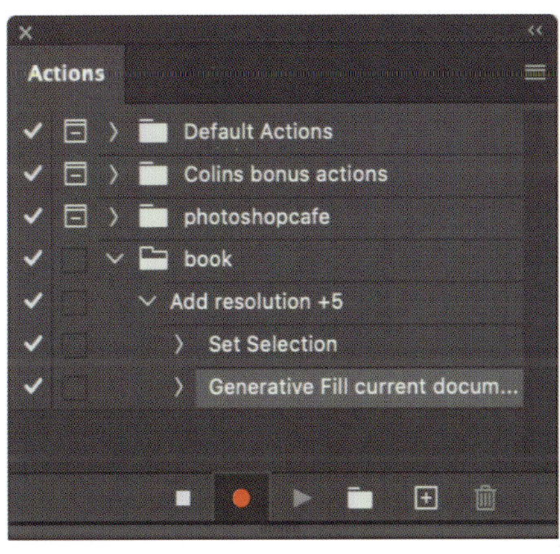

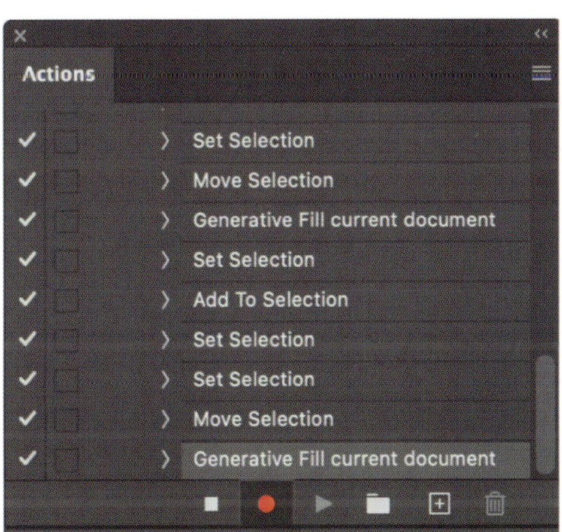

FIGURE 3.26

5. When you have finished, click the square stop button to the left of the record button.

The action will be recorded, and you will have completed the image again. The results will look different each time because Generative Fill produces unique pixels each time. I like this result better than the previous one (**FIGURE 3.27**).

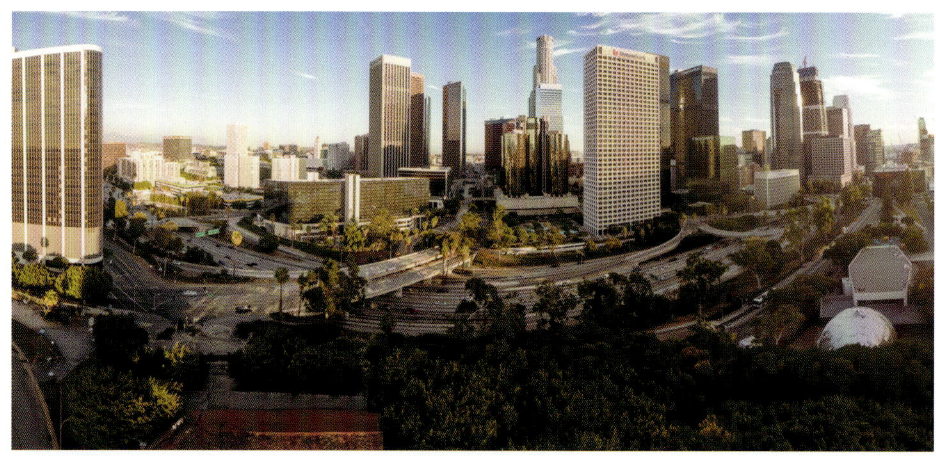

FIGURE 3.27

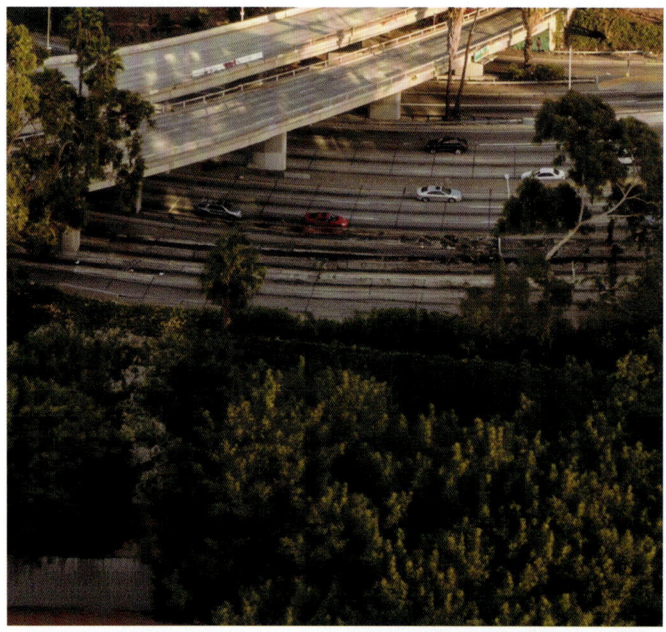

If we zoom in close, notice the resolution looks nice and it matches the rest of the image (**FIGURE 3.28**).

FIGURE 3.28

Using Actions

Now that we've created an action, we can play it back to automatically go through the whole process again and get a different result.

1. To play back the action, select its name in the Actions panel (**FIGURE 3.29**).

2. Press the play button at the bottom of the Actions panel.

The action will now run and complete all the steps on the image by itself. Automating AI—now that's something!

And once again, we get a unique result (**FIGURE 3.30**).

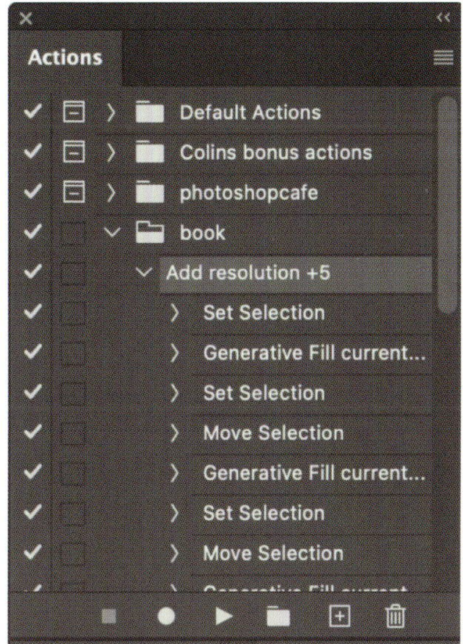

FIGURE 3.29

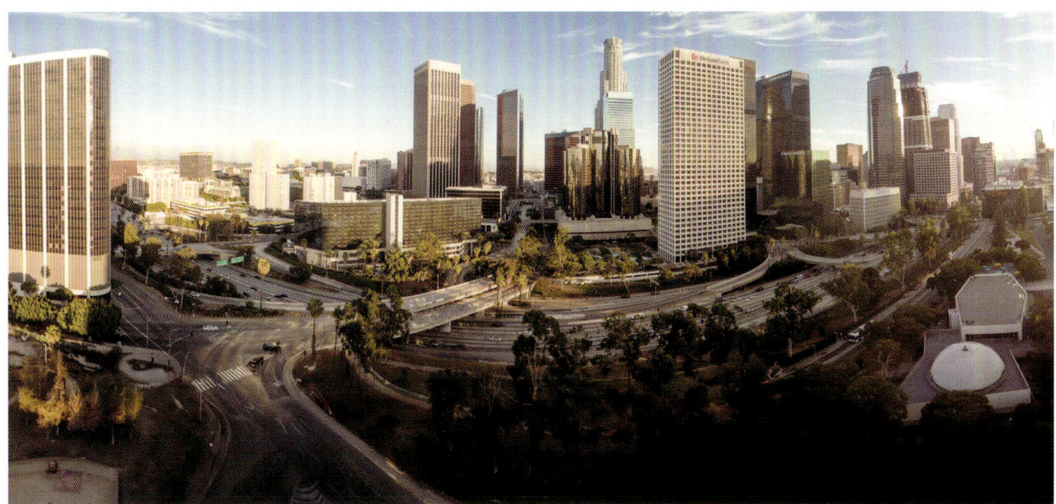

FIGURE 3.30

Outcropping to a Specific Size

We can use Generative Expand to help us resize an image to a specific size. Say we want a final size of 8 inches x 10 inches at 300ppi—that's easy!

1. Choose the Crop Tool.

2. Set the Fill menu to Generative Expand.

3. Change the menu on the left end of Options Bar to W x H x Resolution (Width x Height x Resolution; **FIGURE 3.31**).

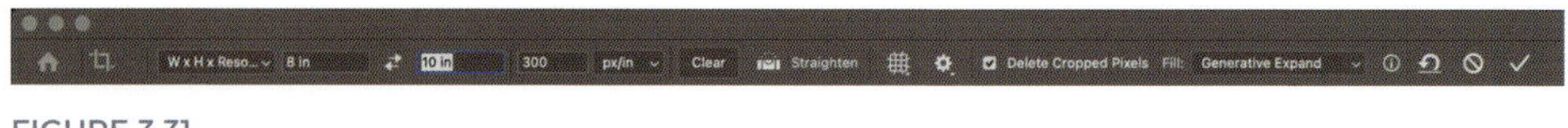

FIGURE 3.31

4. In the next field over, enter "8 in" for the width, followed by "10 in" for the height, and "300" for the resolution, so it will be print resolution. Set the drop-down menu to the right of the measurement fields to px/in. (You can choose, cm, mm, px, etc., for the unit of measurement depending on what you prefer to work with.)

The crop shield will appear in the aspect ratio (8x10) that we selected in the Options Bar (**FIGURE 3.32**).

In the past, you would have to crop into the photo to make it fit the aspect ratio, thus losing some of the photo, or do manual compositing.

5. Drag the crop to enlarge and widen the photo (**FIGURE 3.33**).

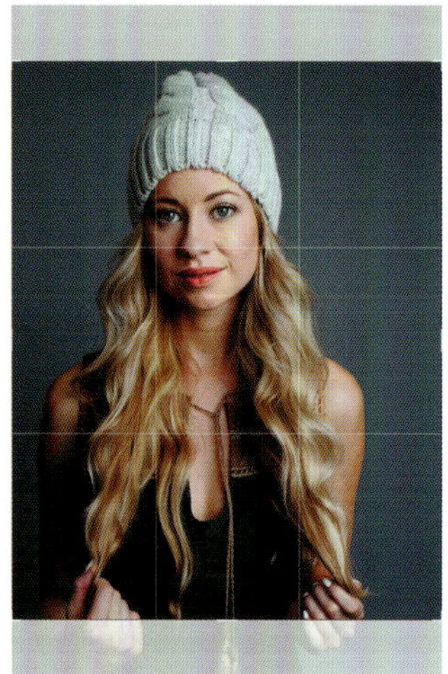

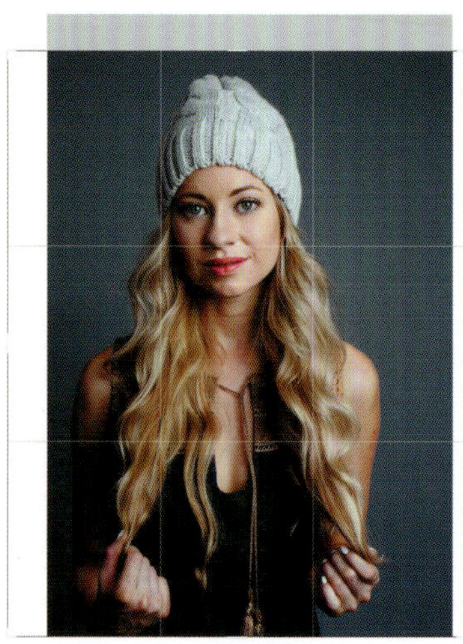

FIGURE 3.32 © Colin Smith   FIGURE 3.33

6. Apply the crop by pressing enter on your keyboard.

Photoshop expands the photo and fills it with the background (**FIGURE 3.34**). It will also change the size of the photo to 8x10 inches at 300ppi. This saves a lot of time.

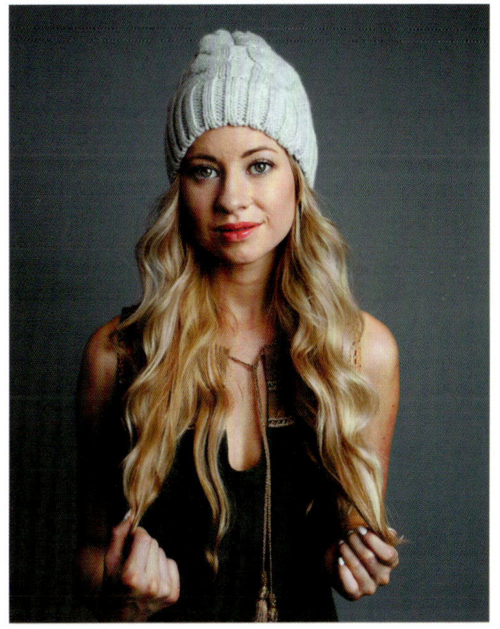

FIGURE 3.34

Changing the Aspect Ratio of an Image

Have you ever had a horizontal image that you need to be vertical? It could be for social media, or for a magazine or poster. The method we'll cover in this section is a big help and I use it often! Even if you're not a designer, it could save a sale if a client wants to use your photo, but needs it tall for a magazine or book cover.

One thing to be aware of is resolution. If you're working with a solid area of color, or out-of-focus bokeh, it's not as much of an issue as it is when you are working with fine detail. For large images, use the tip in the section titled "A Resolution Hack" and generate in blocks.

Here is our wide image of talented violinist Taylor Davis (YouTube: @taylordavisviolin) in a California Super Bloom (**FIGURE 3.35**).

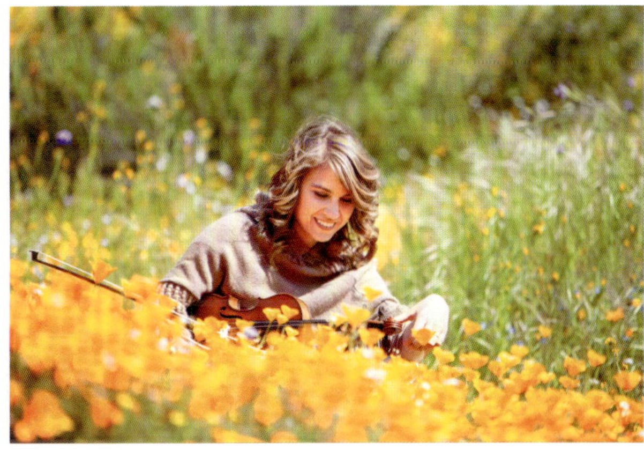

FIGURE 3.35 © Colin Smith

1. Choose the Crop Tool from the Tools panel, choose Generative Expand in the Fill Menu, and change the image shape to vertical by dragging with the Crop Tool (**FIGURE 3.36**).

   > **TIP** Tap the X key to toggle the crop between wide and tall (but not while you are dragging the crop).

2. Select Generative Expand in the Task Bar. If you have something specific you want to generate, type it into the text field (**FIGURE 3.37**). Otherwise, leave the prompt field blank and click Generate, or press the enter key.

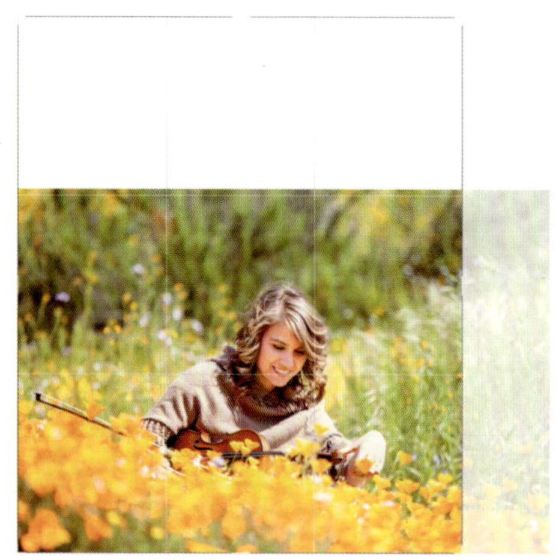

FIGURE 3.36

FIGURE 3.37

Generative Expand will use the existing pixels and generate new pixels. Now we have a vertical image with lots of space to put text at the top of the image, and it still looks like a field of flowers (**FIGURE 3.38**).

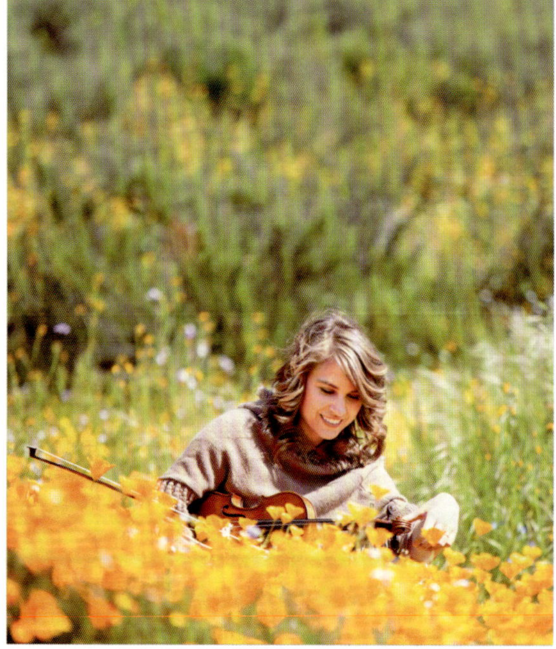

FIGURE 3.38

Fixing a Panorama

When we create panoramas, we end up with non-rectangular edges because of the projection. Usually, to remedy this issue, the edges are cropped and some of the image is lost. What if you want to keep all the details around the edges? This is a great use case for Generative Fill.

Let's quickly merge a panorama, and then we will fix the edges. There are multiple ways to make panoramas in Photoshop; we will use the quickest method. We won't cover shooting and merging panoramas in depth, as that isn't the focus of this book.

Make a Panorama

1. Open your photos in Adobe Bridge (comes with Photoshop). We have three photos shot with an overlap.

2. Ctrl-click/command-click (Windows/Mac) on each thumbnail you want to merge to select them all.

3. Right-click and choose Open in Camera Raw (**FIGURE 3.39**).

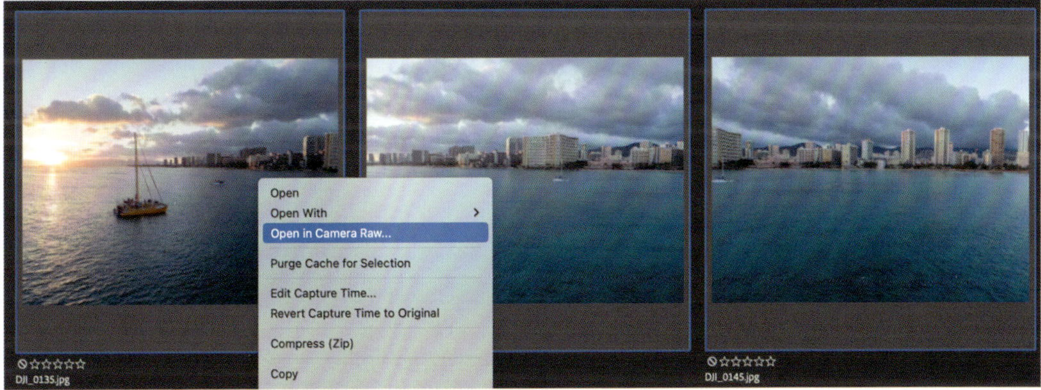

FIGURE 3.39 © Colin Smith

You will now see the images opened in Adobe Camera Raw (**FIGURE 3.40**). If you are using Lightroom, pick up the steps here, they are identical.

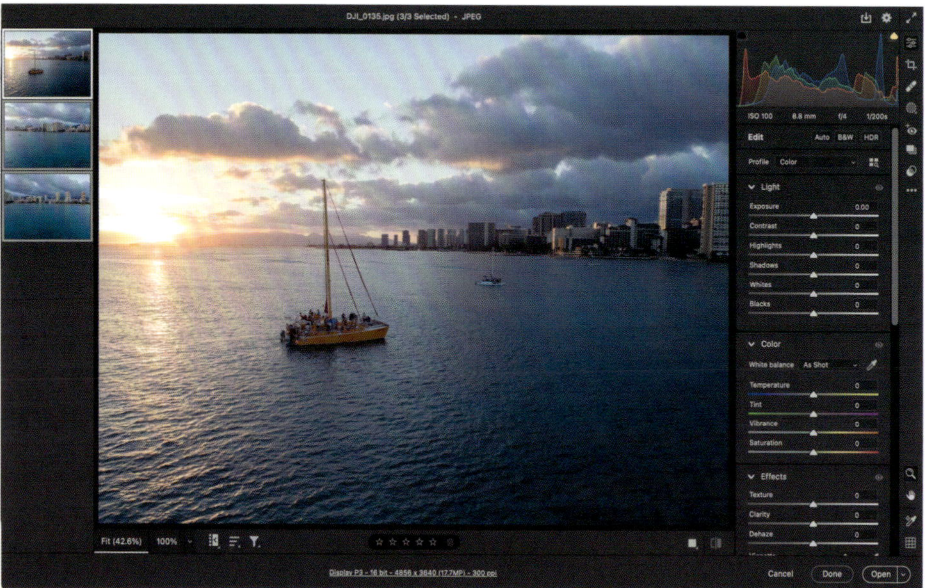

FIGURE 3.40

4. Press Ctrl+A/command+A (Windows/Mac) to select all the images.

5. Click the three-dot menu (meatball menu) on the corner of one of the thumbnails (right-click in Lightroom) and choose Merge to Panorama (**FIGURE 3.41**).

6. Select Spherical under Projection and do not check Auto Crop (**FIGURE 3.42**).

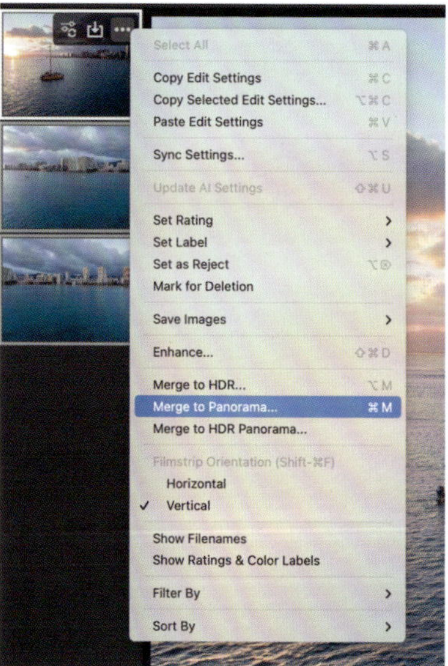

FIGURE 3.41

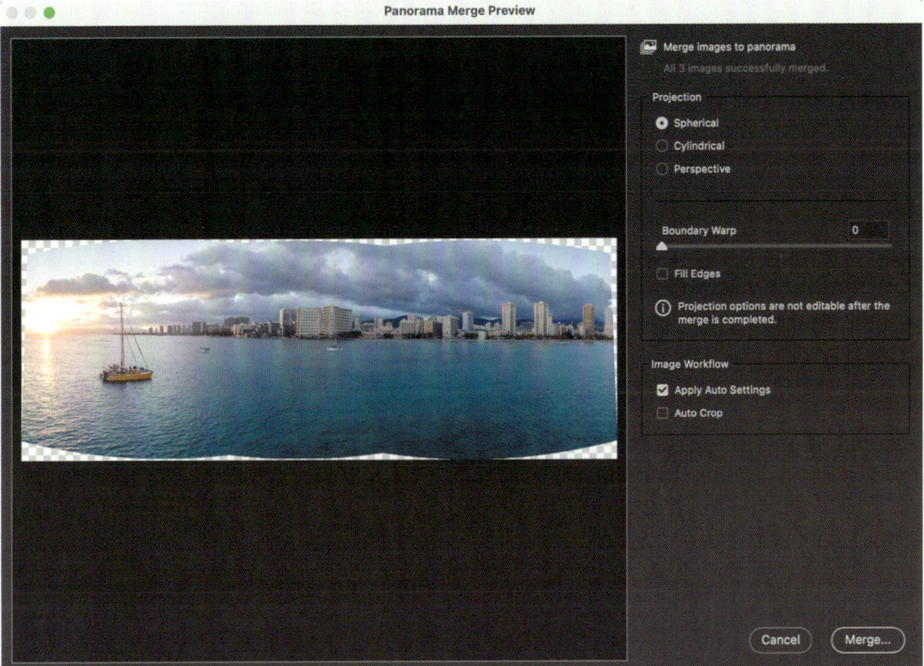

FIGURE 3.42

7.   Click Merge.

A new DNG file will be created. This will be our panorama.

8.   Save the panorama to a location you can find it later (**FIGURE 3.43**).

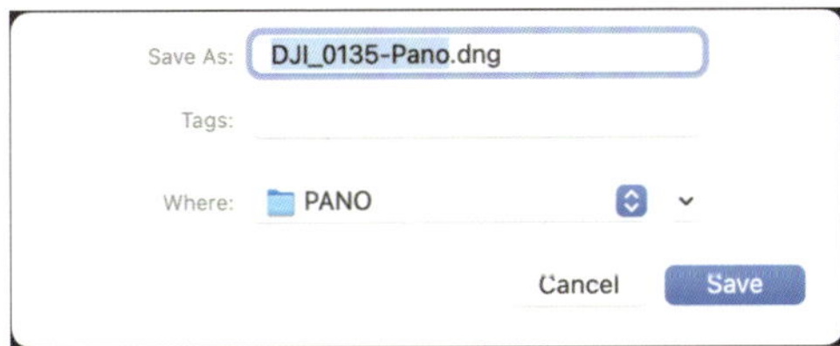

FIGURE 3.43

You will see that Camera Raw merges the images into a seamless panorama. Lightroom works exactly the same way, so you can use that application if you prefer.

9.   Click Open in the bottom-right corner of the Camera Raw interface (**FIGURE 3.44**).

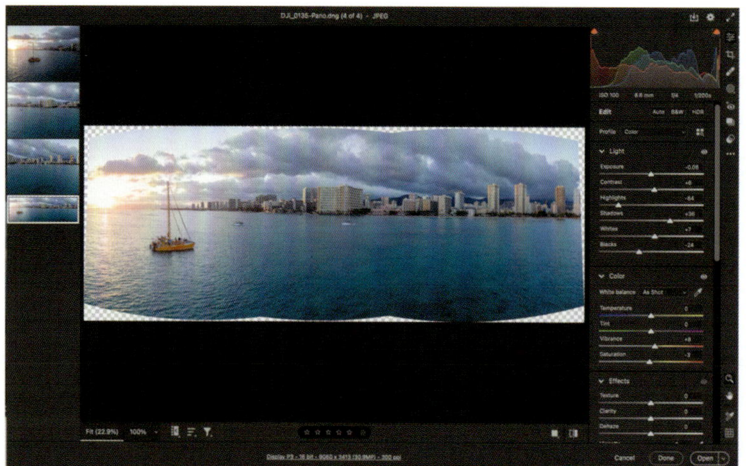

FIGURE 3.44

You will now see your panorama with wavy edges in Photoshop (**FIGURE 3.45**). Fixing this is a perfect job for Generative Fill.

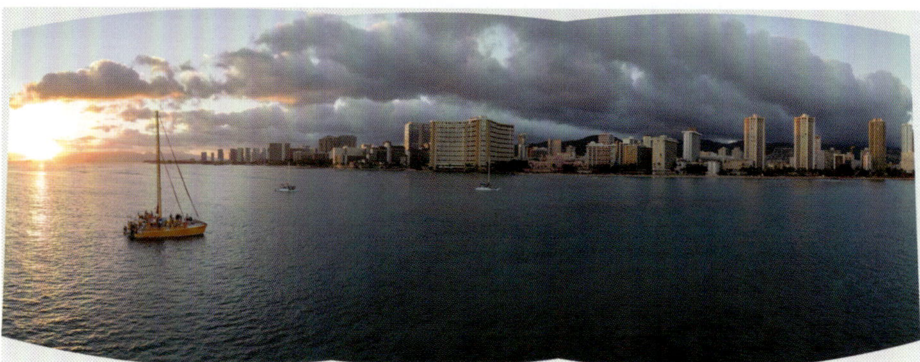

FIGURE 3.45

Fixing the Edges of the Panorama

With the panorama open in Photoshop, let's select the transparency.

1. Hold down the Ctrl/command key (Windows/Mac) and click the thumbnail in the Layers panel. You should see the marching ants selection around the edges of the image.

Let's make sure we have some overlap to work with, so we don't see seams in the final image, although Generative Fill seems to do a good job of this with its mask.

2. Chose Select > Modify > Contract.

3. Set the amount in the Contract By field—2 pixels should be enough (**FIGURE 3.46**).

4. Click OK.

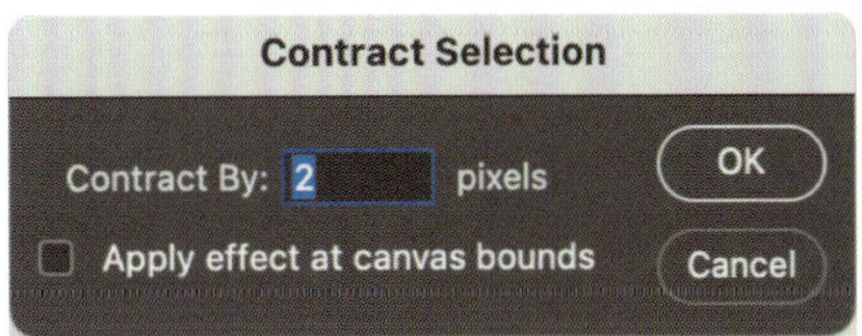

FIGURE 3.46

You will see that the selection is slightly inside the edges of the image now (**FIGURE 3.47**). I exaggerated the effect for this image so you can see what's happening.

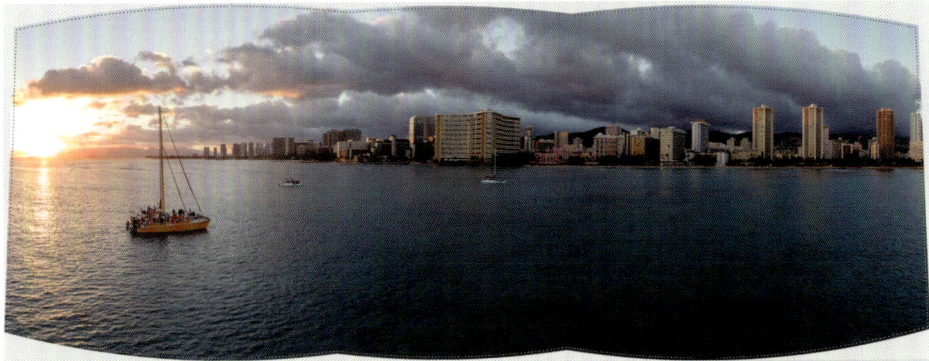

FIGURE 3.47

Now we want to inverse the selection so we are only selecting the transparent areas with the overlap (**FIGURE 3.48**).

5. Choose Select > Inverse.

6. Click Generative Fill in the Task Bar.

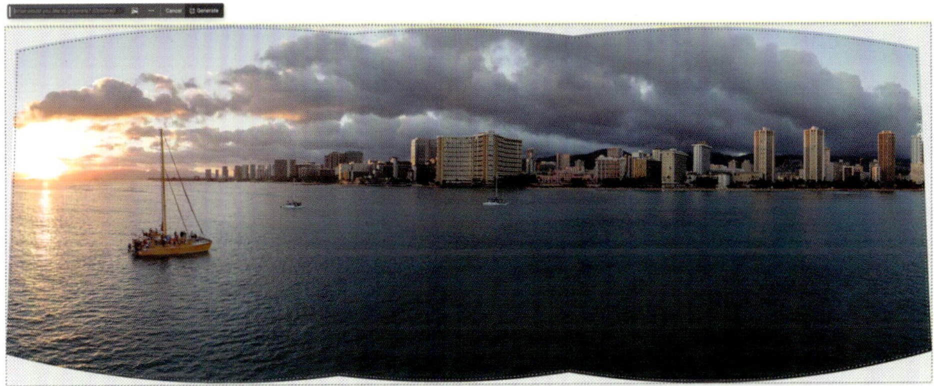

FIGURE 3.48

7. Leave the text prompt blank and click Generate.

Notice the edges are nicely filled up with similar content to the surrounding pixels (**FIGURE 3.49**). We managed to preserve more of the image by using Generative Fill.

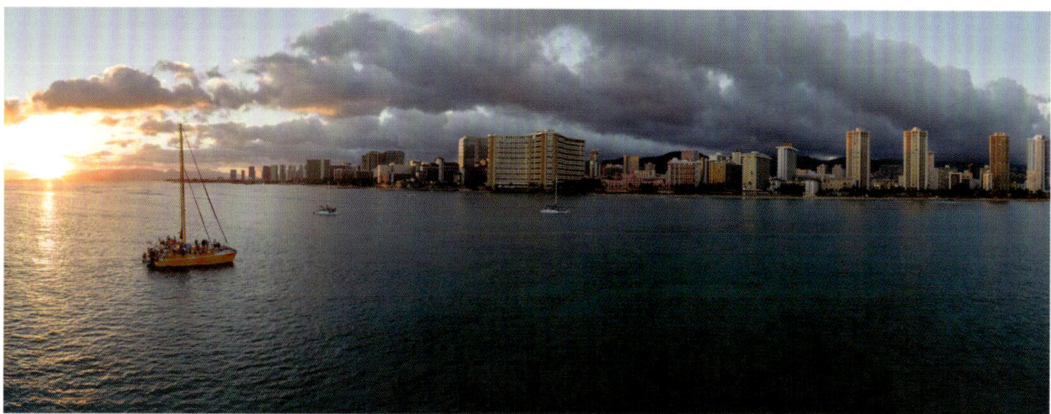

FIGURE 3.49

You may have wondered, "Why you didn't just crop with Generative Expand?" Well, **FIGURE 3.50** shows why—Generative Expand doesn't get all the image.

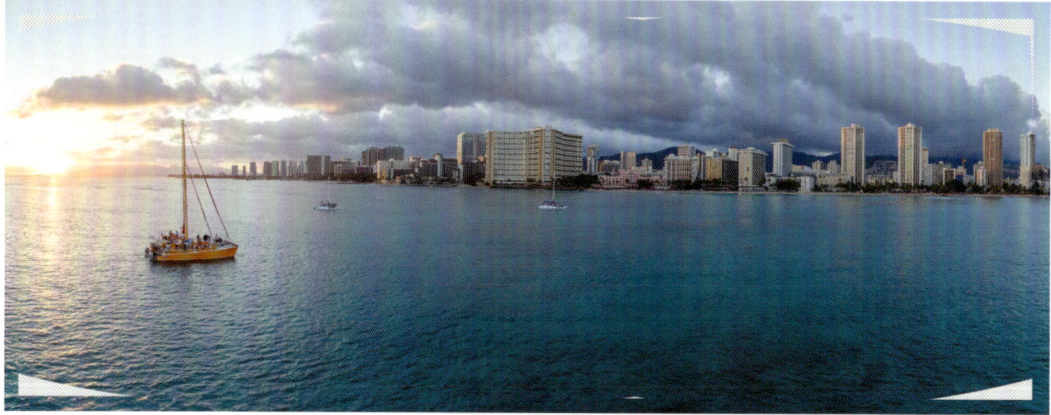

FIGURE 3.50

Fixing Blown-Out Skies

On the panorama we just made, you may have noticed the area around the sun is blown out. Here is another way Generative Fill can help.

1. Make a selection around the blown-out area. The Rectangular Marquee Tool works nicely for this case (**FIGURE 3.51**).

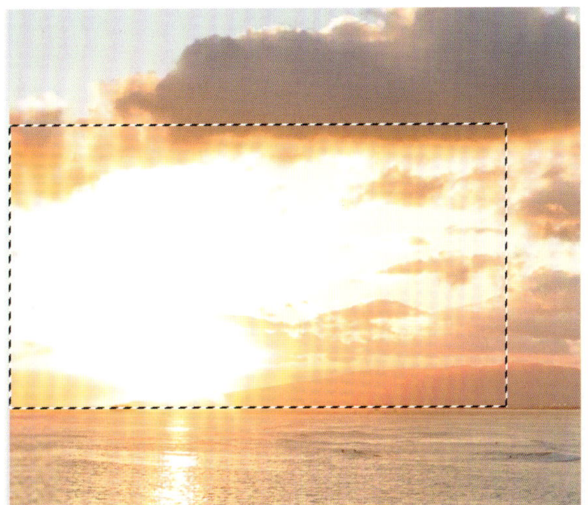

FIGURE 3.51

2. Click on Generative Fill in the Task Bar, type "sun" as the prompt, and click Generate (**FIGURE 3.52**).

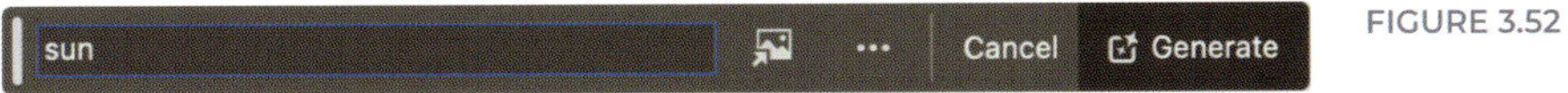

FIGURE 3.52

3. Choose the best variation in the Properties panel (**FIGURE 3.53**).

Notice how much better this looks, and it looks totally natural (**FIGURE 3.54**).

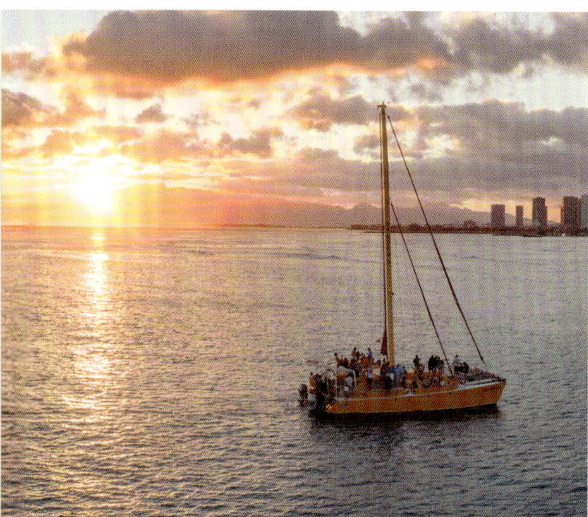

FIGURE 3.53

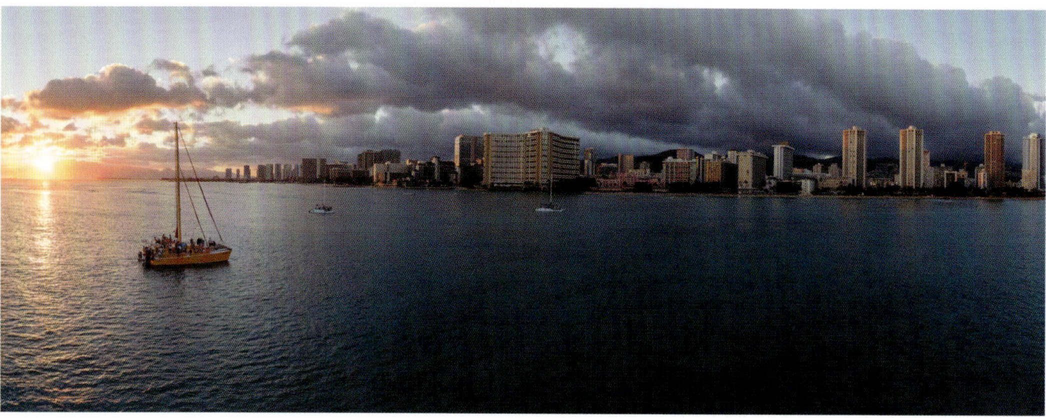

FIGURE 3.54

Fixing Crooked Photos

It happens to us all, especially me, apparently. We are all excited when taking a photo and we forget to level the camera.

We will need to straighten this photo (**FIGURE 3.55**). There used to be a compromise with some methods, and you'd lose a chunk of the photo, but not anymore. There are different ways to straighten an image in Photoshop; we will use the most common way.

1. Choose the Crop Tool from the Tools panel, and make sure Fill is set to Generative Expand in the Options Bar.

2. Drag on the outside corner to rotate the crop. This is the most common way of straightening a photo.

In the past, we were limited to the bounds of the photo. Yes, we can straighten it, but look at what we would be losing; the sides would feel really squeezed (**FIGURE 3.56**).

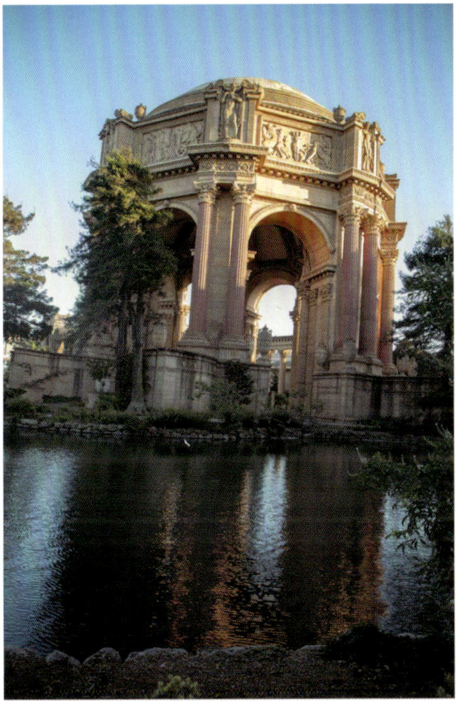

FIGURE 3.55 © Colin Smith

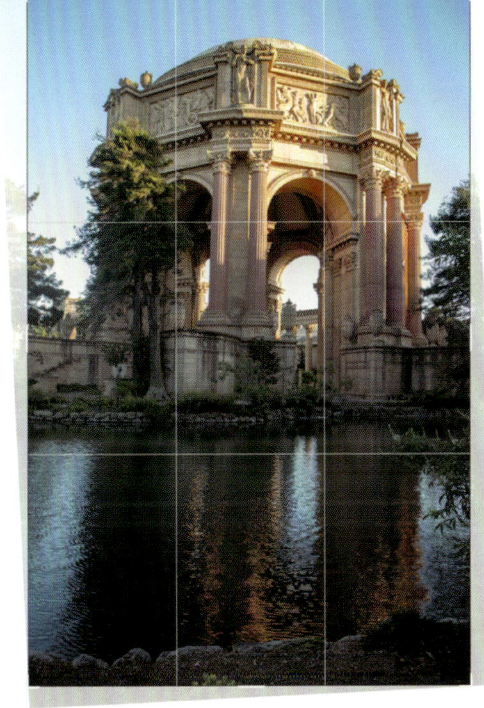

FIGURE 3.56

3. If you want to maintain the original aspect ratio, choose Ratio in the Task Bar (**FIGURE 3.57**). You can choose a specific size if you prefer (covered in a previous tutorial on page 95).

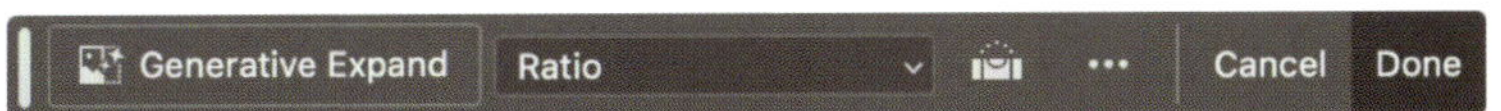

FIGURE 3.57

With Generative Expand, we can outcrop the image as we straighten it.

4. Drag out to enlarge the image frame (**FIGURE 3.58**).

5. Hit the enter key to apply the crop.

Generative Expand will fill up the corners and give us the space we like for a more flexible and spacious crop (**FIGURE 3.59**).

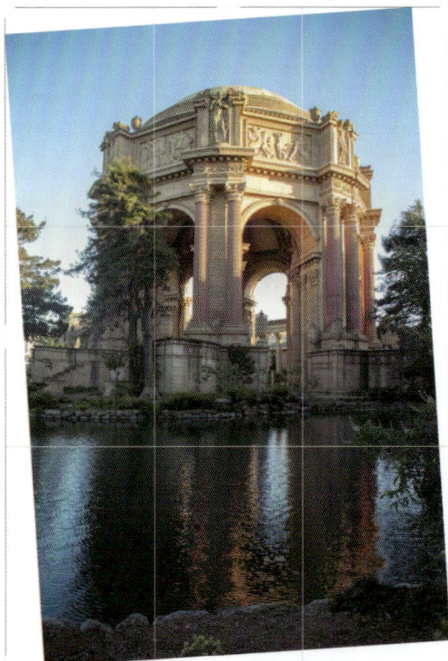

FIGURE 3.58

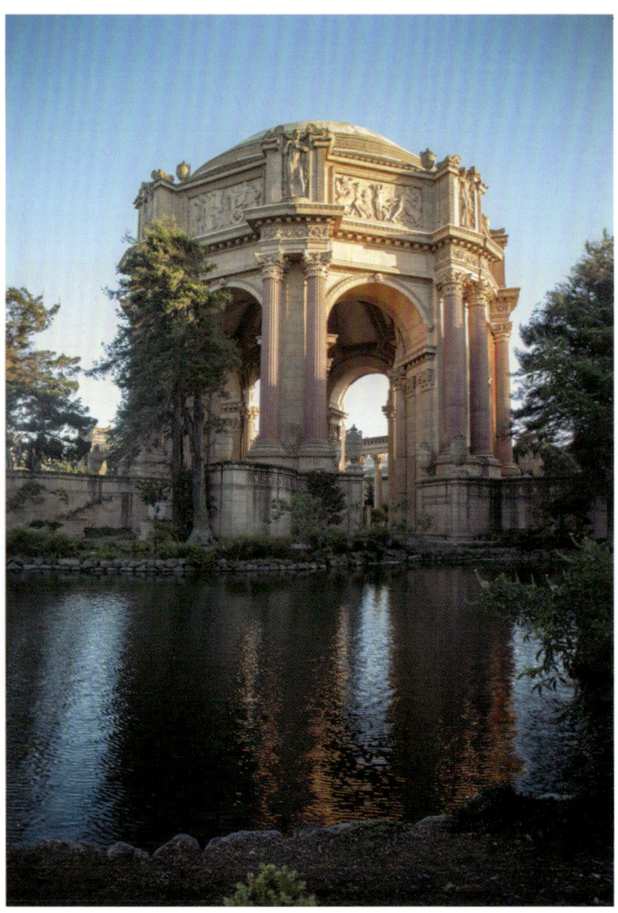

FIGURE 3.59

Enhance the Image on the Edges

You may find the generated edges look a little softer than the rest of the image.

In the Properties panel, roll over your variation thumbnail and you will see an icon with an arrow (**FIGURE 3.60**). This is the Enhance Detail button, which we used on page 74.

6. Click the Enhance Detail button, and Photoshop will use Super Resolution to enhance the details (**FIGURE 3.61**). It enhances the pixels and doesn't use any generative credits.

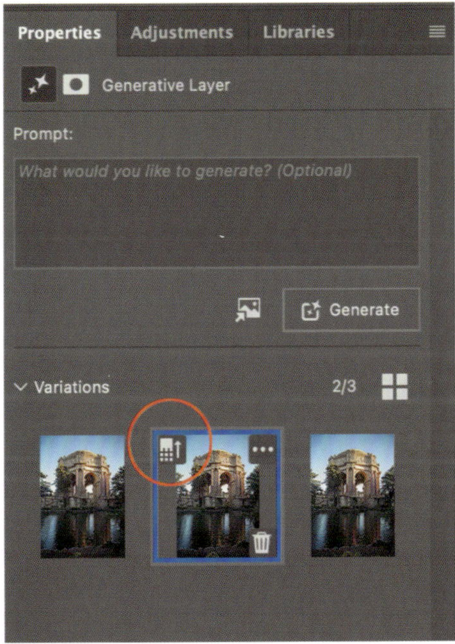

FIGURE 3.60

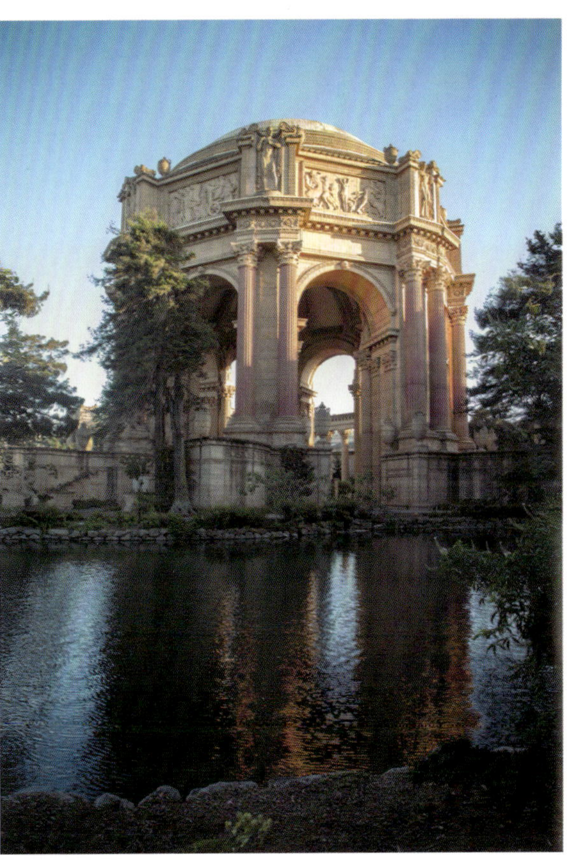

FIGURE 3.61

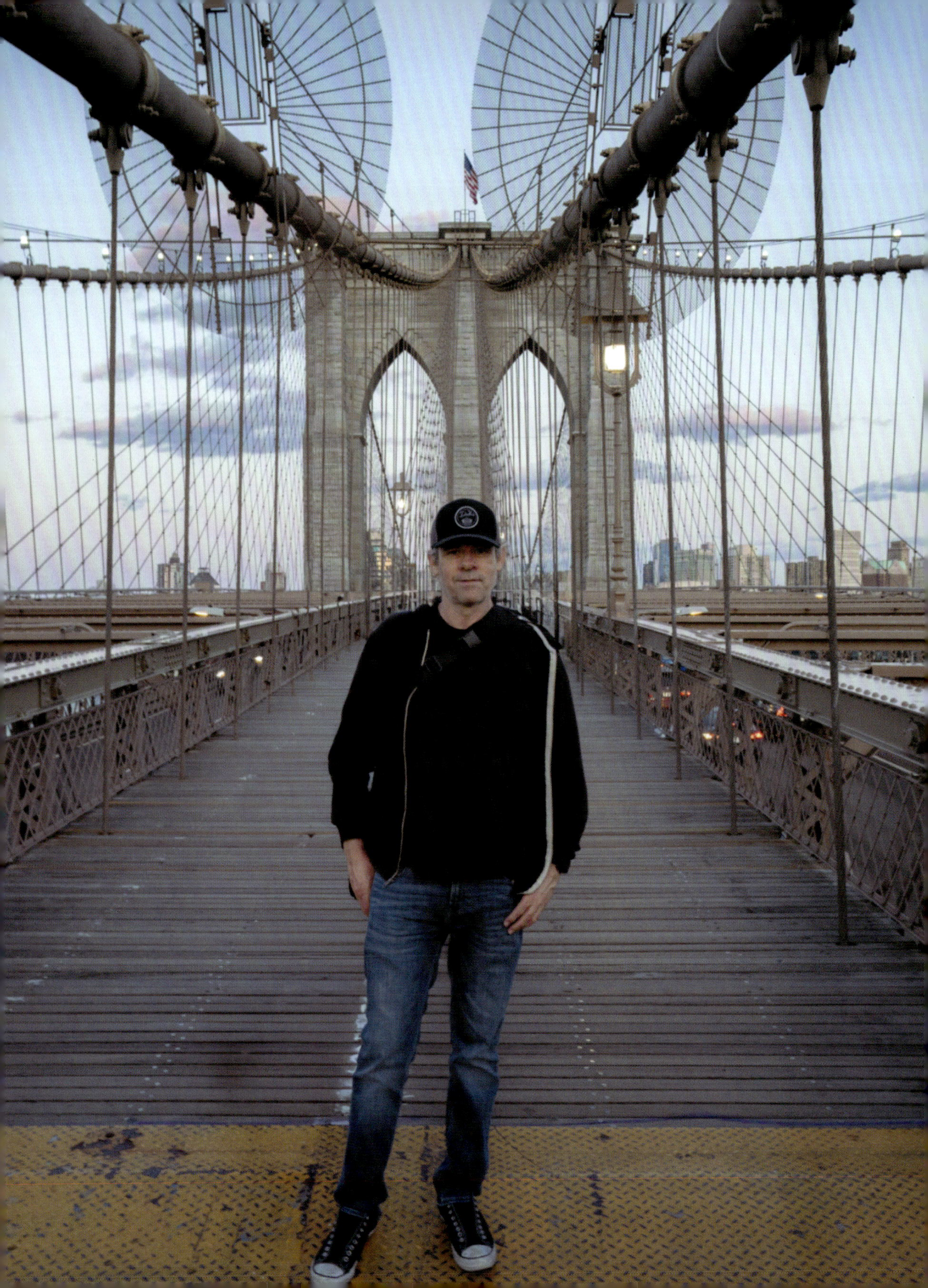

4

REMOVE

This chapter is all about fixing photos. You will learn how to improve your images and fix common problems we face as photographers.

A powerful function of Generative Fill is removing things from images. We have other tools in Photoshop that can handle this task, of course, including the Remove Tool and Content-Aware Fill. Then there are the old standbys, the Patch and Healing Tools and the Clone Stamp. While there is a place for these other tools, Generative Fill will be doing a lot of the heavy lifting going forward, especially as a replacement for Content-Aware Fill.

Here are a couple of useful tips when using Generative Fill to remove things from your images:

- Unless you are trying to replace a selection with something specific, leave the prompt blank. Generative Fill analyzes the surroundings, lighting direction, color, context, and other properties of the photograph and will account for all of these when it generates new pixels. If the results aren't what you desire, you can add the word "remove" to the prompt. This is a reversal from Adobe's previous guidelines, which said not to use instructional prompts. Now they are telling us to use them in Firefly v3.

- If you are finding that Gen Fill is recreating your object instead of completing the desired removal, make certain to completely cover the object you want to remove with the selection. If part of it isn't selected, Gen Fill will reconstruct the object instead.

Removing Anything with Generative Fill

I remember one time I traveled for hours to get to Death Valley, stayed the night, and woke up before sunrise. I hiked out into the dunes to get that pristine shot of the sand dunes at first light.

To my horror, as light began to reveal the dunes, I could see that a couple of other people had the same idea. These people had trampled on the pristine sand, leaving behind massive trails of footprints on top of the ridges on their way to ruin everyone's photos of another spot, wearing bright-orange jackets.

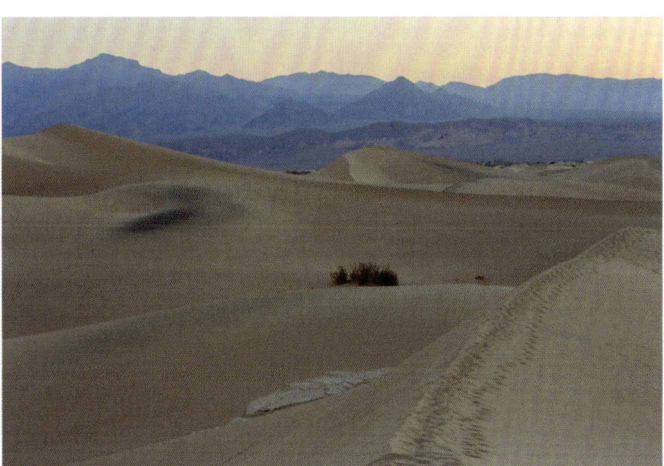

I've heard some people say, "Generative AI has ruined photography." Actually, people like those orange-jacket-clad photobombers ruined it a long time ago. In this case, Generative Fill can save photography. All joking aside, let's remove the footprints from this dune shot.

FIGURE 4.1 © Colin Smith

1. Choose the Lasso Tool from the Tools panel (**FIGURE 4.2**). (Alternatively, you could use the Selection Brush Tool at 100% Opacity, as explained in chapter 2.)

2. Make a selection around the main footprints on the peaks (**FIGURE 4.3**). If you are working on a high-resolution image, select smaller pieces at a time to maximize the resolution limits of Generative Fill.

3. Choose Generative Fill from the Contextual Task Bar (**FIGURE 4.4**).

4. Leave the text prompt field empty.

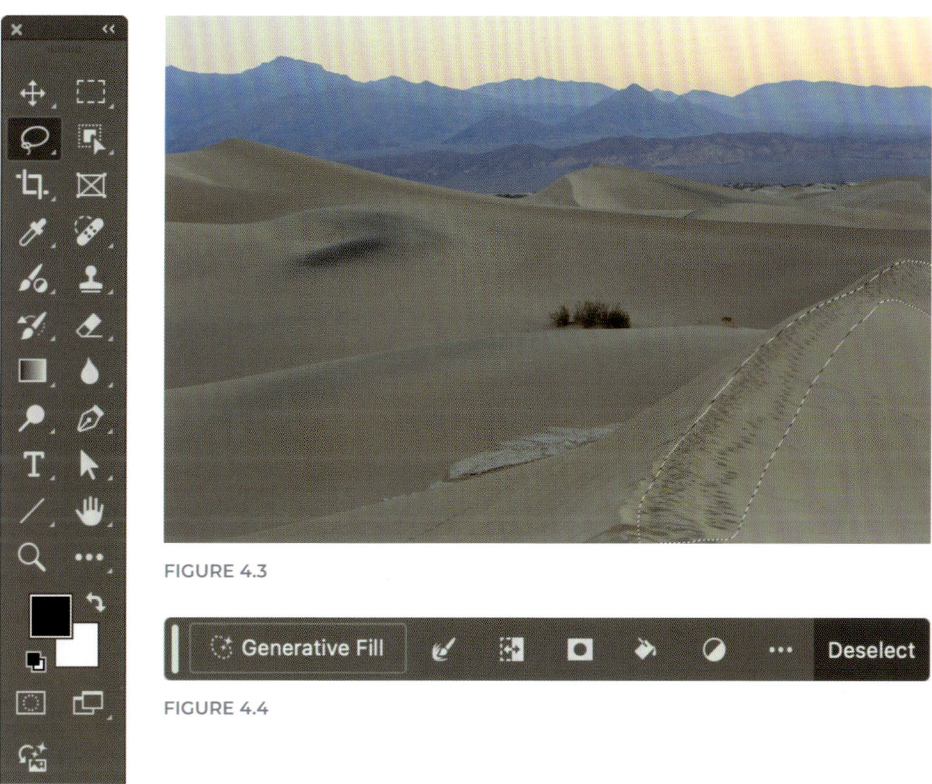

FIGURE 4.3

FIGURE 4.4

FIGURE 4.2

5. Click Generate.

Generative Fill will create a new Generative Layer and blend it into the existing image (**FIGURE 4.5**).

6. Look at the three variations in the Properties panel and choose the one you like the best. If you don't like any of them, click the Generate button again to get three different variations.

7. Repeat these steps on the other footprints lower down on the dune (**FIGURE 4.6**).

It's a good strategy to get the big stuff first, and then move on to the smaller details, such as secondary footprints on other parts of the image.

Don't be afraid to work with multiple Generative Layers. **FIGURE 4.7** shows the image all cleaned up after five different passes.

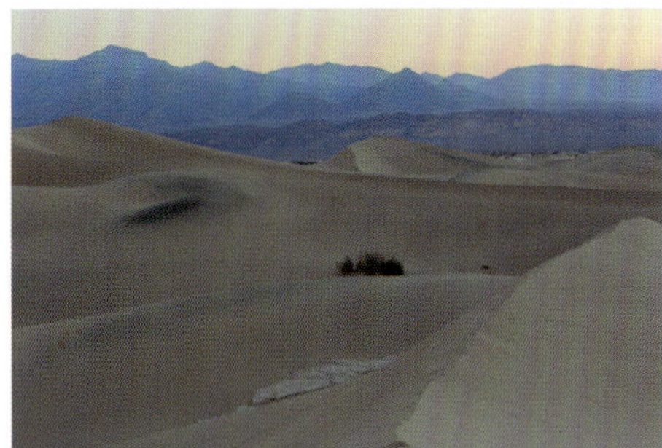

FIGURE 4.5

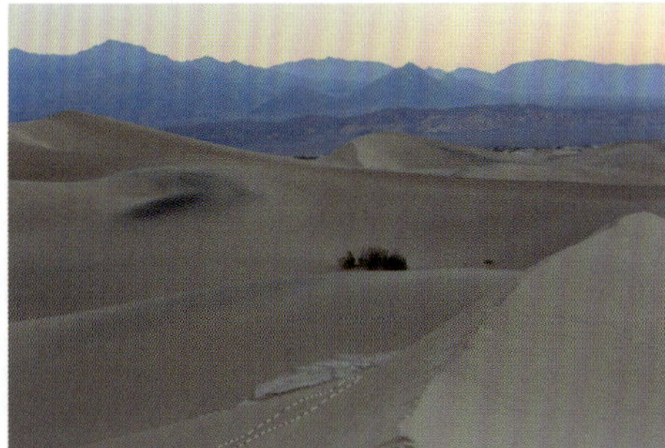

FIGURE 4.6

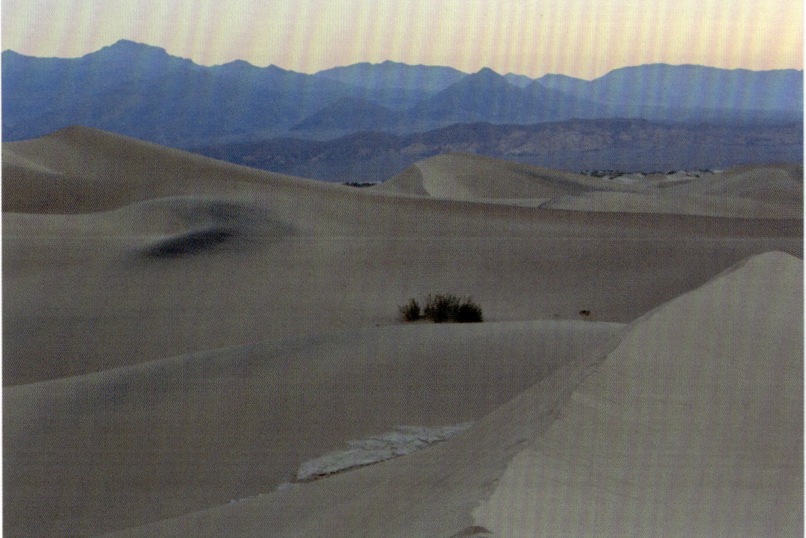

FIGURE 4.7

Removing People from a Photograph

As travel hot spots get more and more crowded, I imagine a lot of people will be using AI tools to remove crowds. Let's do a basic crowd removal right now.

Here I am at the famed (and ever crowded) Brooklyn Bridge (**FIGURE 4.8**). Let's remove all the people for a clean shot of the bridge.

There are two methods to remove the people. There is an automated method using the AI-powered Remove Tool, and a second method that involves using selections and Generative Fill. We'll walk through both methods here.

Method 1: The Remove Tool with Find Distractions

1. Best practice is to create a new layer first and work on this layer (**FIGURE 4.9**). This will allow us to modify the results with masks.

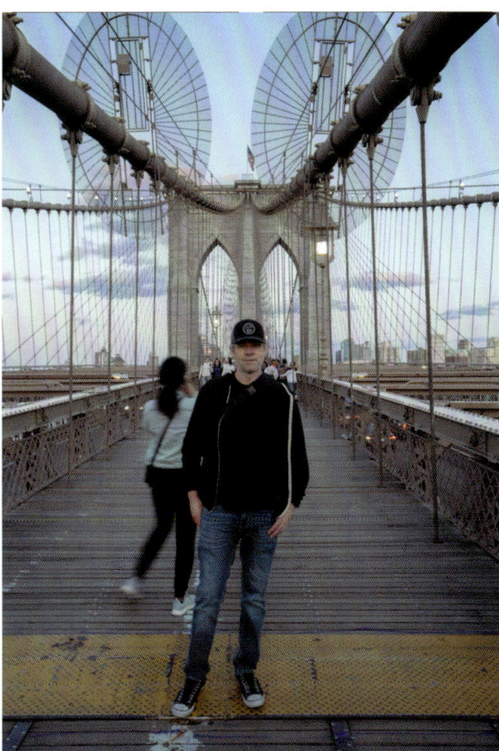

FIGURE 4.8 © Colin Smith

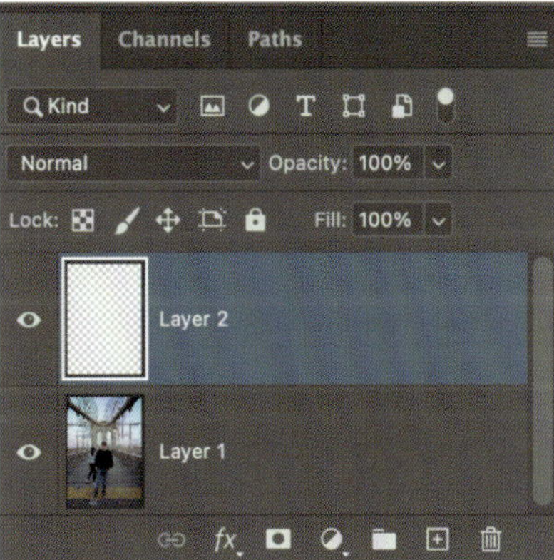

FIGURE 4.9

2. Choose the Remove Tool from the Tools panel (**FIGURE 4.10**). It is nested under the Spot Healing Brush Tool.

3. Turn on Sample All Layers in the Options Bar at the top of the interface (**FIGURE 4.11**); otherwise, the tool won't see anything on the blank layer.

4. Click on Find Distractions in the Options Bar and choose People (**FIGURE 4.12**).

Photoshop will look for people and highlight them. Usually, any people in the background will be highlighted, and the primary subject will be left alone (**FIGURE 4.13**). We can also add to or remove from the selection. We will come back to that soon.

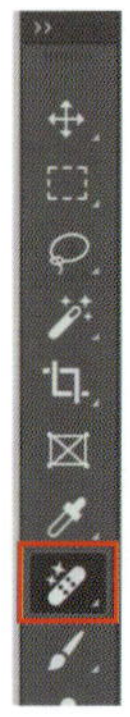

FIGURE 4.10

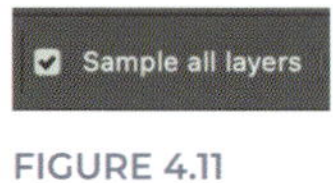

FIGURE 4.11

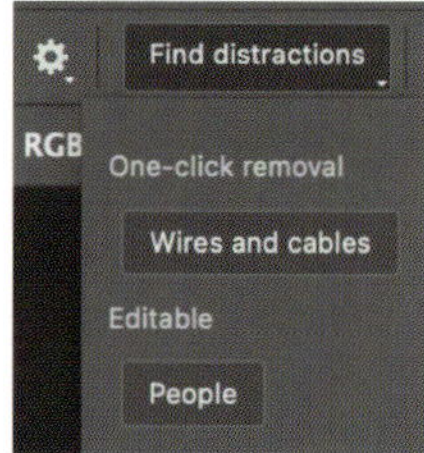

FIGURE 4.12

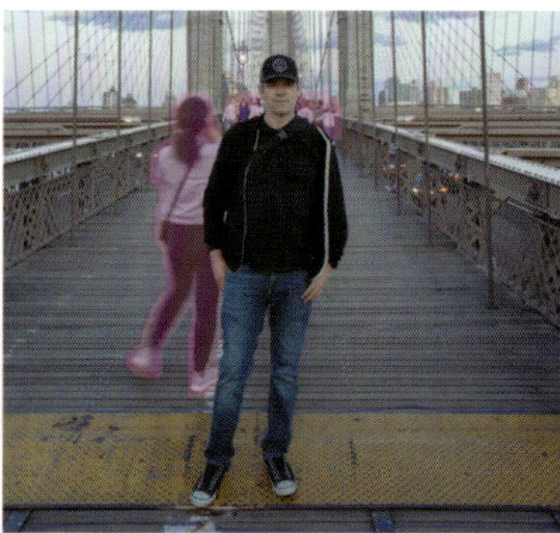

FIGURE 4.13

5. Press Enter or click the check mark in the Options Bar to apply the removal. The selected people will vanish, as if by magic (**FIGURE 4.14**).

This removed all the background people and kept the main subject (me). What if you want to remove all of the people?

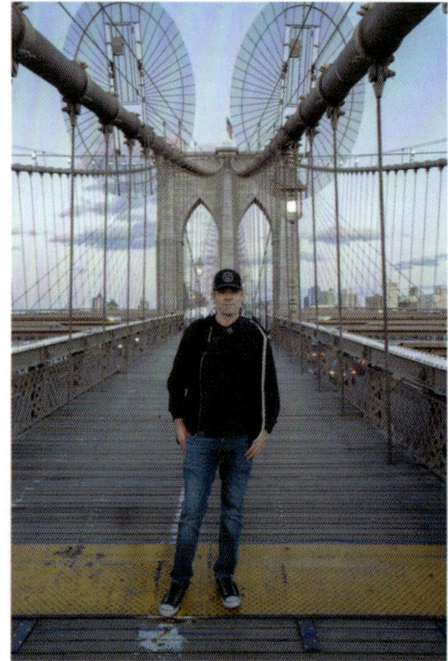

FIGURE 4.14

6. Repeat steps 1–4.

Now we will guide the selection process.

7. Make sure the plus is selected in the Options Bar (**FIGURE 4.15**).

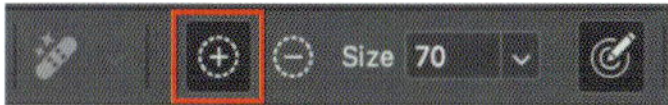

FIGURE 4.15

8. Paint over the other people or objects that you want to remove (**FIGURE 4.16**). If there are areas highlighted that you don't want to remove, hold down Alt/ option and paint to remove the highlight.

9. Press Enter to apply the removal to the selection, and all the people are now gone (**FIGURE 4.17**).

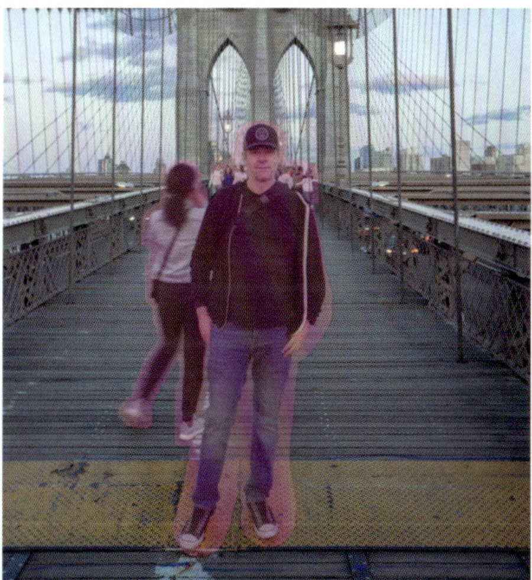

FIGURE 4.16

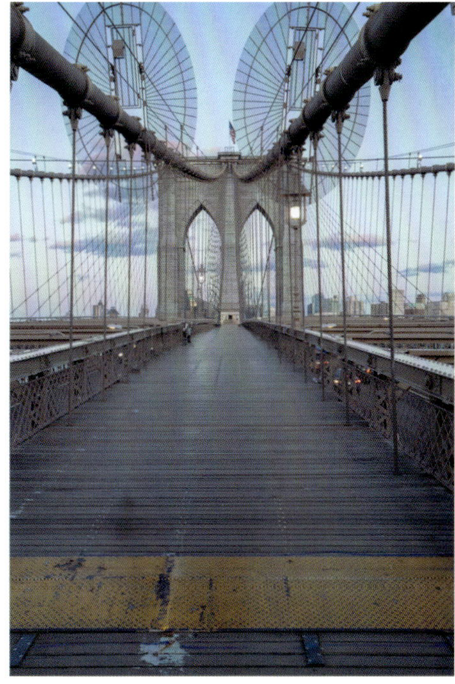

FIGURE 4.17

Method 2: Generative Fill with Selections

Now let's have a look at making the selections manually and using Generative Fill to remove the people. It's good to know multiple methods because sometimes automated things don't work as you'd like them to and you should know how to do it (somewhat) manually. This method also has the advantage of allowing us to choose from different variations.

1. Choose the Lasso Tool from the Tools panel.

2. Make a selection around all the people (**FIGURE 4.18**).

3. Click on Generative Fill in the Contextual Task Bar.

4. Leave the text prompt blank.

5. Click Generate.

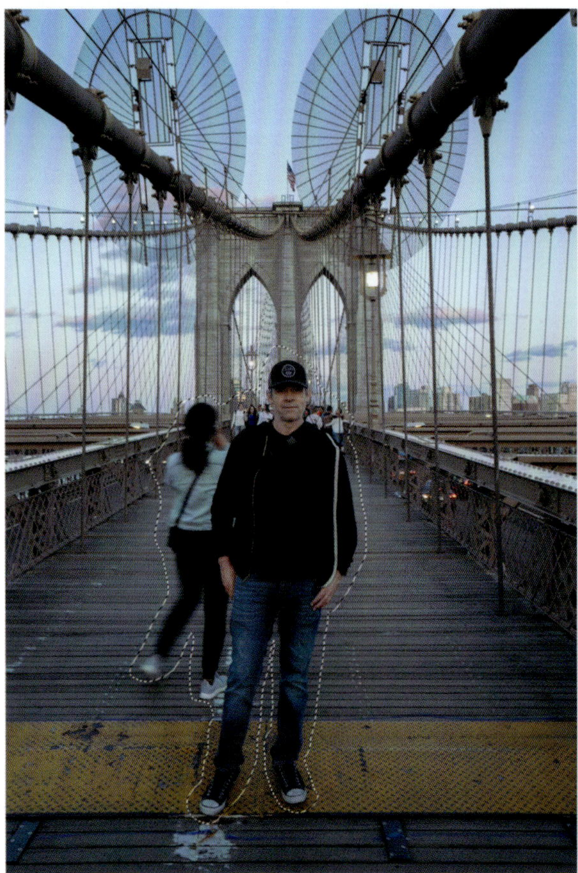

FIGURE 4.18

Notice all the people are removed and it looks great (**FIGURE 4.19**).

If the result isn't what you want, click through the different variations in the Properties panel (**FIGURE 4.20**). If you don't like any of the variations, click Generate to make three more.

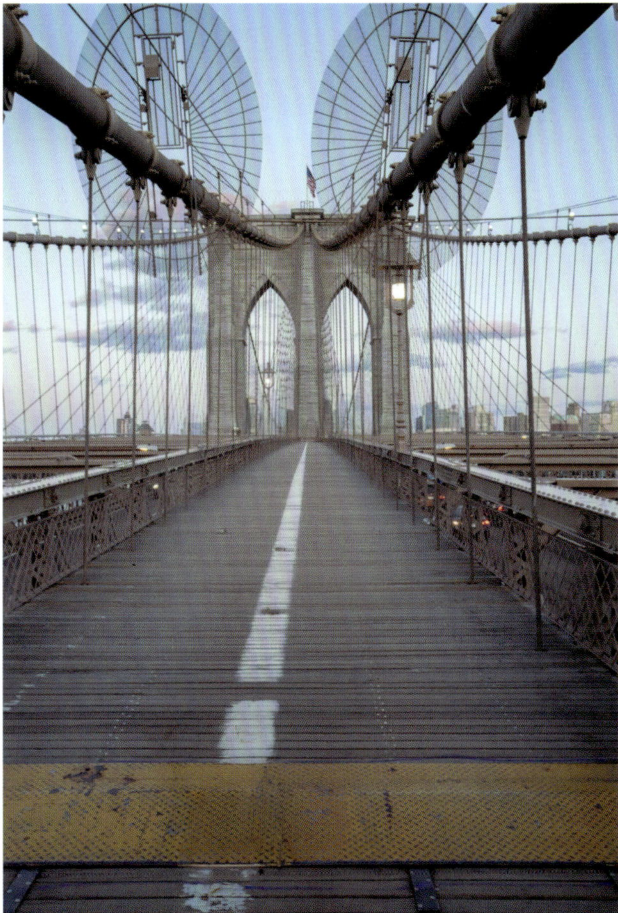

FIGURE 4.19

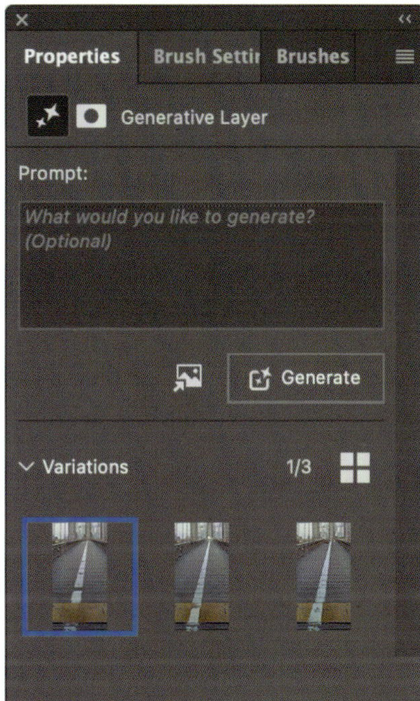

FIGURE 4.20

Remove a Crowd and Keep a Person

Okay, we know we can remove the crowd. What if we want to remove the crowd, but keep the main person in the shot? We need to do a sandwich move here.

Let's perform these steps with that photo of me on the Brooklyn Bridge in New York City (**FIGURE 4.8**).

1. Choose one of the magic tools: either the Magic Wand, the Quick Selection Tool, or the Object Selection Tool (**FIGURE 4.21**).

Once one of these tools is selected, the context-sensitive Options Bar at the top will show Select Subject.

2. Open the Select Subject menu and choose the Cloud option, if you're connected to the internet (**FIGURE 4.22**). The Cloud option will always do a better job because it uses a more advanced algorithm on Adobe's data center (versus being limited to your computer).

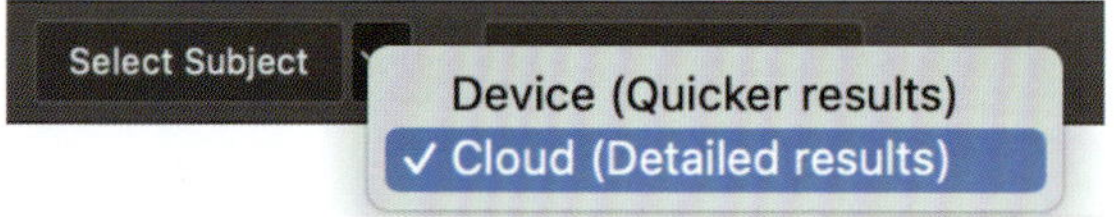

FIGURE 4.21   **FIGURE 4.22**

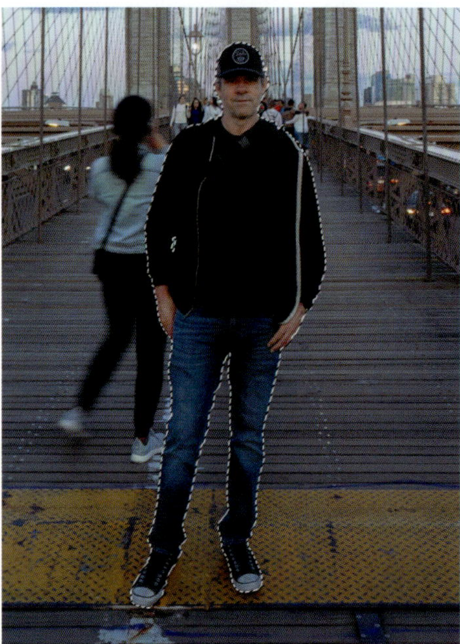

You will see a selection around the person (me) now (**FIGURE 4.23**).

3. Use the Quick Selection and Lasso Tools to fix the selection if you need to.

FIGURE 4.23

4. Press Ctrl+J/command+J (Windows/Mac) to copy the selection to a new layer. Now you have preserved the person and you can apply Generative Fill underneath.

5. Choose the Background layer (**FIGURE 4.24**).

6. Make a selection around the people (**FIGURE 4.25**). Don't worry if you go over the main person, as they are nice and safe on the top layer now.

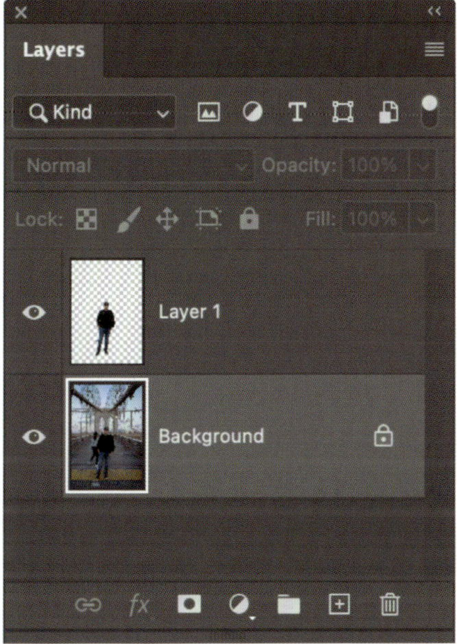

FIGURE 4.24

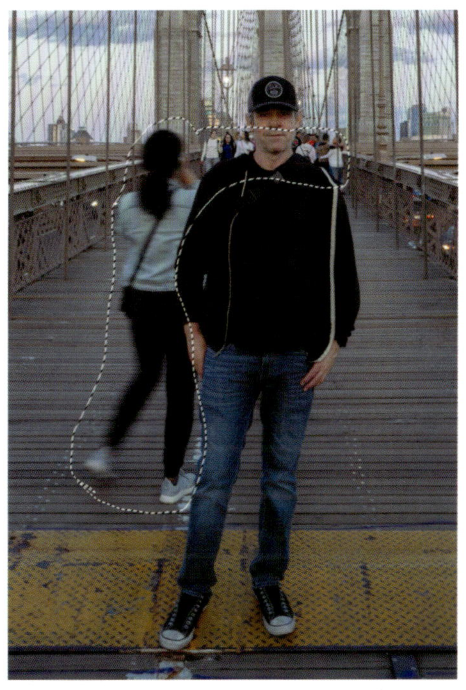

FIGURE 4.25

7. Choose Generative Fill in the Contextual Task Bar.

8. Leave the text prompt field empty.

9. Click Generate.

10. Choose the best variation in the Properties panel, or click Generate again if you don't like any of the variations.

> **TIP** If you generate a few times and still don't like the results, delete the Generative Layer and start again with a different selection.

Now we have achieved our goal (**FIGURE 4.26**).

If you look at the Layer's panel, you will see the Generative Fill sandwiched between the two layers (**FIGURE 4.27**). Use the layer mask to refine the image if you need to.

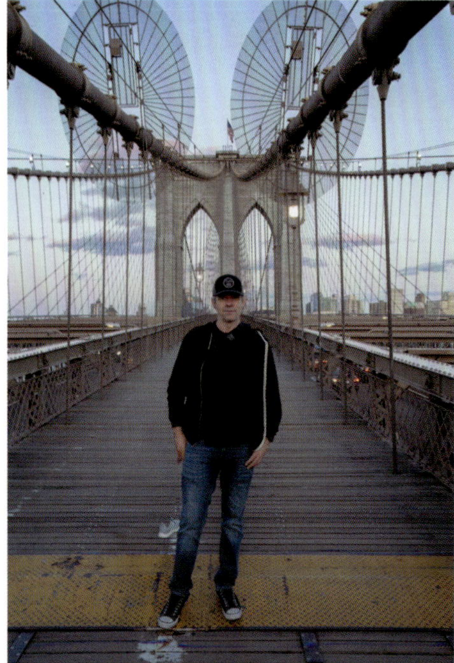

FIGURE 4.26

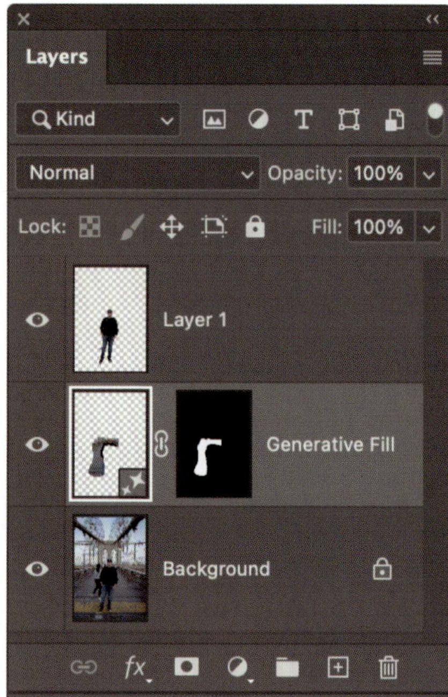

FIGURE 4.27

Using Quick Mask to Make Selections

A different way to make selections is with Quick Mask. Quick Mask is very useful for working with Generative Fill because it's as simple as painting on a selection. Alternatively, you can use the Selection Brush Tool in a similar way. The Selection Brush Tool is easier to use—you simply choose a size and paint with it—but Quick Mask provides more brush options and can be used in combination with other selection tools, whereas the Selection Brush Tool cannot.

1. To enter Quick Mask, press Q or click the icon at the bottom of the Tools panel (**FIGURE 4.28**).

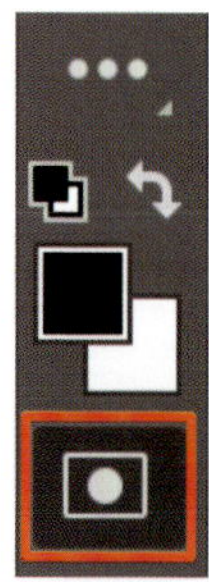

FIGURE 4.28

2. Choose a black brush and paint over the area you would like to select. The area you paint will appear red on the image (**FIGURE 4.29**).

3. Press Q once more, and the mask is converted to a selection (**FIGURE 4.30**).

If you press Q again, it will go back to a mask. This is basically a paintable selection.

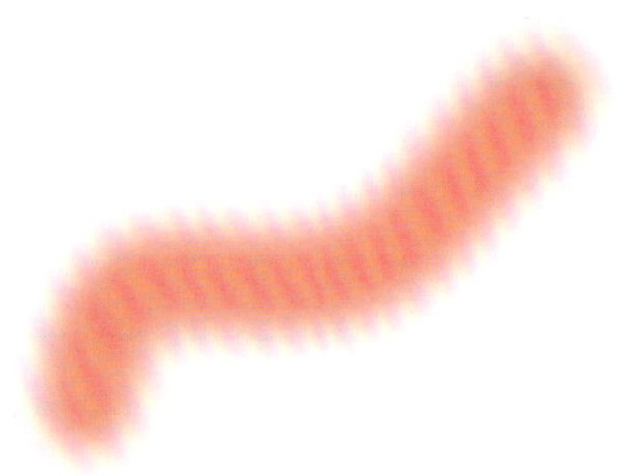

FIGURE 4.29

FIGURE 4.30

Note that there are two different settings for Quick Mask mode—Color Indicates: Masked Areas and Color Indicates: Selected Areas (**FIGURE 4.31**). When you are painting in Quick Mask mode, these appear to be identical. Where they differ is when you exit Quick Mask mode and the selection is made. If Color Indicates: Selected Areas is on, your brushstrokes will become the selection. If Color Indicates: Masked Areas is on, the opposite will happen— everything EXCEPT the brushstrokes will be selected.

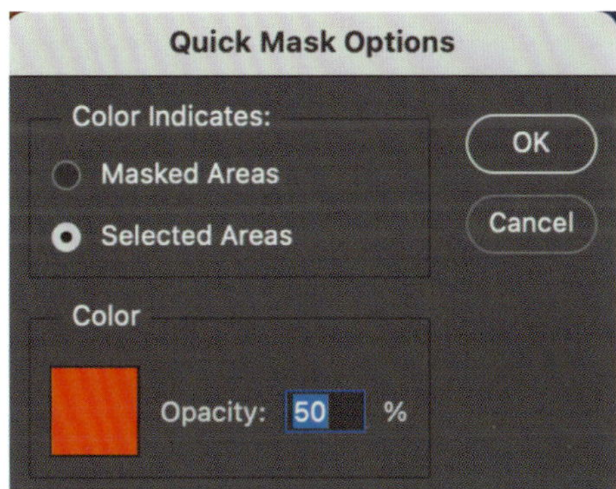

FIGURE 4.31

To access the Quick Mask Options, double-click the Quick Mask button to open the dialog. Here, you can choose an option for Color Indicates, and you can also change the Color and Opacity of the Quick Mask overlay.

If you realize the wrong Color Indicates option was enabled when you made your selection, it's easy to fix—just press Ctrl+Shift+I/command+shift+I (Windows/Mac) to inverse the selection.

In the Tools panel, the Quick Mask icon indicates which mode you are in (**FIGURES 4.32 AND 4.33**). To toggle the mode without opening the Quick Mask Options dialog, Alt-click/option-click (Windows/Mac) on the Quick Mask icon.

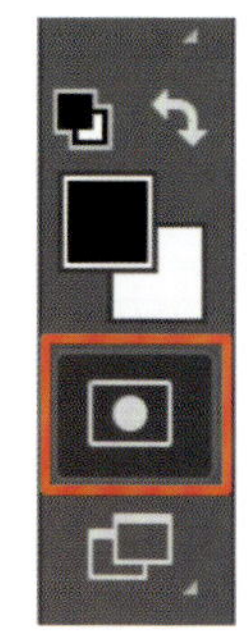

FIGURE 4.32 Color Indicates: Selected Areas

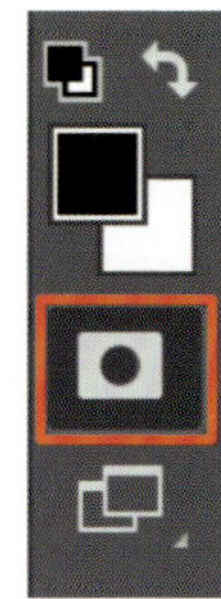

FIGURE 4.33 Color Indicates: Masked Areas

Retouching: Removing a Tattoo

Generative Fill is a great tool for performing tasks like removing tattoos. This used to be a difficult task, but not anymore.

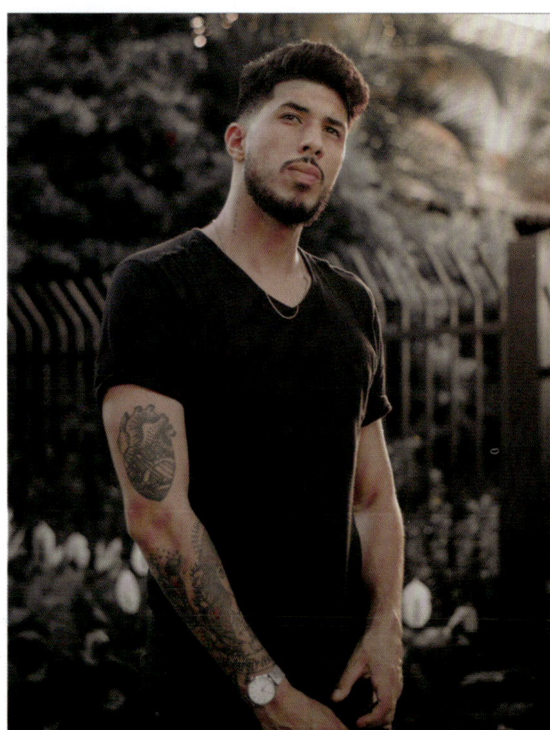

FIGURE 4.34 © Allef Vinicius – Unsplash

Let's remove the tattoos from the arm of the model in **FIGURE 4.34**. This would be very difficult without Generative Fill.

1. Choose the Quick Selection Tool (**FIGURE 4.35**).

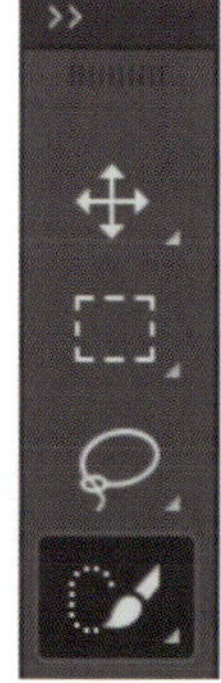

FIGURE 4.35

2. Make a selection of the arm (**FIGURE 4.36**).

> **TIP** If you select too much, hold down Alt/option (Widows/Mac) and click to remove from the selection.

3. Press the Q key. This puts us into Quick Mask mode and the selection is now a mask (**FIGURE 4.37**).

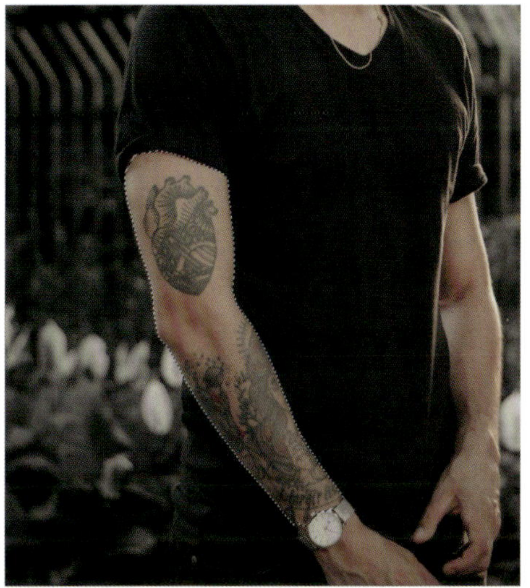

FIGURE 4.36

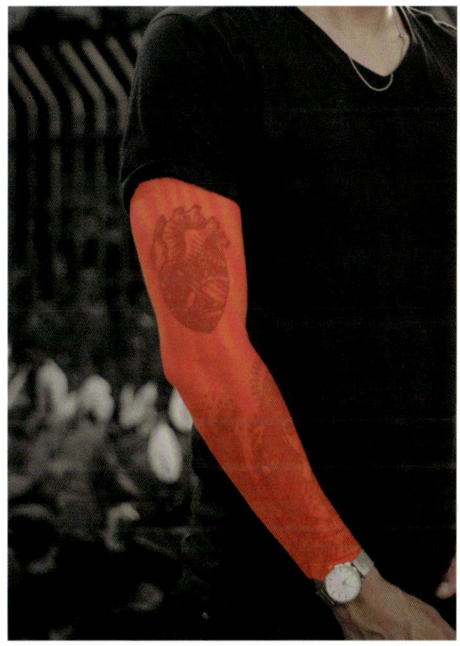

FIGURE 4.37

4. Choose a brush with a hard edge to help us get the fine details. To adjust the Hardness of the brush, go to the Options Bar at the top of the interface and click on the drop-down menu next to the size of the brush (**FIGURE 4.38**). Set the Hardness to 100%.

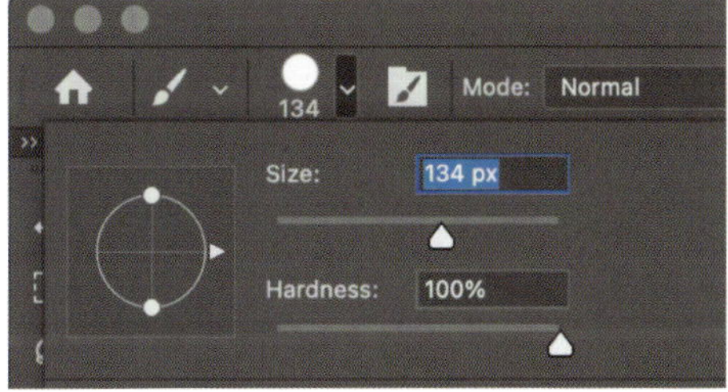

FIGURE 4.38

5. In the Tools panel, set the foreground color to white. White removes from the mask while black adds to it.

6. Paint away the areas that don't have a tattoo (**FIGURE 4.39**). The Quick Mask makes it easy to work with selections.

7. Tap the Q key to convert the mask to a selection (**FIGURE 4.40**).

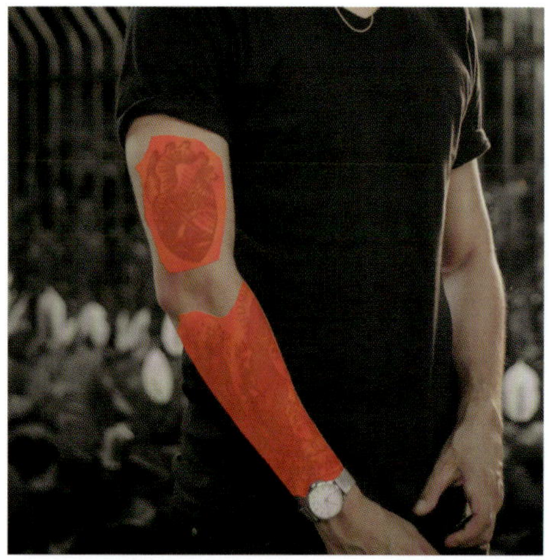

FIGURE 4.39

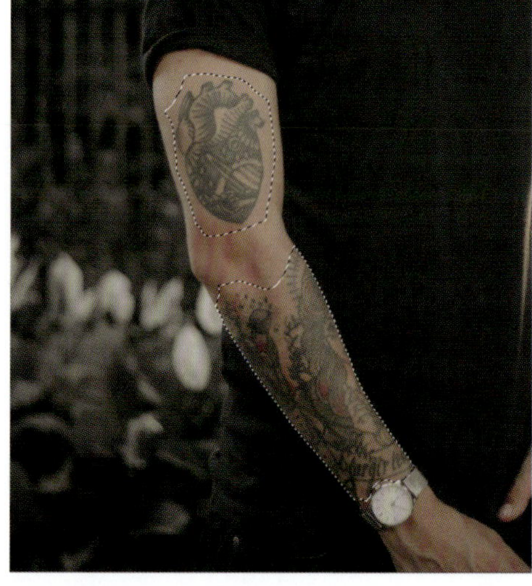

FIGURE 4.40

8. In the Contextual Task Bar, click Generative Fill (**FIGURE 4.41**).

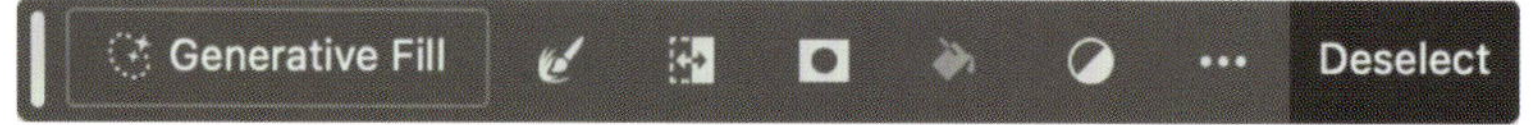

FIGURE 4.41

9. Leave the text prompt blank because we want Generative Fill to be completely influenced by the existing image.

10. Click Generate.

Notice the tattoos are entirely removed (**FIGURE 4.42**).

This next step is completely optional. Often, the result will look great, but sometimes it looks a little too smooth. In this case, we'll change the layer blending mode.

11. In the Layers panel, click on the word Normal and you will see the other blending modes. Choose Lighten (**FIGURE 4.43**).

This allows some of the brighter contour from the original arm to show through, while still hiding the darker areas. This maintains a more natural appearance (**FIGURE 4.44**).

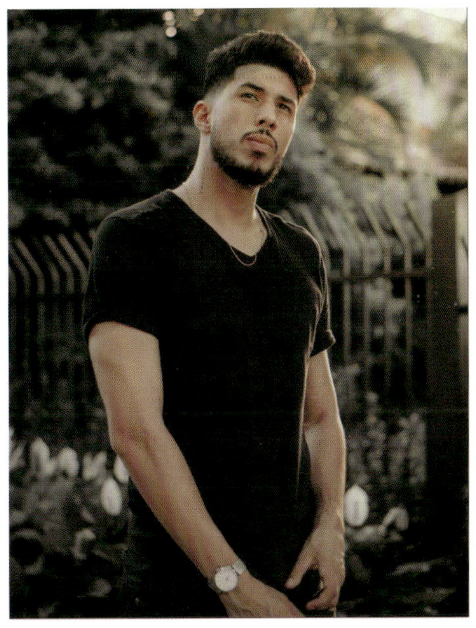

FIGURE 4.42

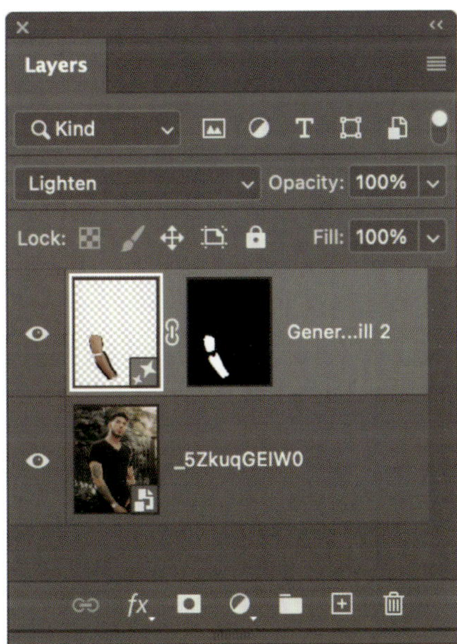

FIGURE 4.43

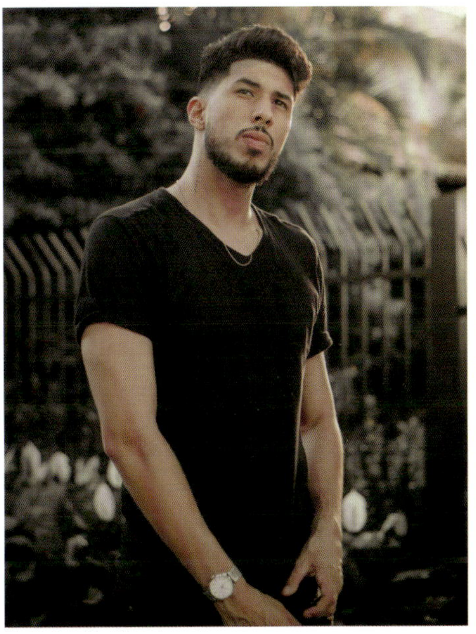

FIGURE 4.44

Removing Reflections from Glasses

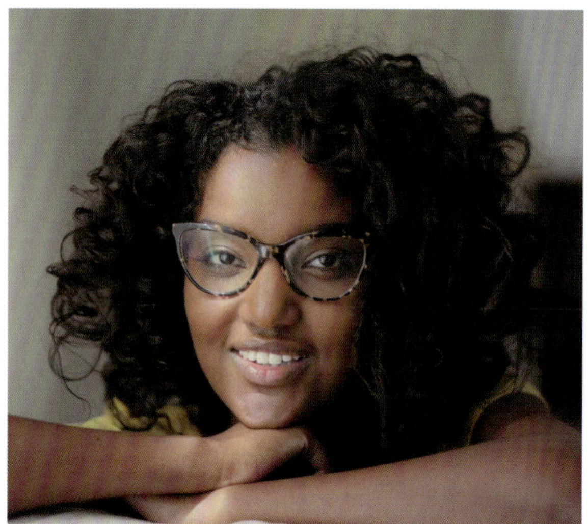

Many of us are going to face reflections on glasses at some point. Let's use Generative Fill to fix the reflections in this example image (**FIGURE 4.45**).

TIP To minimize reflections on glasses while photographing a person with an elevated light source—like a studio light or the sun—tilt the glasses down slightly.

FIGURE 4.45 © Andrea Piacquadio – Pexels

We'll start with the Selection Brush Tool (Quick Mask or the Lasso Tool would work well too):

1. Paint over the first reflection (**FIGURE 4.46**). It's best to tackle them one at a time, rather than trying to remove all the reflections at once.

2. Click Generative Fill in the Contextual Task Bar.

3. Leave the text prompt field empty and click Generate.

4. Choose the best variation in the Properties panel.

The worst reflection is now gone (**FIGURE 4.47**).

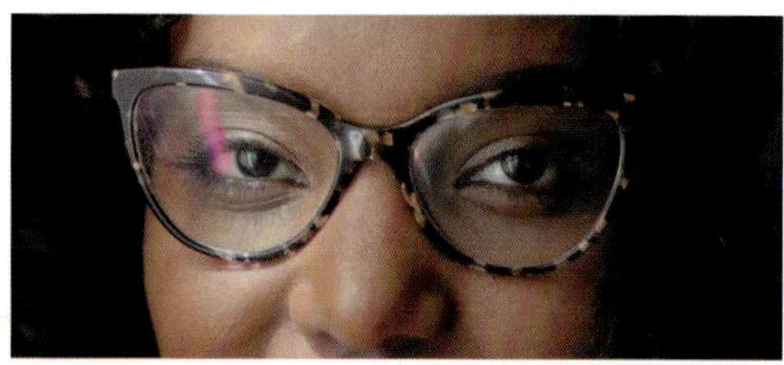

FIGURE 4.46

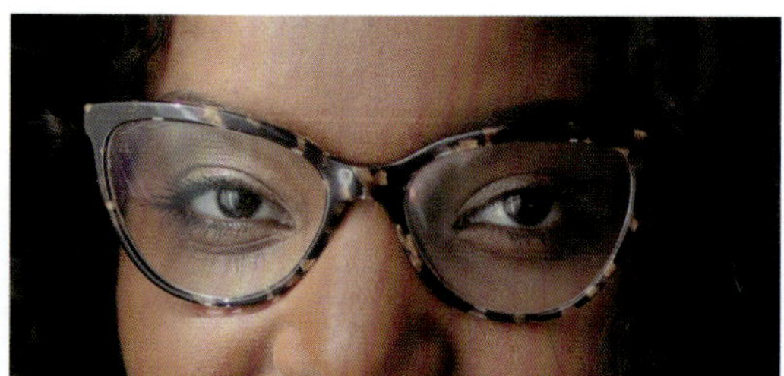

FIGURE 4.47

5. Paint over the next reflection (**FIGURE 4.48**). We started with the worst reflection, and we'll work your way through them from worst to least.

6. Click Generative Fill in the Task Bar.

7. Leave the text prompt field empty and click Generate.

8. Choose the best variation in the Properties panel (**FIGURE 4.49**).

Let's work on the other lens.

9. Paint over the top reflection (**FIGURE 4.50**). Be careful to select the entire reflection, but avoid selecting the frames from the glasses.

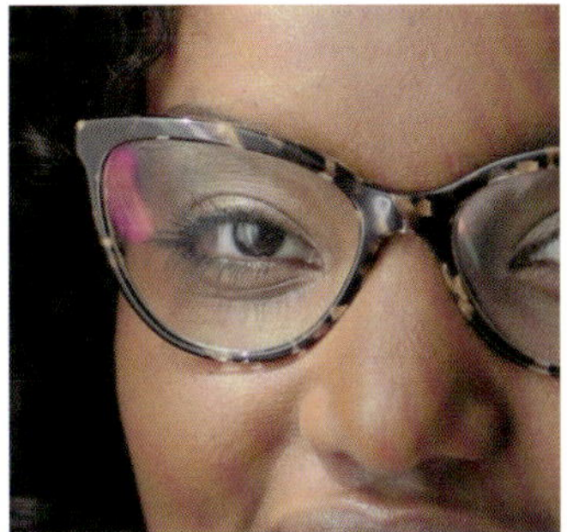

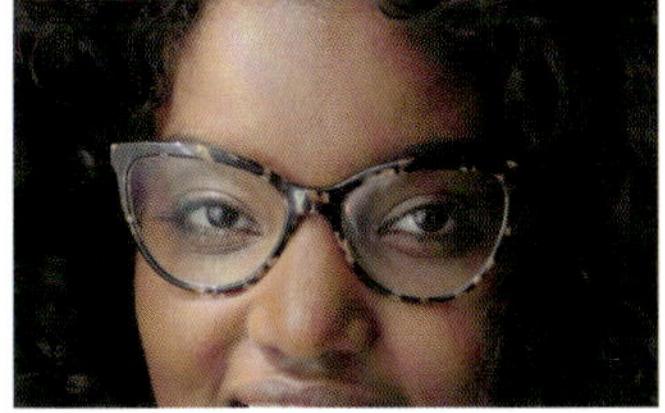

FIGURE 4.49

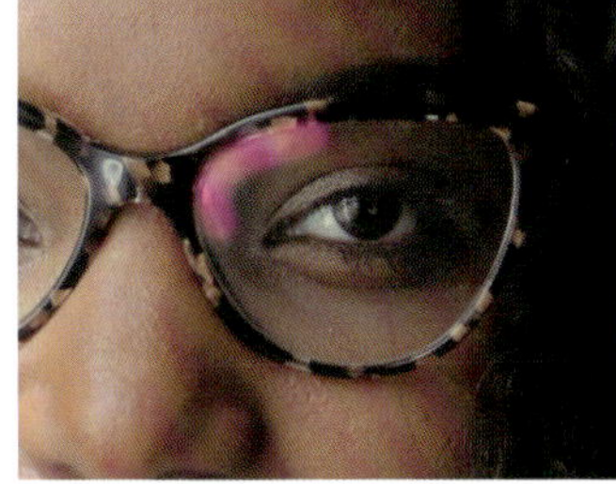

FIGURE 4.50

FIGURE 4.48

Click Generate and see how much better the glasses look (**FIGURE 4.51**).

You don't have to remove all the glare and make it look like there is no glass in the frames, but you do want to remove the distracting reflections.

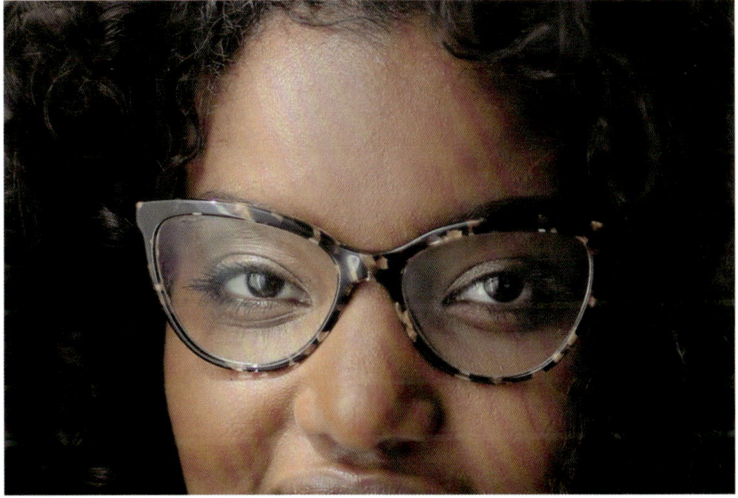

FIGURE 4.51

Combining Different Variations

Every time you apply Generative Fill, you get a different result. Sometimes it's close to what you're looking for; other times, it's wildly different. A common occurrence is when part of a variation looks perfect, but another part doesn't. Sometimes the perfect result is shared across two or more variations. We can use this to our advantage and combine different variations.

Here we have a number of people climbing the steps to the top of Diamond Head Summit Trail (**FIGURE 4.52**). You will almost never find these stairs without people on them. Let's remove the people.

1. Choose the Lasso Tool and make a selection around the group of people (**FIGURE 4.53**).

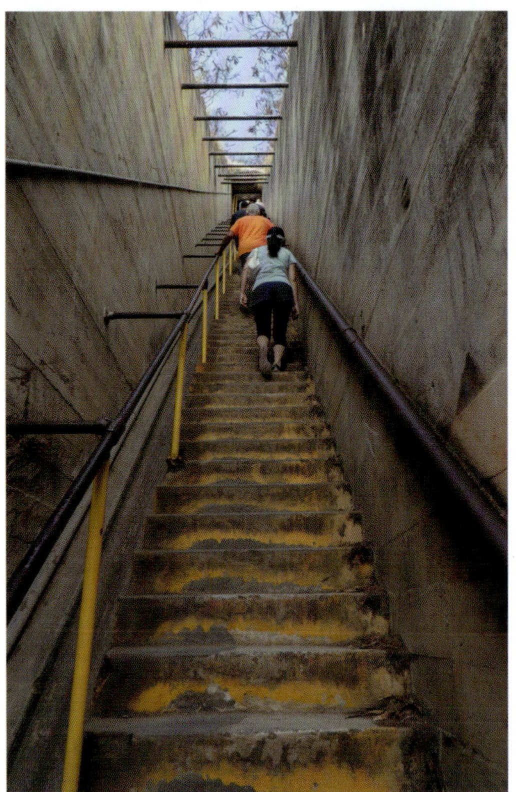

FIGURE 4.52 © Colin Smith

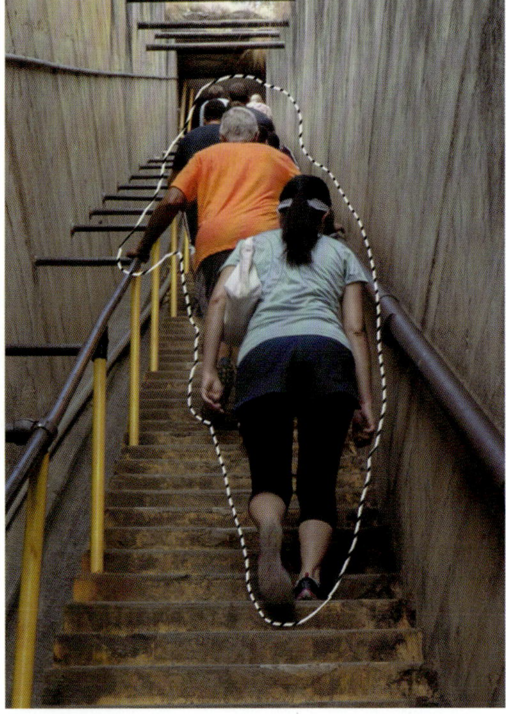

FIGURE 4.53

> **NOTE** I've tried using Select Subject and the Object Selection Tool and haven't had consistently great results when removing objects. I suspect, because Generative Fill is influenced by the shape of the selection, if it's a recognizable silhouette, it tends to try and create the object that fits the silhouette. At least for now, I try to make the selection more of a blob. This will probably change over time.

2. Click on Generative Fill in the Task Bar.

3. We want to remove the people, so leave the text field blank and click Generate.

As always, three variations will be generated. If you don't like any of them, press Generate once again to make three more.

In my Properties panel, variation number 3 has the best version of the opening at the top, but the rail on the left is crooked (**FIGURES 4.54 AND 4.55**).

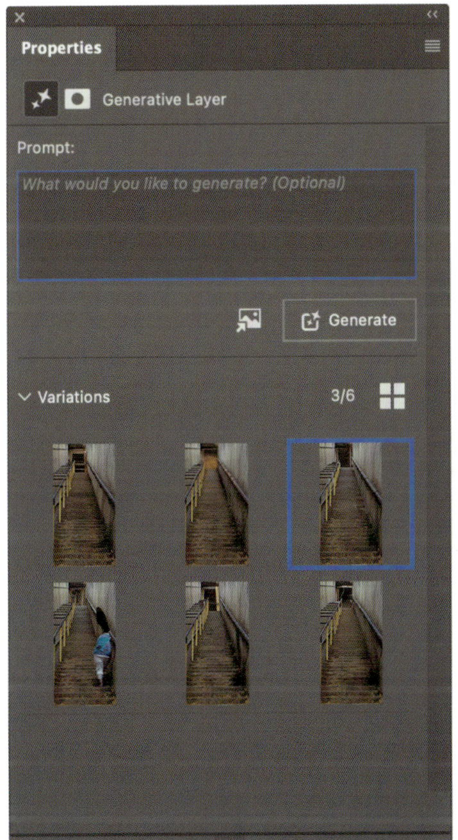

FIGURE 4.54

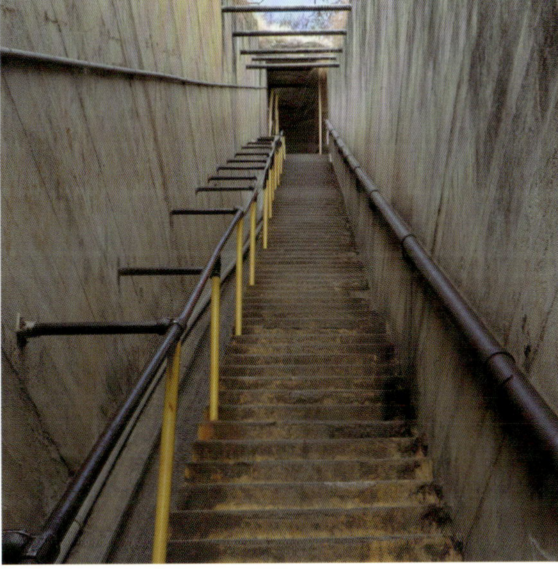

FIGURE 4.55

Variation number 6 has a nice unbroken handrail on the left; however, there are now extra stairs at the top (**FIGURE 4.56**).

The solution is to combine variation 6 with the top of variation number 3.

4. With variation 6 selected in the Properties panel, duplicate the Generative Layer by pressing Ctrl+J/command+J (Windows/Mac), or by dragging the layer onto the New Layer icon in the Layers panel (**FIGURE 4.57**).

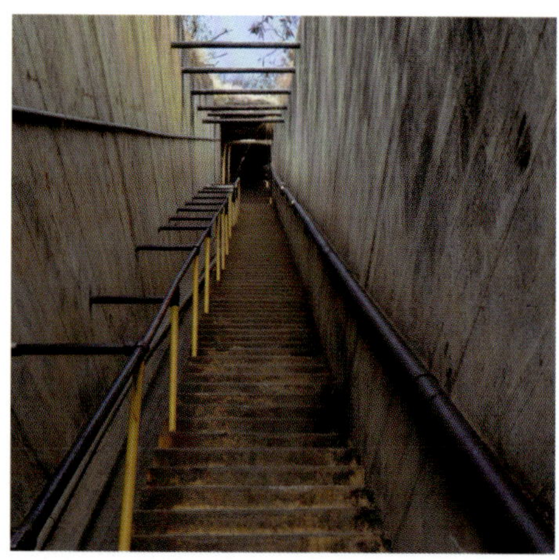

FIGURE 4.56

Because these are Generative Layers, all the variations are a part of the layer, even after we duplicate it. We can change the variation on any of the Generative Layers.

5. With the top layer selected in the Layers panel, head to the Properties panel and click on variation 3 (**FIGURE 4.58**).

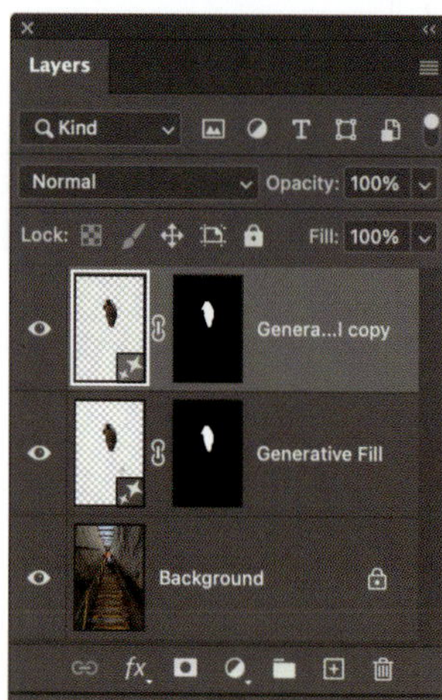

FIGURE 4.57

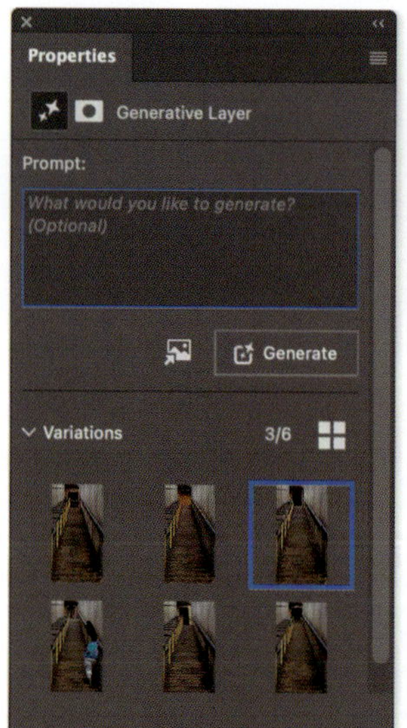

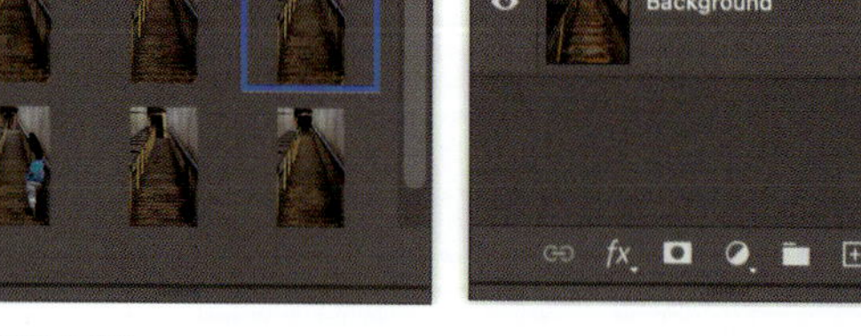

FIGURE 4.58

Now we need to use a Layer Mask to combine the variations. It just so happens that the Generative Layer already gives us a Layer Mask.

6. Choose that mask by clicking on it in the Layers panel (**FIGURE 4.59**). You will see a white border around the mask thumbnail to indicate that it's selected.

A Layer Mask shows or hides its contents based on its darkness. If we add white, the corresponding areas of the layer will be revealed, and the underlying layers will be hidden. If we add black, the layer will be hidden and we will see the pixels underneath.

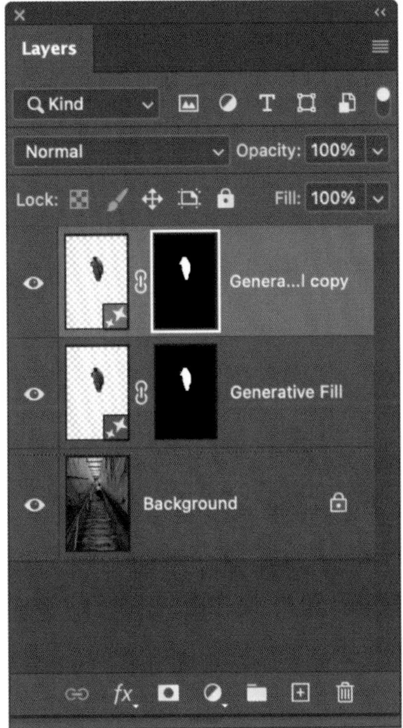

FIGURE 4.59

> **NOTE** It's been said, "White Reveals and Black Conceals." I find this saying confusing—it reveals or conceals what? The layer or the underlying layers? I have an easier way to remember masking. If you turn on the lights, you can see—it's white light and you can see that layer. Turn off the lights and it's black and you cannot see the layer.

What we want to do is hide part of the top layer and allow the layer underneath—the layer with the nice handrail—to show through.

7. Choose a soft-edged brush from the Tools panel. The B key chooses the Brush Tool.

8. Choose black as the foreground color (to turn off the lights where we paint; **FIGURE 4.60**).

9. Paint away the bottom part of the layer with the mask. If you make a mistake and need to paint back some of the layer, paint with white to show (turn on the lights) that part of the layer.

Now we have combined the two variations, and no one knows there used to be people obstructing our photo of the steps (**FIGURE 4.61**).

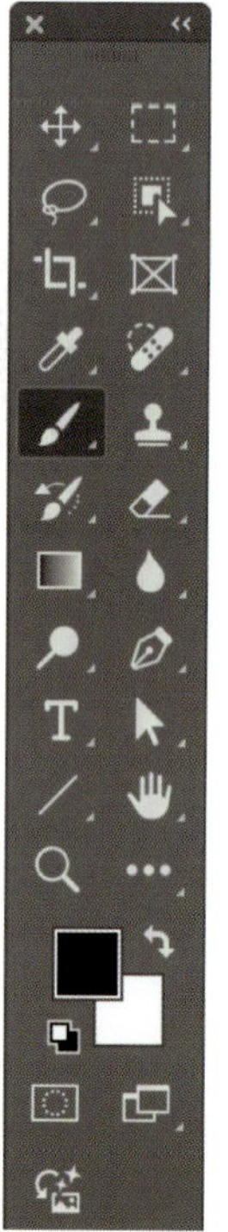

FIGURE 4.60

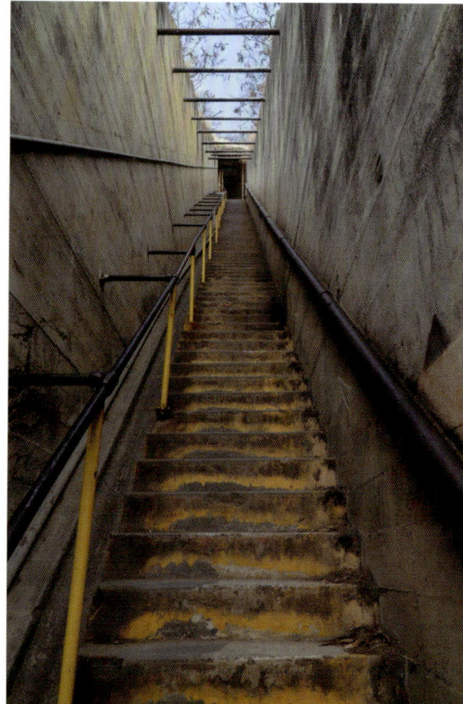

FIGURE 4.61

Removing a Seam

When you join images together, sometimes there is an unsightly seam. Some of the common scenarios in which I've encountered this issue are:

- Scanning a large image that is too big to fit on the scanner bed, so I have to scan it in parts and join them.

- Scanning a book or magazine spread.

- Panoramas where the stitching went bad.

Generative Fill is godsend for these types of image problems.

The example here is a panorama that went bad when stitching (**FIGURE 4.62**). Notice something weird went on with the buildings in the background—they don't match up. It's so easy to fix now.

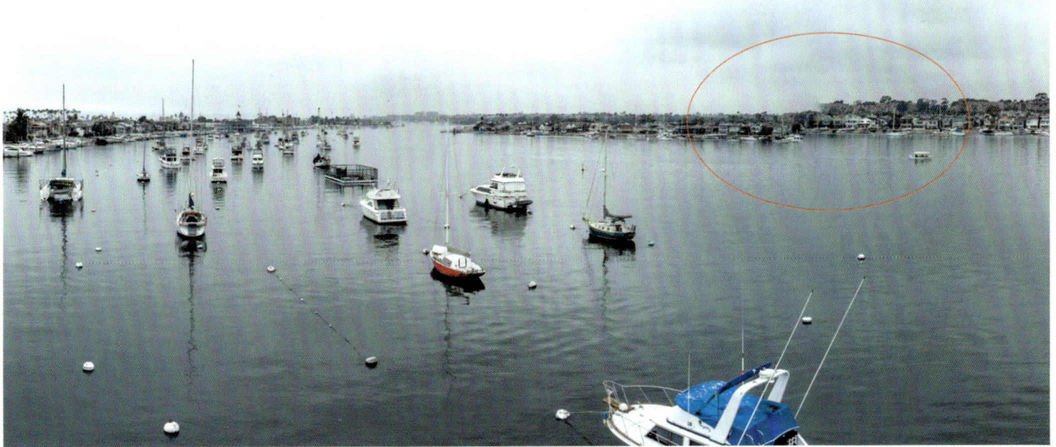

FIGURE 4.62 © Colin Smith

1. Choose the Lasso Tool or Selection Brush Tool and make a selection around or paint over the area to be repaired (**FIGURE 4.63**).

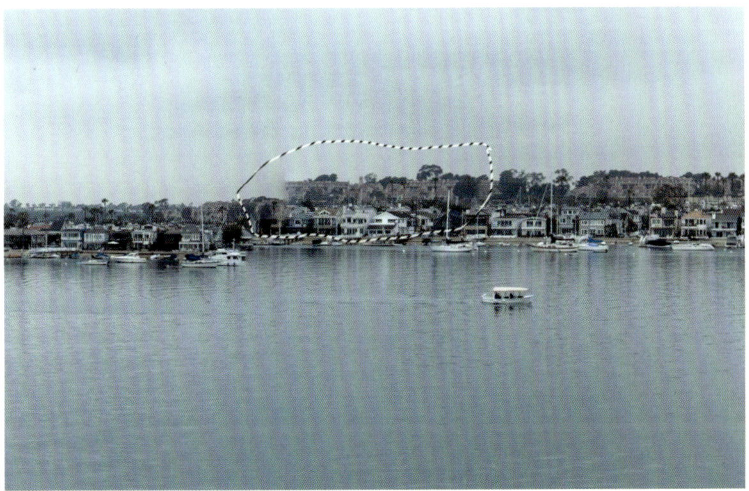

FIGURE 4.63

2. Choose Generative Fill from the Task Bar.

3. Leave the text prompt field blank and click Generate.

4. Choose the best variation in the Properties panel.

Now our panorama is saved (**FIGURES 4.64 AND 4.65**). It's such a small detail no one will notice. But they certainly would have noticed before.

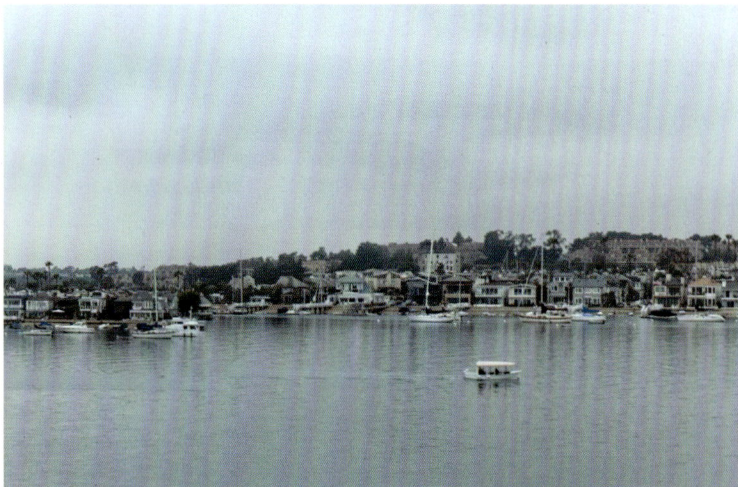

FIGURE 4.64

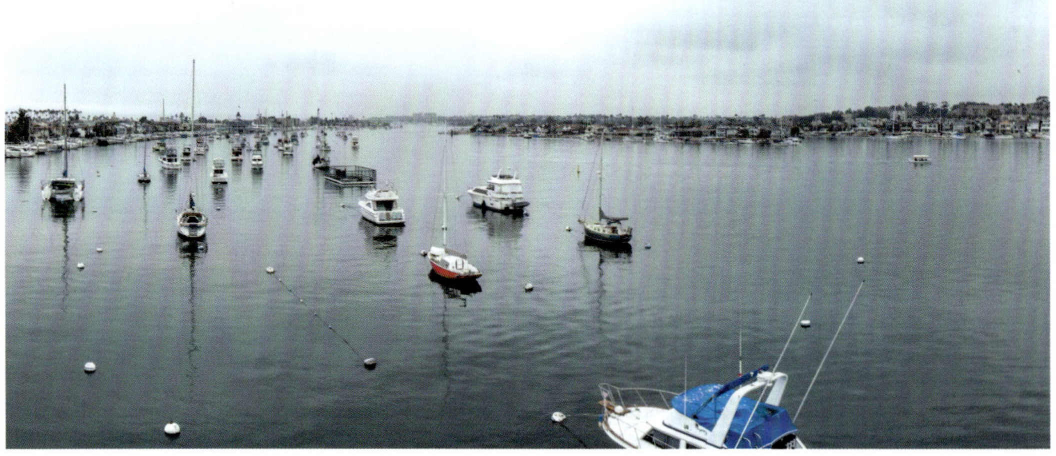

FIGURE 4.65

The Remove Tool

I'd be remiss if I didn't discuss the AI-powered Remove Tool in Photoshop (**FIGURE 4.66**), which we touched on earlier in this chapter. The Remove Tool is a brush that uses AI to remove things in Photoshop. It works extremely well, but is limited compared to Generative Fill because it doesn't provide variations and doesn't always work as well as Generative Fill. You also have the option to use it with or without Generative AI (**FIGURE 4.67**).

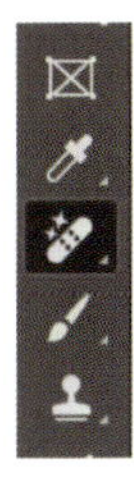

FIGURE 4.66

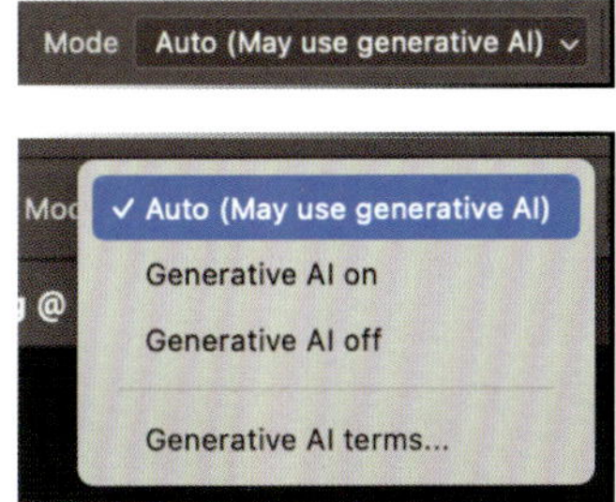

FIGURE 4.67

The Remove Tool with Generative AI turned off has a few advantages:

- It's a local tool (on your computer in the Photoshop install) and doesn't require an internet connection.

- Remove is faster than Generative Fill.

- Because it's local, it doesn't use Generative Credits.

- It performs at full resolution.

The disadvantages of the Remove Tool with Generative AI turned on are:

- There are no variations to choose from.

- It doesn't always generate as well as Generative Fill.

Here is a quick look at how to use the Remove Tool:

1. Choose the Remove Tool from the Tools panel (**FIGURE 4.68**). It is nested under the Spot Healing Brush Tool.

    The best way to use this tool is on a new layer so that it's nondestructive and we can use a Layer Mask if we want to blend it.

2. Create a new layer (**FIGURE 4.69**).

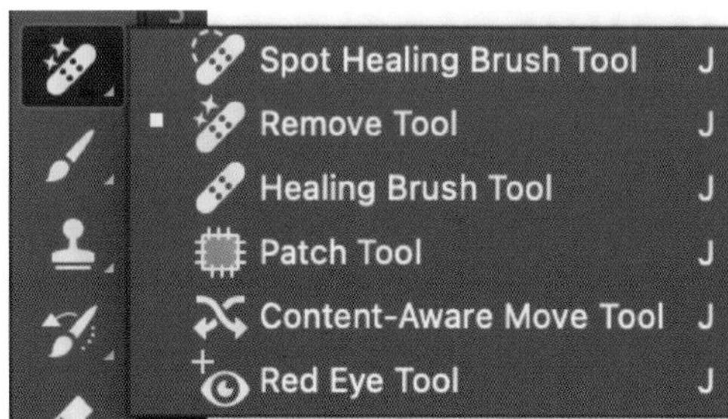

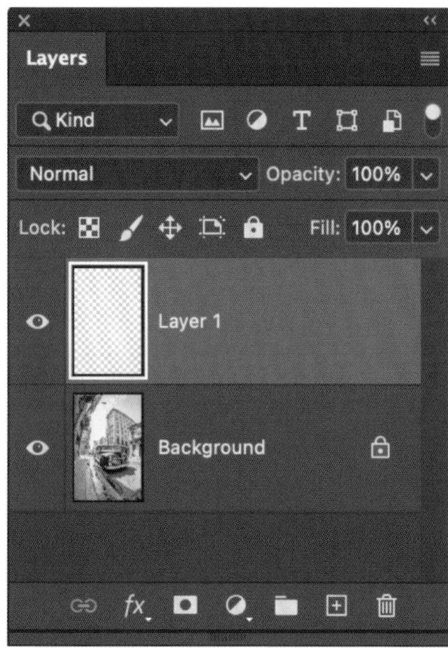

FIGURE 4.68

FIGURE 4.69

3. Choose Sample All Layers in the Options Bar at the top of the interface (**FIGURE 4.70**). If this is not selected, nothing will happen.

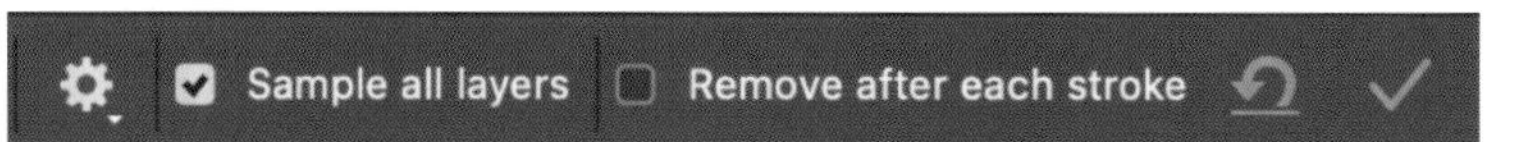

FIGURE 4.70

4. Set Mode to Auto, where it will use Generative AI on larger selections.

5. Decide if you want to enable Remove After Each Stroke. If this is on, as soon as you lift your finger off the mouse button, it will apply. I prefer to turn this option off; this way I can apply all my strokes and press the enter key (or click the check mark in the Options Bar) to apply the tool.

Let's try it out on this image (**FIGURE 4.71**).

6. Paint over the man next to the car (**FIGURE 4.72**). Note, you can circle him, like with Google Magic Eraser, and the brush will fill the circle.

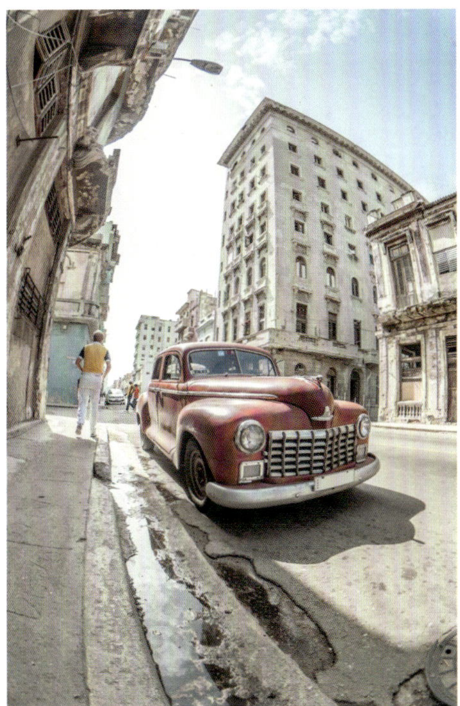

FIGURE 4.71 © Adobe Stock

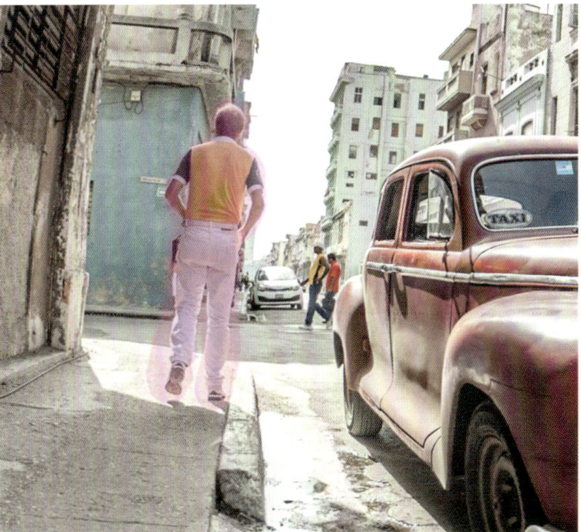

FIGURE 4.72

7. Press the enter key to apply the tool.

Notice the man is gone (**FIGURE 4.73**).

8. Paint over the car and its shadow (**FIGURE 4.74**). I also painted over the people crossing the road in the background.

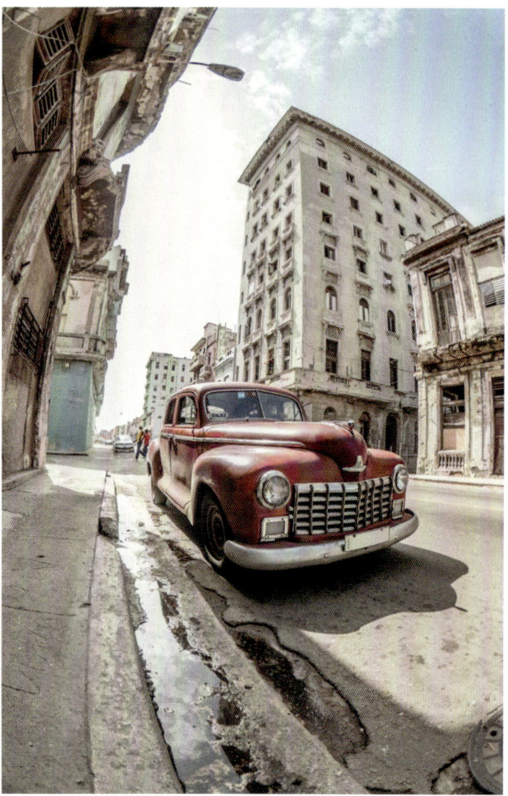

FIGURE 4.73

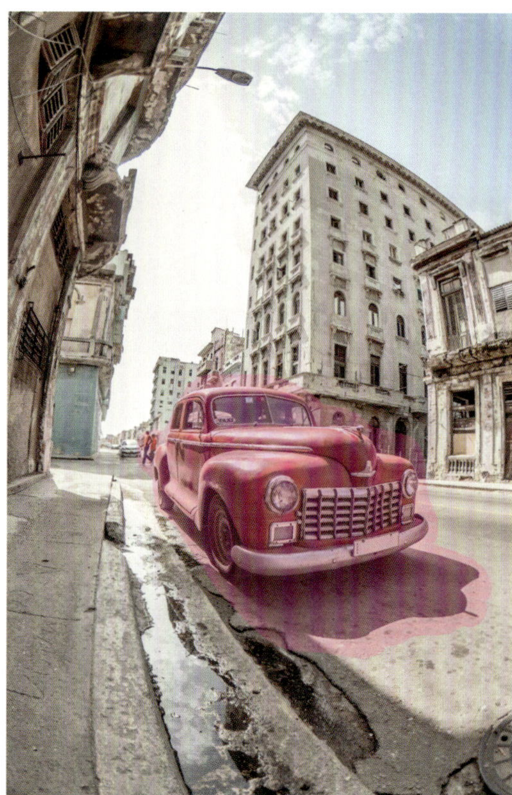

FIGURE 4.74

The car is now gone, but there are some objects on the road, including a badly rendered car (**FIGURE 4.75**).

After applying the tool again, I was able to easily remove the objects from the road (**FIGURE 4.76**). I think it did a pretty decent job and it will only get better over time.

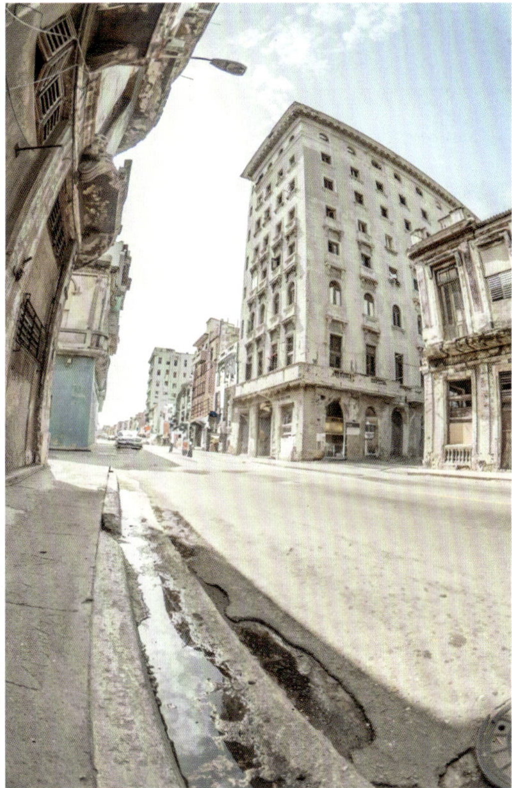

FIGURE 4.75

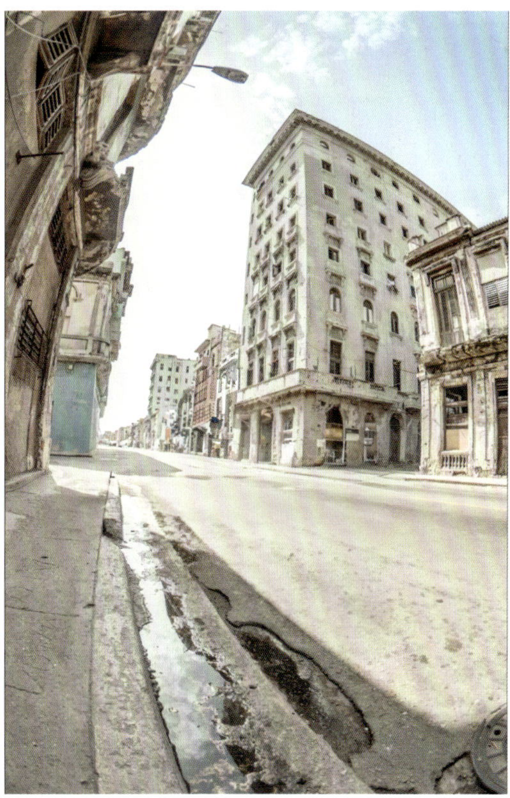

FIGURE 4.76

Removing Wires and Powerlines

The Find Distractions feature in the Remove Tool is a great time-saver. We already used the People removal earlier in this chapter. Another option is the ability to remove wires and cables.

To demonstrate how well this tool works, let's use an absolutely impossible image (**FIGURE 4.77**).

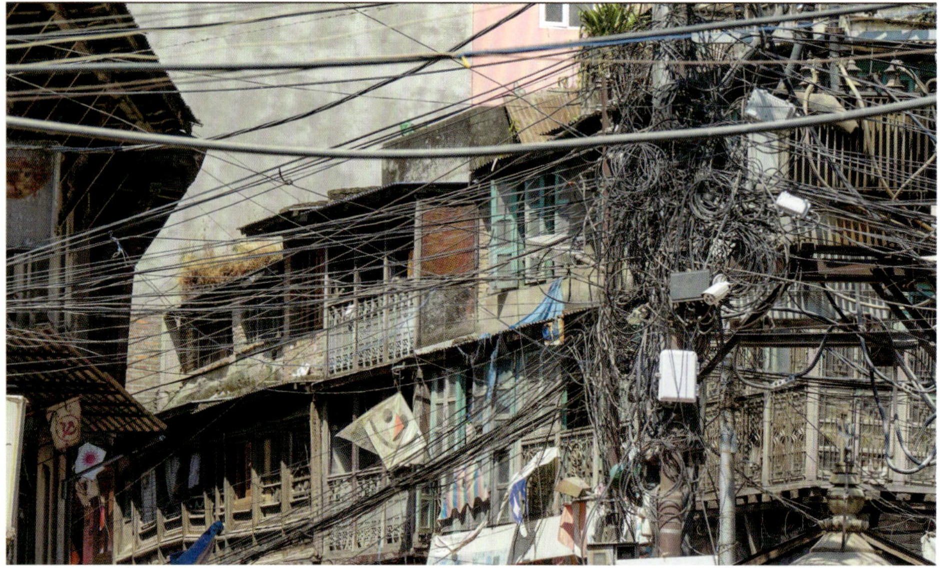

FIGURE 4.77 © Adobe Stock

1. Choose the Remove Tool from the Tools panel.

2. This works directly on the image, but best practice calls for us to create a new layer to work on (**FIGURE 4.78**).

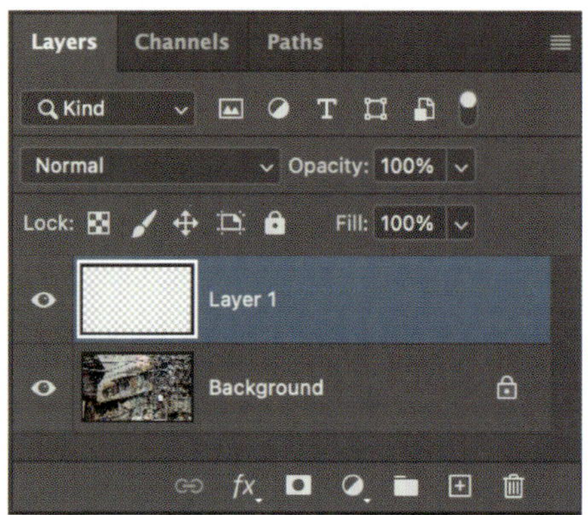

FIGURE 4.78

3. Choose Sample All Layers in the Options Bar at the top of the interface.

4. Choose Find Distractions in the Options Bar and select Wires and Cables (**FIGURE 4.79**).

This option doesn't have any settings. Photoshop looks at the image and decides where the wires are. It then removes them, without any further interaction from us.

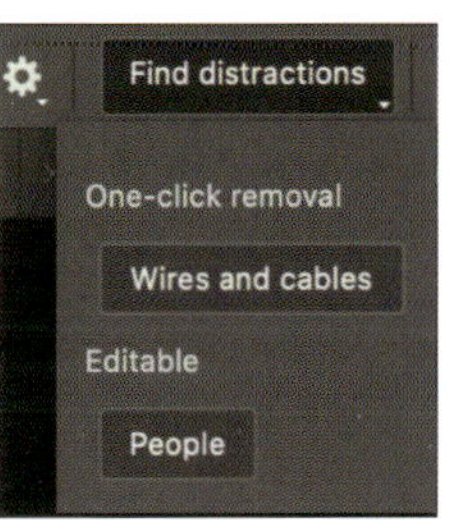

FIGURE 4.79

As you can see, the results are mind-blowing, even on this very difficult image (**FIGURE 4.80**). It's not perfect, but it's pretty close to it. On less-complicated images it is pretty much perfect.

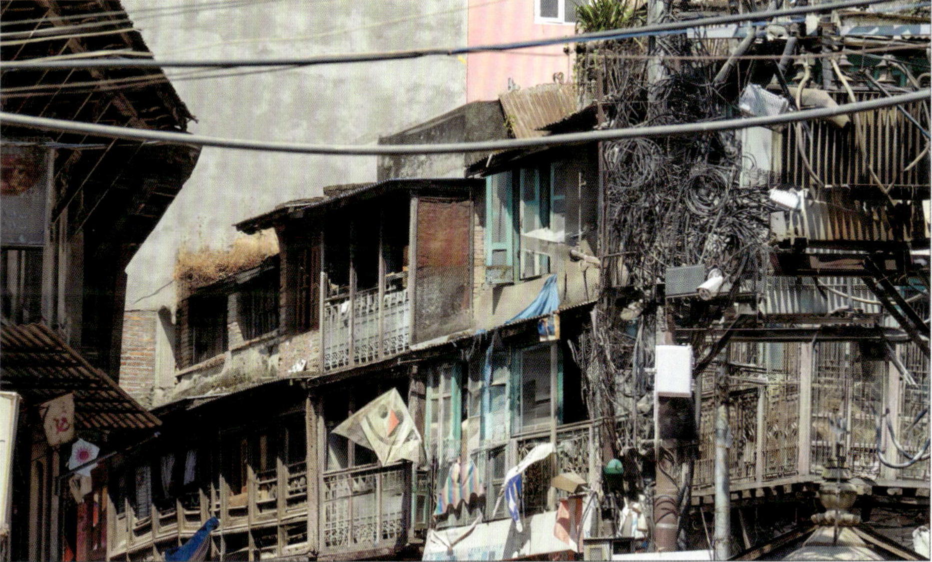

FIGURE 4.80

I think this gives you an idea of what the Remove Tool is able to do. I do encourage you to try it out. It's a really great tool for certain tasks.

In this chapter, we have looked at removing all kinds of things. Of course, this isn't an exhaustive list of everything that Generative AI can remove in Photoshop. I hope you are starting to see what a useful tool it is and how you can use it alongside other Photoshop tools to perform work that frankly doesn't look like AI or replace photography at all.

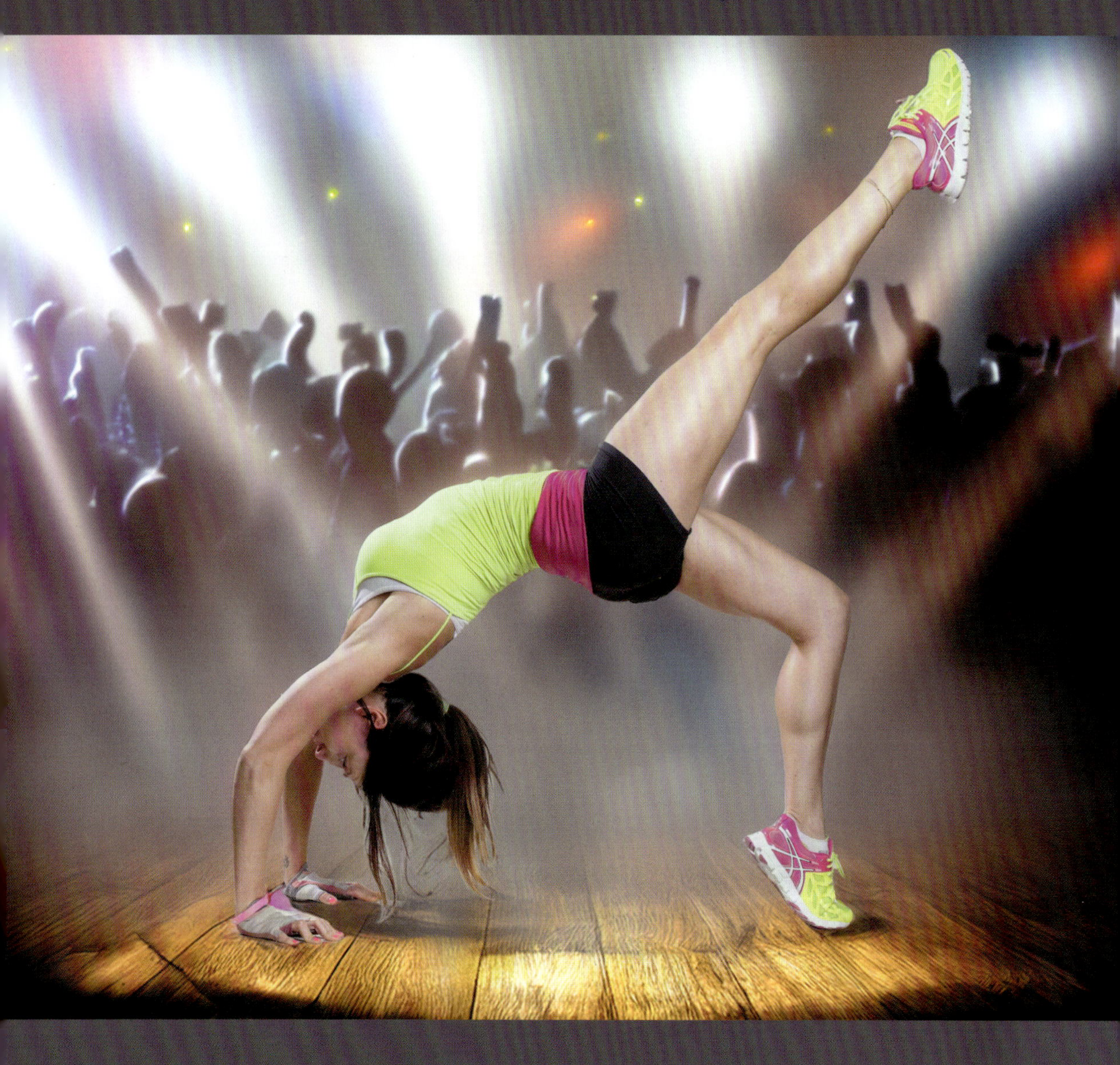

5

CHANGE

In this chapter, we will explore how Generative Fill changes aspects of photos. This is perhaps the most impressive ability of Generative Fill, allowing us to perform virtual magic on our images. I remember the first time I saw it change the clothing on a person in such a realistic way—suddenly Photoshop could do the things my non-Photoshop friends thought it could do!

Using Generative Fill to Change Objects and Environments

Let's use Generative Fill to completely change the context of this photo (**FIGURE 5.1**). We are starting with a woman in an office environment in the city.

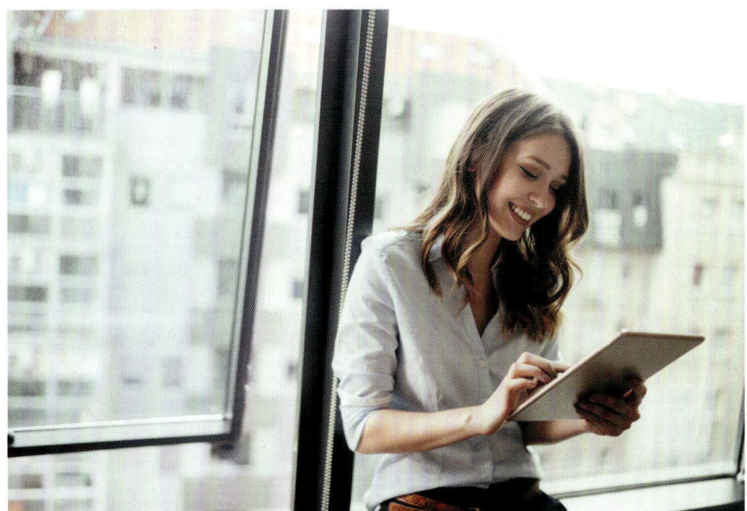

FIGURE 5.1
© Adobe Stock

Changing the Environment

Our first task is to change the environment. Let's get out of the city and move everything into the woods. We will start by selecting the glass in the windows.

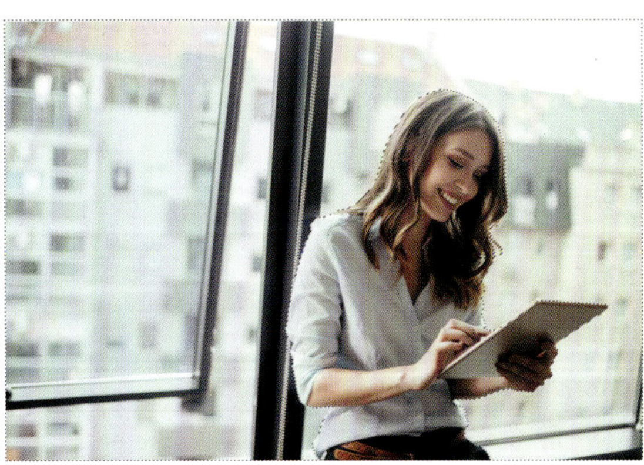

FIGURE 5.2

1. Choose the Object Selection Tool in the Tools panel.

2. Click on Select Subject in the Task Bar. Our woman is now selected.

3. Choose Select > Inverse to inverse the selection. Now everything but the woman is selected (**FIGURE 5.2**).

We want to remove the window frames from the selection so that we just have the glass selected.

4. Choose the Polygonal Lasso Tool from the Tools panel (**FIGURE 5.3**).

5. Hold down the Alt/option (Windows/Mac) key to remove areas from the selection. Click around the window frame edges to remove the frames from the selection (**FIGURE 5.4**).

With just the windows selected, let's change the content outside.

6. Click on Generative Fill in the Task Bar and type in a new environment. Let your imagination be the limit. Here we will do "wilderness in winter" (**FIGURE 5.5**).

7. Click Generate.

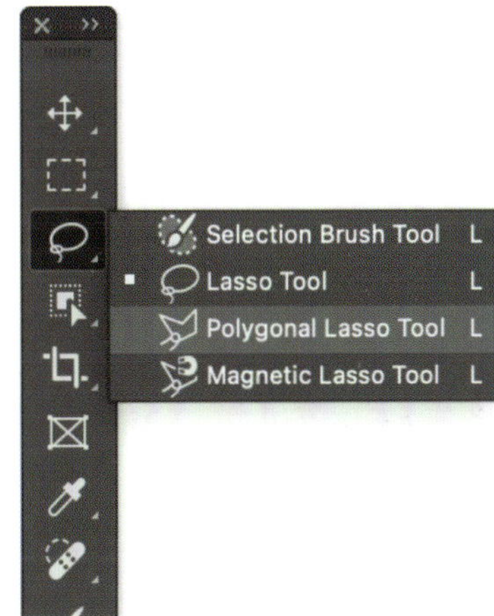

FIGURE 5.3

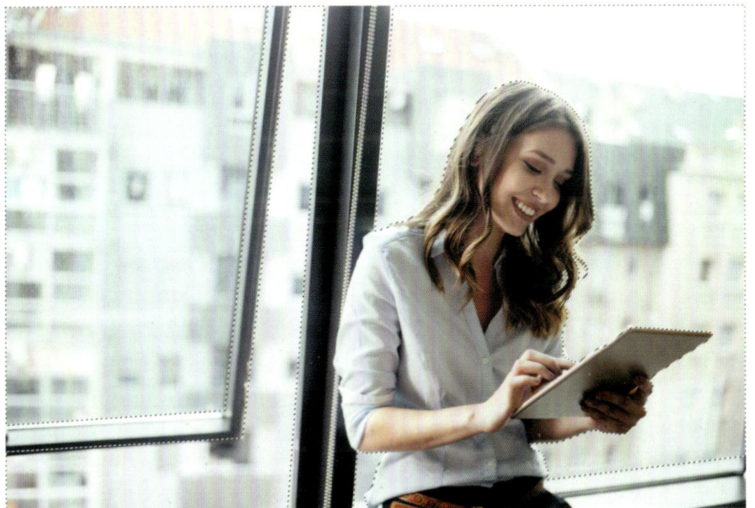

FIGURE 5.4

FIGURE 5.5

8. Choose your favorite variation in the Properties panel, or click Generate again until you see something you are happy with. You may need to modify the text prompt if you aren't getting what you want.

Here we have the great outdoors in a cooler season (**FIGURE 5.6**).

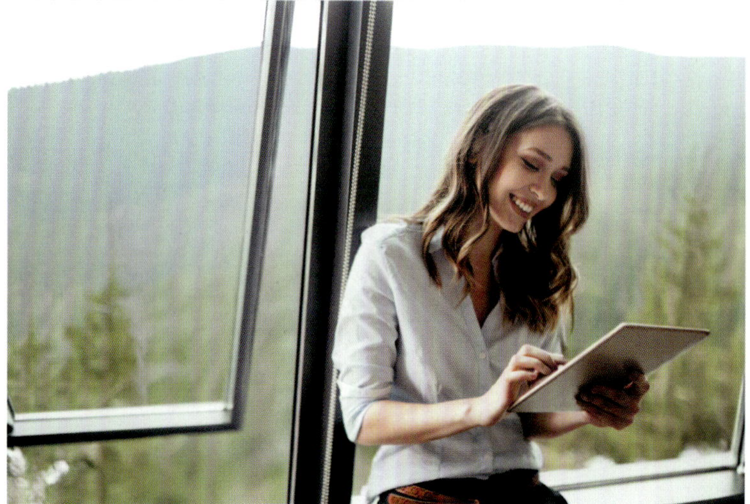

FIGURE 5.6

Changing Clothing

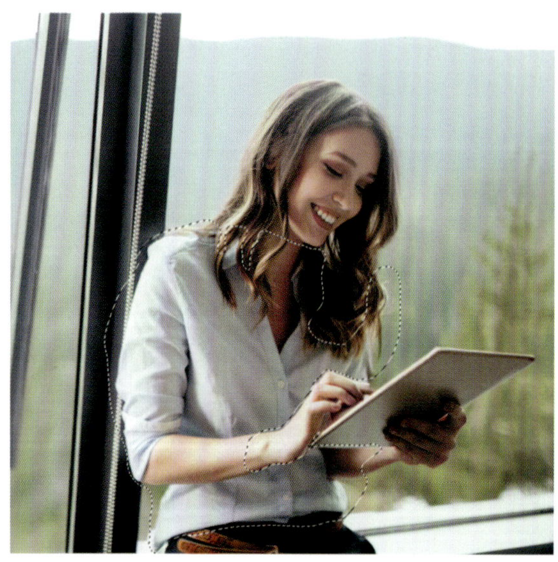

FIGURE 5.7

Our subject must be freezing by now. Let's change her blouse into a nice warm sweater.

1. Make a selection that completely covers the woman's blouse (**FIGURE 5.7**). Be careful to exclude her hair from the selection, or her hairstyle could change. I included part of her arms in the selection, so sleeves can be generated.

> **TIP** When you want to replace an object, it's important that you fully cover it with the selection. Traditionally, a selection in Photoshop has to be tight and precise. In the case of Generative Fill, however, this isn't the case. Gen Fill doesn't use the selection to cut out; it uses it as a guide to tell it what can be replaced and what can't. **Remember, Generative Fill cannot generate pixels outside the selection.**

2. Click on Generative Fill in the Task Bar and type in "wool sweater" for the text prompt (**FIGURE 5.8**). If you have a color in mind, add that to the prompt.

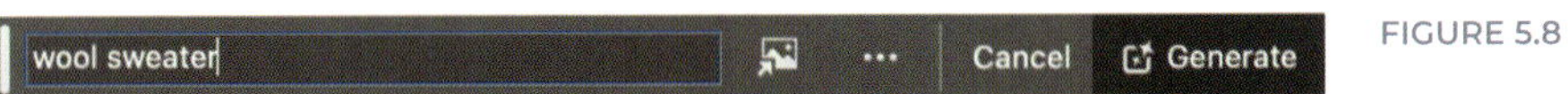

FIGURE 5.8

3. Click Generate.

> **TIP** I find it's best to keep prompts as concise as possible. Start simple and add words to the prompt if you don't get what you want.

And now the woman is wearing a sweater, just like magic (**FIGURE 5.9**).

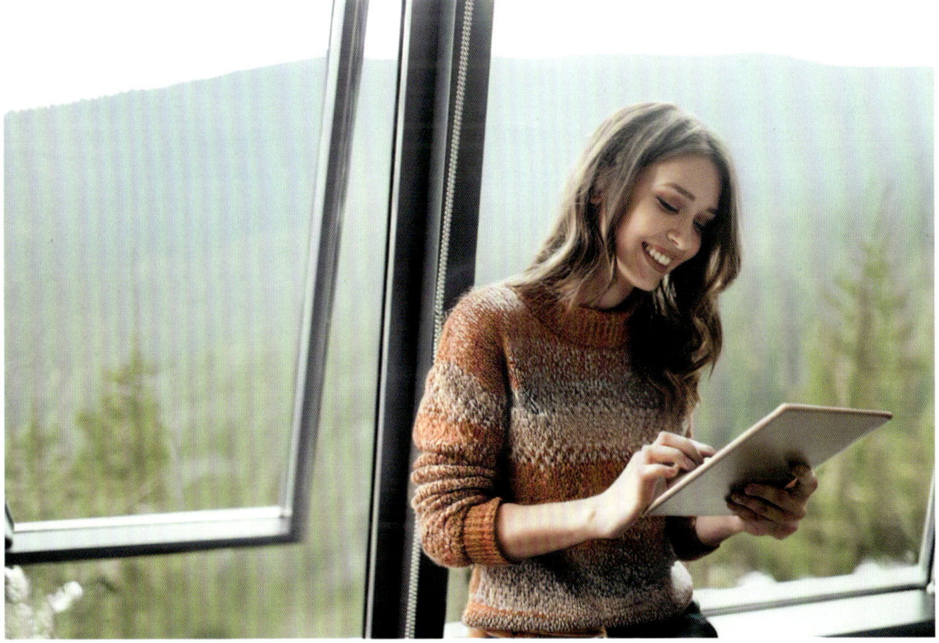

FIGURE 5.9

Changing an Object

Just to see how far we can go, let's swap out the iPad for something different.

1. Make a selection around the iPad.

2. Choose Generative Fill and type "journal" in the text prompt field.

3. Click Generate.

Now the woman is holding a journal (**FIGURE 5.10**).

Let's change the style of the window frame too.

4. Make a selection around the frame with the Polygonal Lasso Tool (**FIGURE 5.11**).

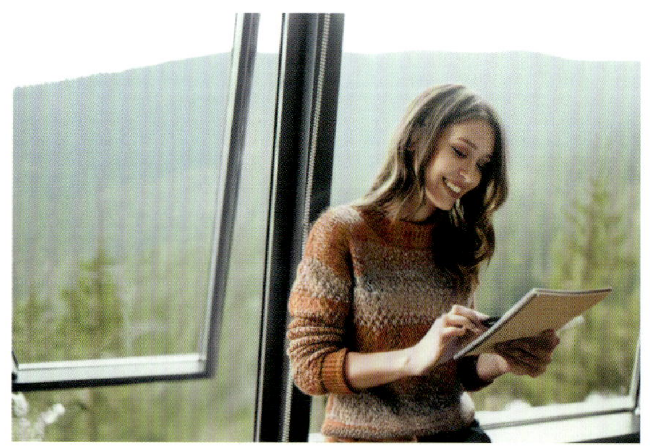

FIGURE 5.10

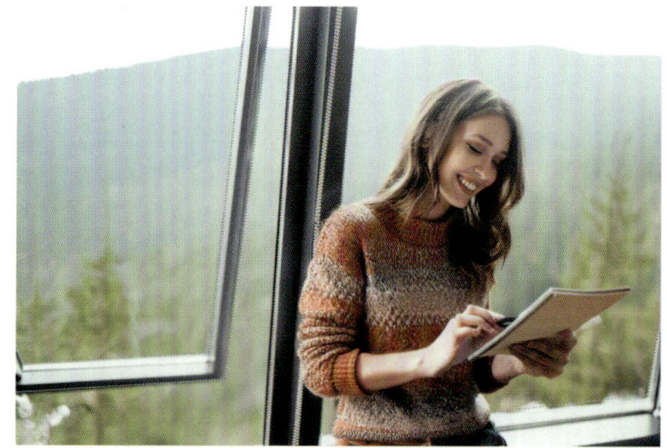

FIGURE 5.11

5. Choose Generative Fill from the Task Bar and type "wooden window frame" in the text prompt field.

6. Click Generate.

Now the window has a wooden frame instead of an aluminum one (**FIGURE 5.12**).

As you can see, Generative Fill can change anything in a picture. Let your imagination be the guide.

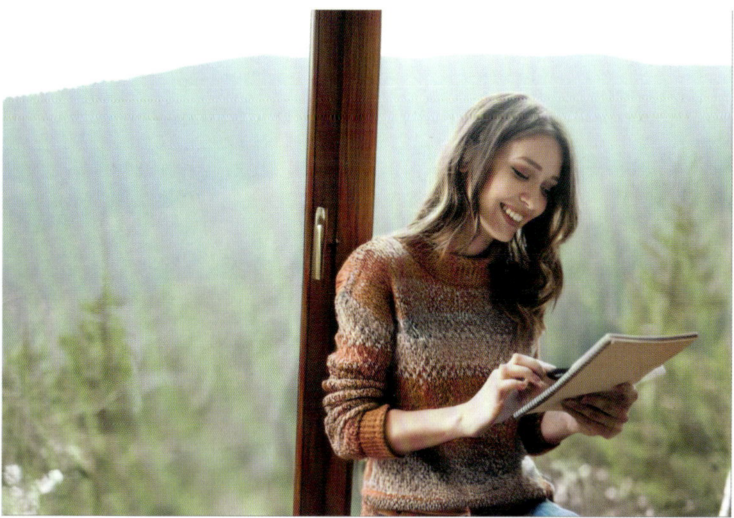

FIGURE 5.12

Changing Backgrounds

Changing backgrounds is a very common thing people do. This is now easier than ever, with more creative options at your fingertips.

I did a photo shoot with Brooke, who is a yoga guru and was my marketing director at the time. Her poses are quite amazing, but the setting was not so exciting (**FIGURE 5.13**). Let's see what we can do that change that.

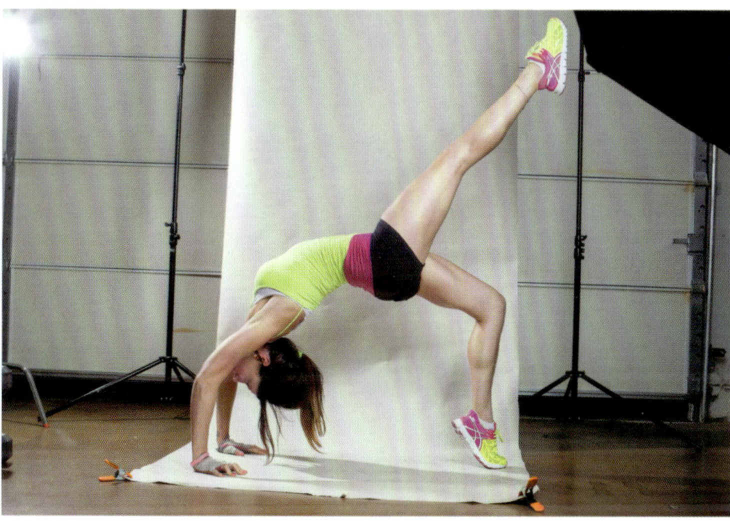

FIGURE 5.13
© Colin Smith

1. Choose the Object Selection Tool (**FIGURE 5.14**).

2. Click on Select Subject in the Task Bar.

Now, you see the marching ants selection around Brooke (**FIGURE 5.15**).

3. Choose Generative Fill from the Task Bar and leave the text prompt field empty.

4. Click Generate to remove Brooke and create an empty scene (**FIGURE 5.16**).

This scene can be used as a background plate to achieve all kinds of effects with compositing, or even mixed with video. If you use background plates, you know what I mean; otherwise, let's save this exploration for another time.

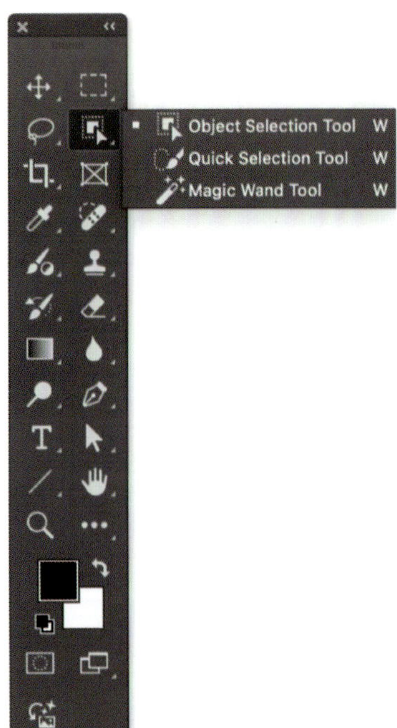

FIGURE 5.14

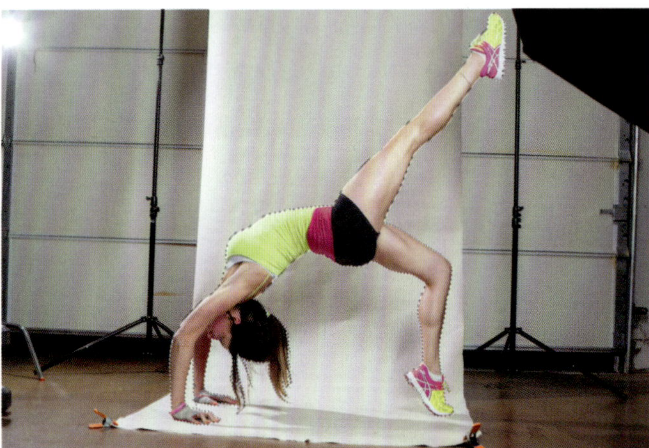

FIGURE 5.15

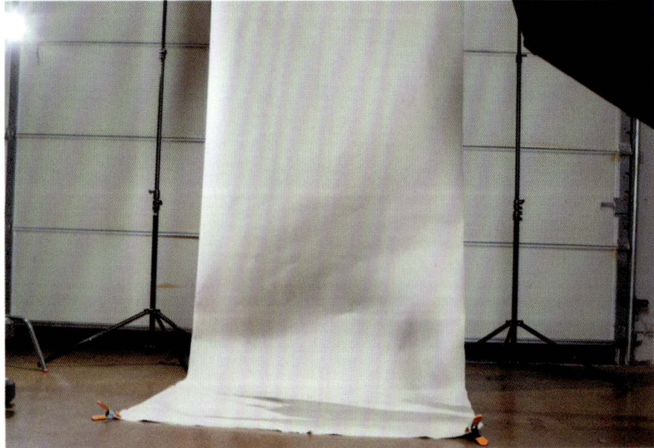

FIGURE 5.16

Let's back up a step to where we had the selection around Brooke.

5. Choose Select > Inverse to select everything except our yogi (**FIGURE 5.17**).

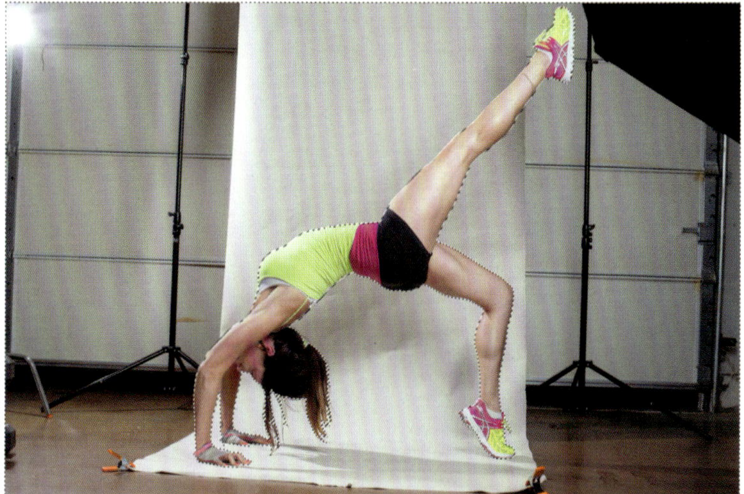

FIGURE 5.17

6. Choose Generative Fill and leave the text prompt blank to allow Gen Fill to add whatever background it thinks is appropriate.

7. Click Generate.

Now we have a new room, complete with accurate shadows (**FIGURE 5.18**).

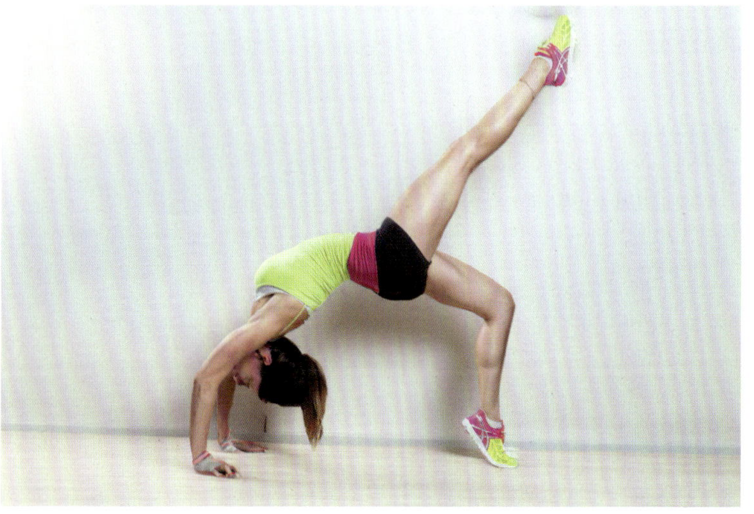

FIGURE 5.18

8. If you want to try guiding it, type "beach" into the text prompt field (**FIGURE 5.19**).

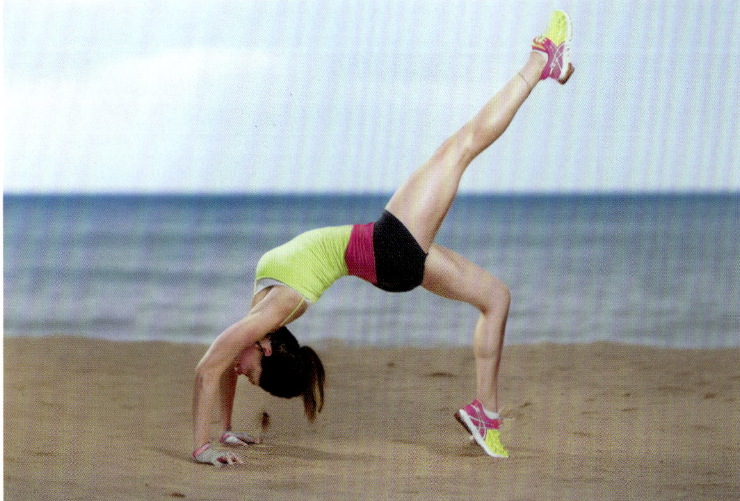

FIGURE 5.19

Enhance Detail

If you look closely at the edges of the generated layer, you will notice pixelation. This is because the resolution generated is less than the original image. Depending on when you are reading this, this may or may not be a problem, as Adobe is updating Generative Fill at a rapid pace. Let's address this now.

1. Head over to the Properties panel and roll over the selected variation. You will see an icon that includes an arrow—this is the Enhance Detail button (**FIGURE 5.20**).

2. Click the button to apply the enhancement. Enhancement does not use Generative Credits.

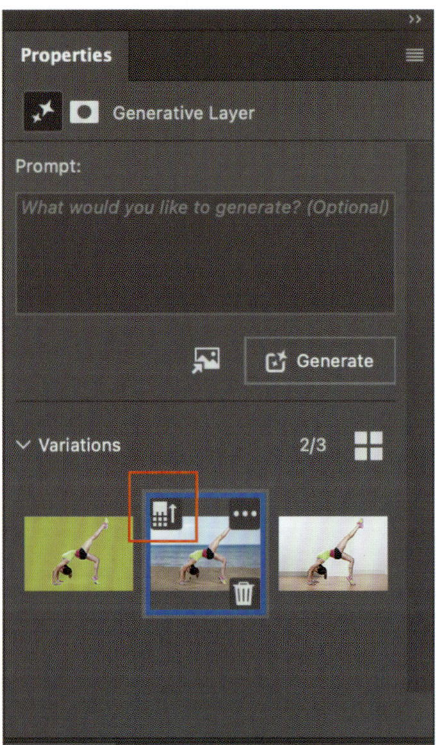

FIGURE 5.20

We can clearly see the difference Enhance Detail makes to the image. **FIGURE 5.21** shows the image before Enhance Detail was applied, and **FIGURE 5.22** shows the image after.

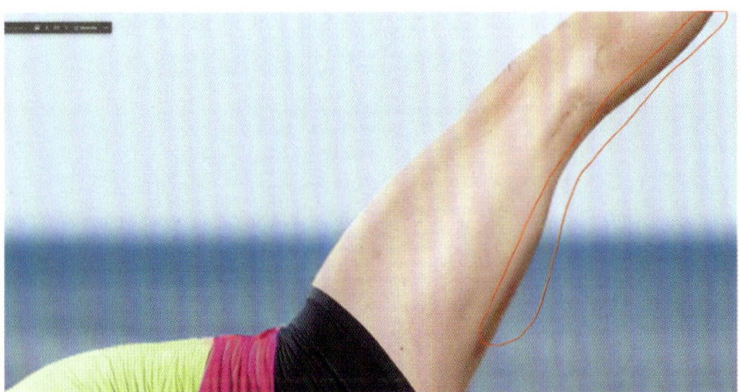

FIGURE 5.21

FIGURE 5.22

Generate Background

There is an easier way to change the background of an image by using Generate Background. Let's start with the same photo we just used (**FIGURE 5.13**). We will get a similar result, via a different route.

1. Choose the Move Tool, then click Remove Background in the Task Bar (**FIGURE 5.23**).

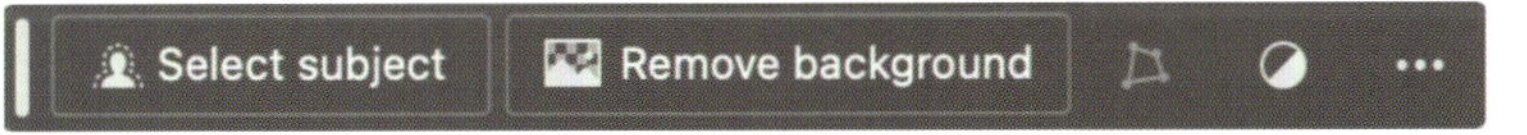

FIGURE 5.23

The background will be removed, and you'll see the checkerboard transparency behind Brooke (**FIGURE 5.24**).

Look at the Layers panel, and you'll notice that a layer mask has been created and the mask is selected (**FIGURE 5.25**).

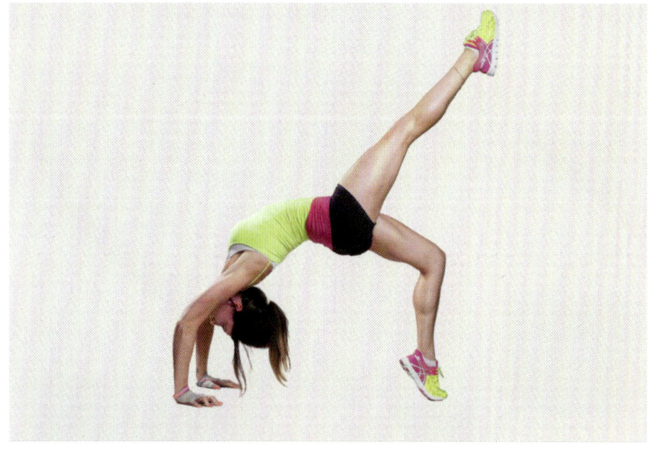

FIGURE 5.24

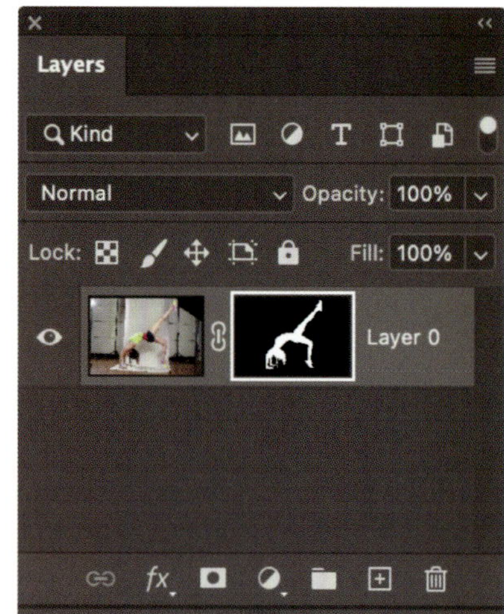

FIGURE 5.25

2. Click Generate Background in the Task Bar (**FIGURE 5.26**).

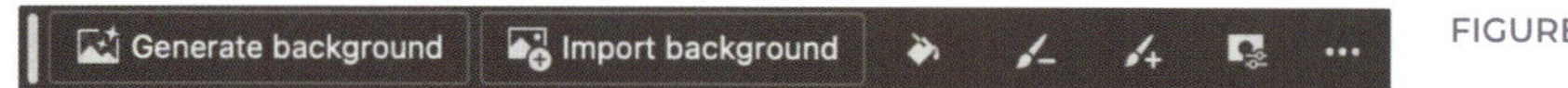

FIGURE 5.26

3. Enter your desired background into the text prompt. Let's go with "yoga studio" for this example.

Now we get a yoga studio, along with a yoga mat that matches Brooke's outfit (**FIGURE 5.27**).

FIGURE 5.27

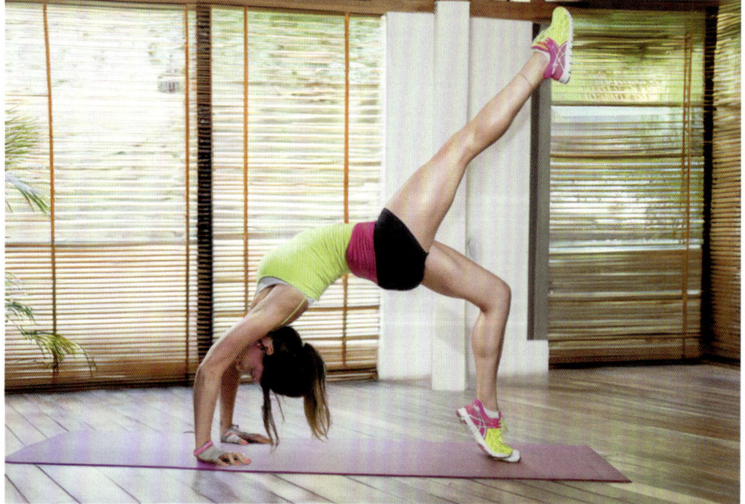

4. Try a different prompt, such as "beach" (**FIGURE 5.28**).

We can generate all kinds of backgrounds, with mixed results (**FIGURE 5.29**).

We can use more complex prompts such as "party, disco lights and crowd cheering" (**FIGURE 5.30**). Or how about "Times Square New York, New Year's Eve, crowds, lights" (**FIGURE 5.31**)?

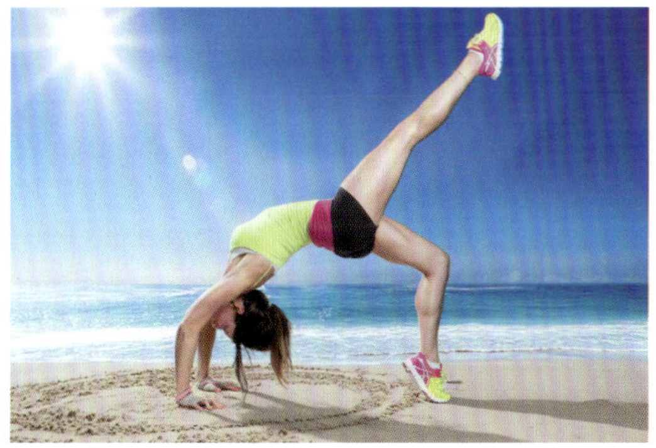

FIGURE 5.28

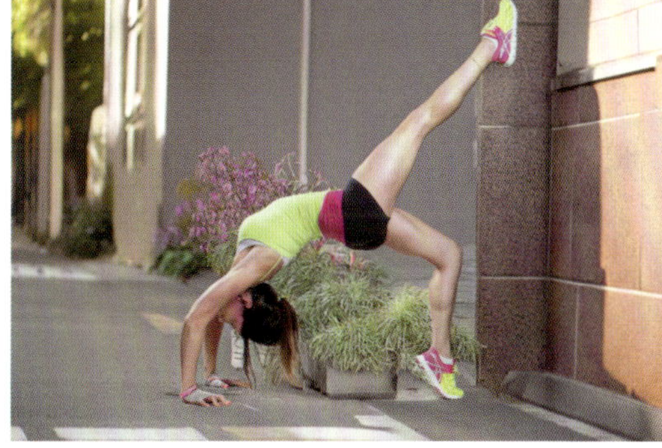

FIGURE 5.29

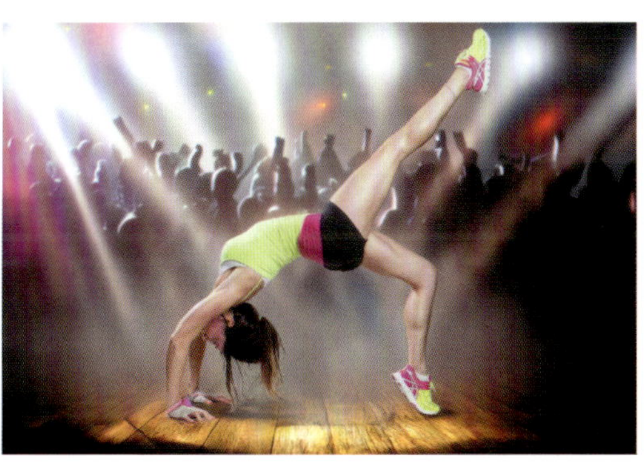

FIGURE 5.30

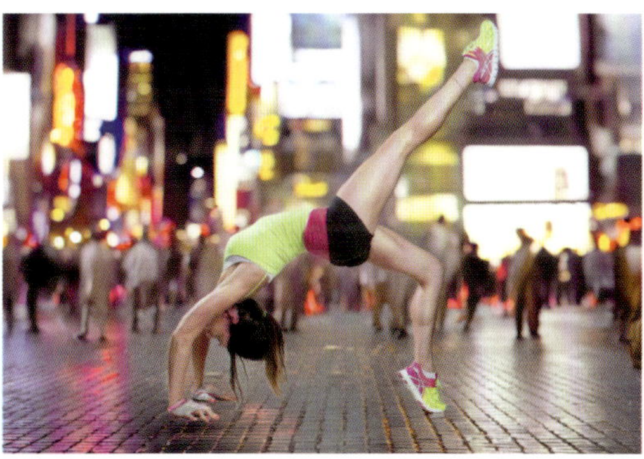

FIGURE 5.31

Changing Colors

I've heard people cry out, "All my Photoshop skills are worthless because of AI."

"Codswallop!" I say.

All your skills are still useful, and I'd even say more so than ever. Generative AI is unpredictable and often needs a little help from its friends. That's you and I with the conventional tools.

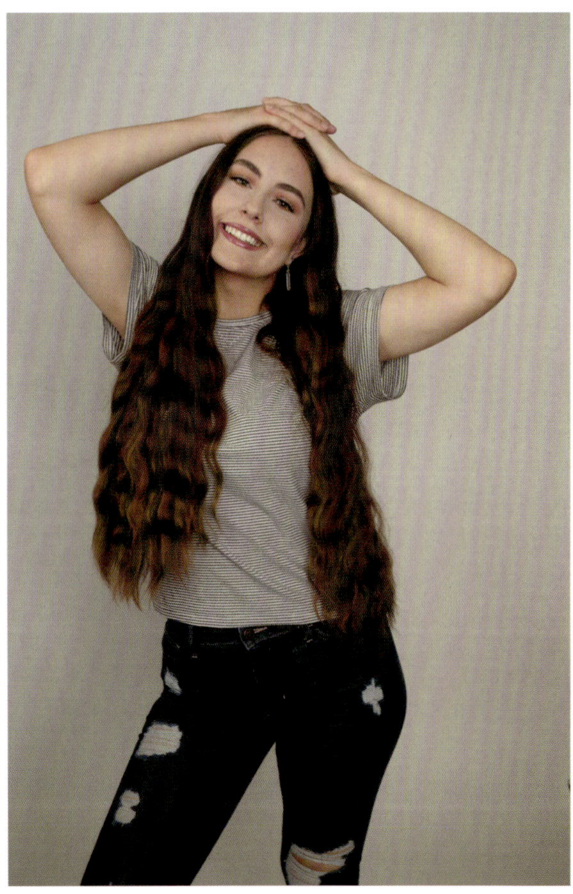

FIGURE 5.32 © Colin Smith

A perfect example of this is changing colors. So often your favorite variation is the wrong color, and try as you might, you can't seem to generate a variation as good in the correct color.

Example time.

Let's start with this photo of Meghan, and we'll change her shirt to a solid color (**FIGURE 5.32**).

1. Choose the Lasso Tool from the Tools panel.

2. Make a selection around the shirt (**FIGURE 5.33**). Hold down the shift key while using the Lasso Tool to make multiple selections to capture the body and sleeves of the shirt. Make sure you completely select all of the shirt, or you will get weird results. One big reason things don't get removed is because the selection didn't cover the entire object. If your person has long hair, make sure the majority of the hair isn't selected, or it will probably change when you generate.

3. Click on Generative Fill in the Task Bar and enter something like "green T-shirt" into the prompt.

4. Click Generate.

5. Choose your favorite variation from the Properties panel (**FIGURE 5.34**).

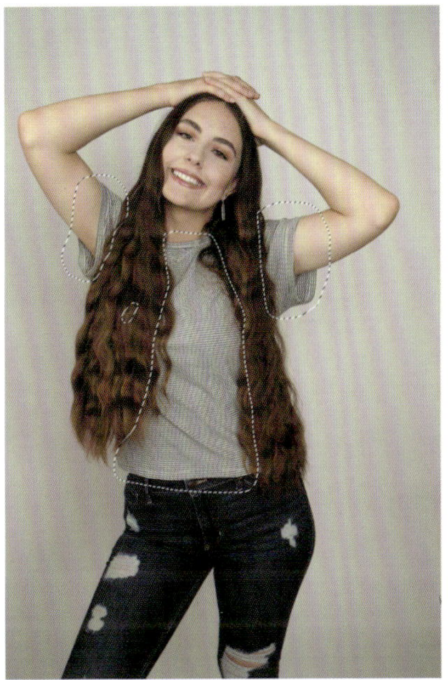

FIGURE 5.33

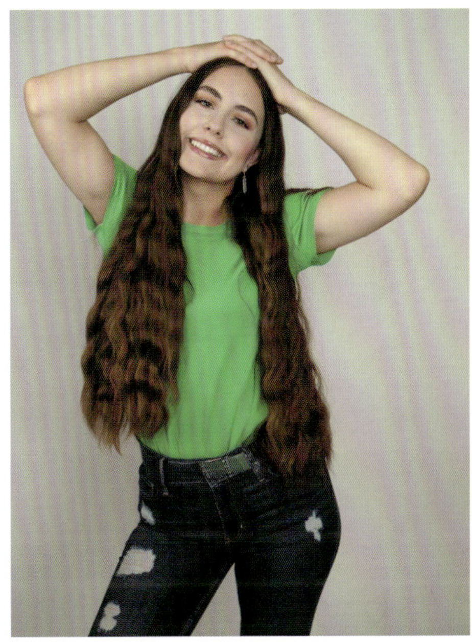

FIGURE 5.34

Let's say we like this shirt the best, but it's not quite the shade of green we wanted. We are using a shirt as the example, but this could apply to anything from a bird to a couch.

Rather than generate something similar, let's simply change the color.

1. Create a Hue/Saturation adjustment layer in the Layers panel (**FIGURE 5.35**).

2. In the Properties panel, click on the finger tool, directly under Preset (**FIGURE 5.36**).

3. Position the dropper over the image and click on the color you want to change—in this case, the shirt.

Notice at the bottom of the Properties panel there are sliders between the two color bars positioned at the chosen color (**FIGURE 5.37**).

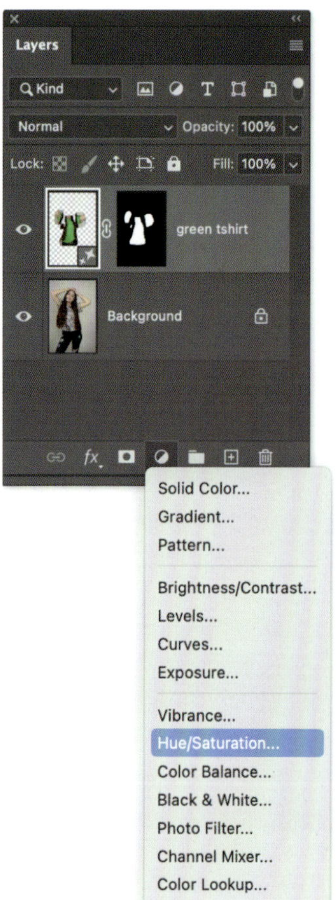

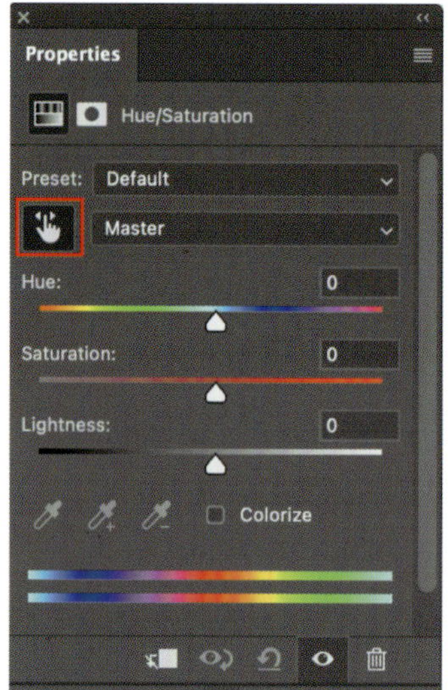

FIGURE 5.36

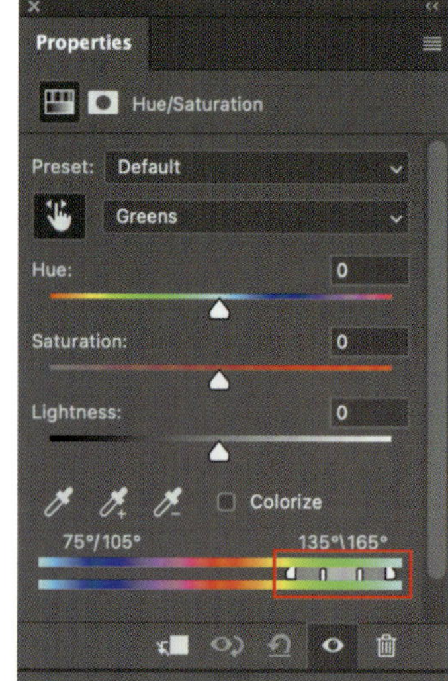

FIGURE 5.37

FIGURE 5.35

4. Move the Hue slider until the color changes, and note the change on the image (**FIGURE 5.38**). Initially, we are changing the slider so we can see the areas that are selected. We will choose the exact color we want after we have refined the selection.

5. Now drag on the sliders at the bottom of the Properties panel to refine the color selection, making sure only the shirt is being affected and nothing else. These will be minor adjustments.

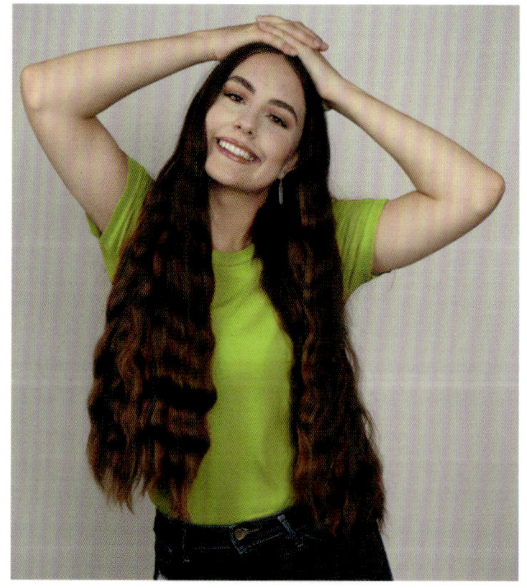

FIGURE 5.38

If additional parts of the photo with similar colors are also selected, you can paint them away in the mask later.

6. Once you have a good color selection, change the Hue to make it a different color without shifting the entire image (**FIGURE 5.39**).

7. Change the Saturation and Brightness to achieve almost any color, even black or white.

Here we have exactly the shade of green we want (**FIGURE 5.40**).

Have a look at the Layers panel (**FIGURE 5.41**). If other parts of the image have shifted in color, click on the Hue/Saturation layer mask. Grab the Brush Tool and set it to black to hide the adjustment where you paint on the image.

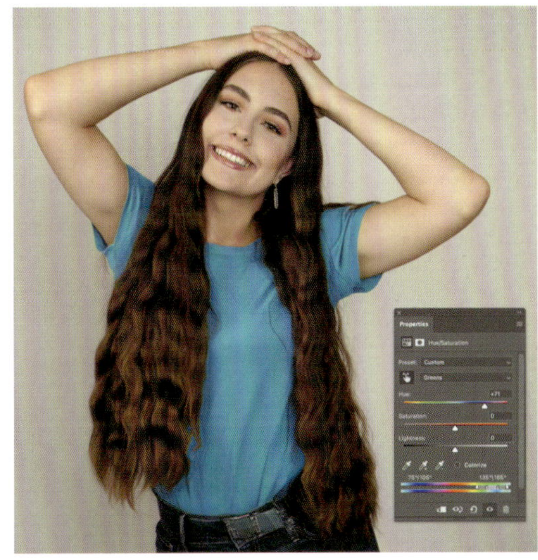

FIGURE 5.39

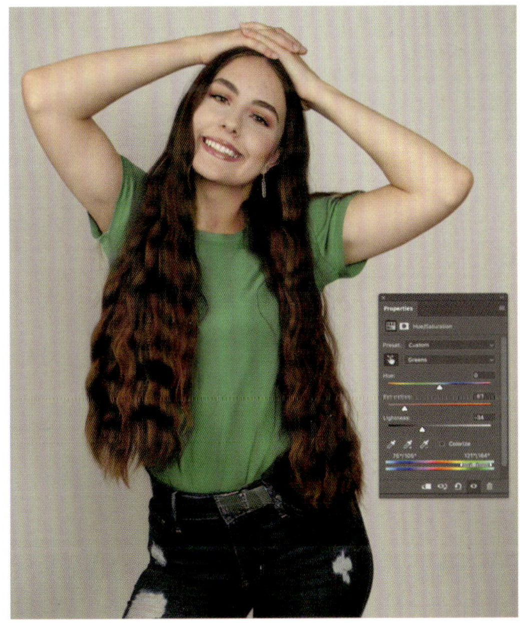

FIGURE 5.40

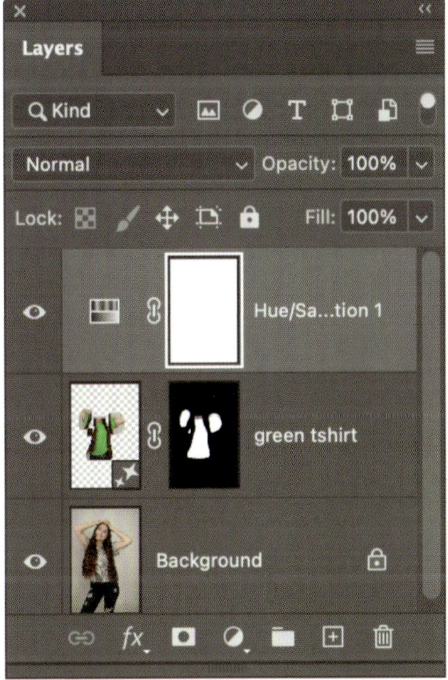

FIGURE 5.41

Repairing and Restoring Photos with Generative Fill

Traditionally, photo restoration is a very tricky task. While there is still plenty of need for precision clone stamping and brushing, Generative Fill can tackle a large part of the heavy lifting.

Let's fix this damaged photo (**FIGURE 5.42**).

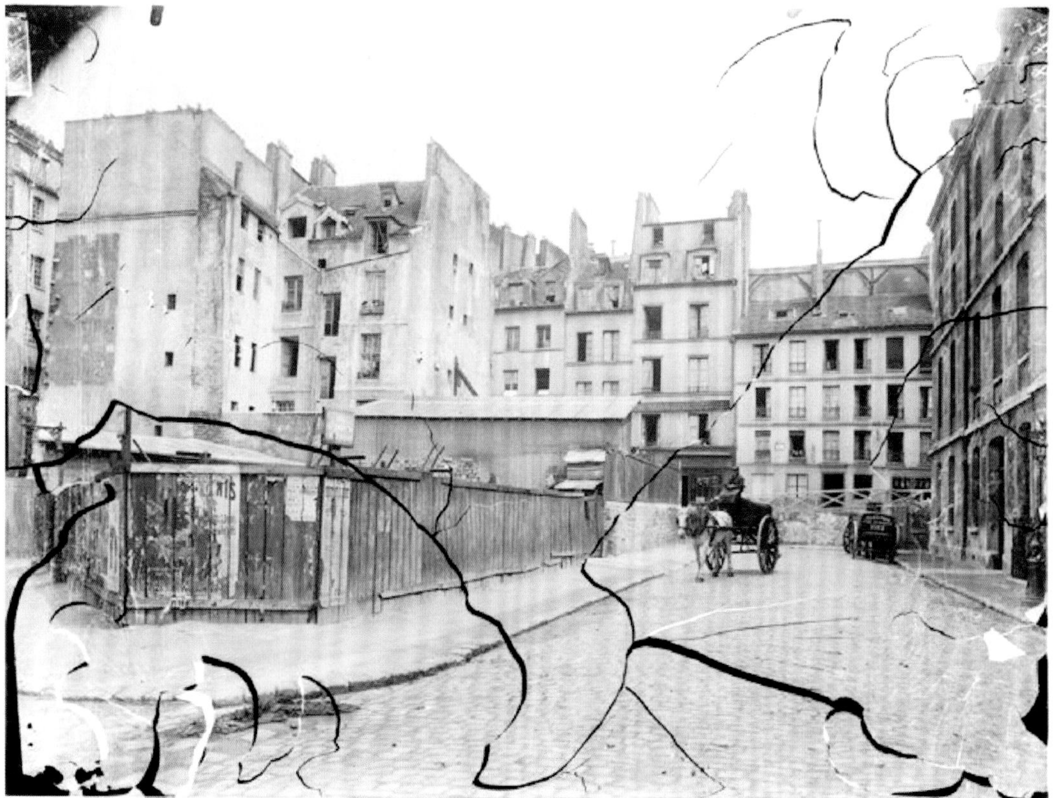

FIGURE 5.42 public domain

1. Grab the Selection Brush Tool and choose a hard-edged brush (**FIGURE 5.43**). Remember, you can access the brush Hardness slider by clicking on the drop-down menu next to the brush size in the Options Bar at the top of the interface.

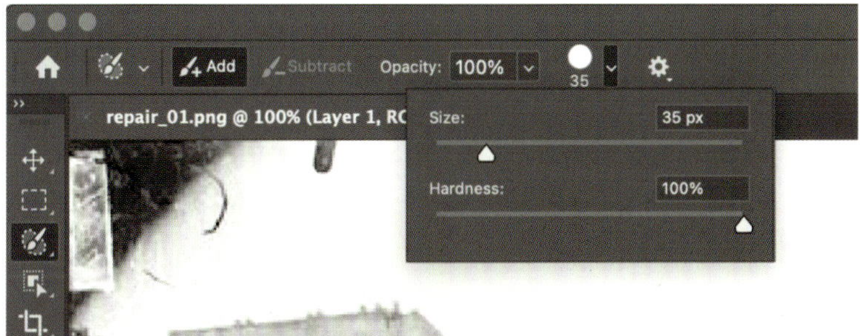

FIGURE 5.43

2. Use the] key to make the brush size a bit larger than the cracks in the image.

3. Paint over all the areas you want to fix (**FIGURE 5.44**). You can see the pink brush strokes as you paint; you don't need to convert it to a selection.

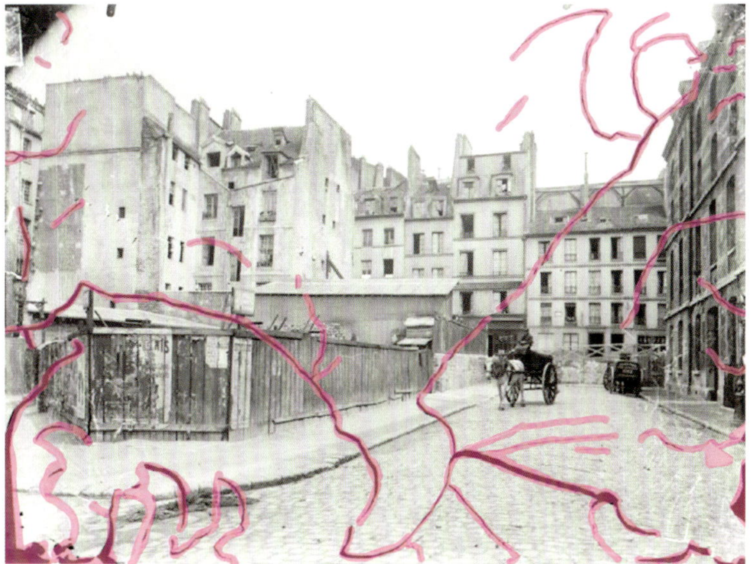

FIGURE 5.44

TIP Be careful to fully cover the cracks. If they are only partly selected, Generative Fill will mistake them for an image feature and try to incorporate them into the new generation.

4. Click on Generative Fill in the Task Bar.

5. Leave the prompt blank and click Generate.

6. Choose the best variation in the Properties panel (**FIGURE 5.45**).

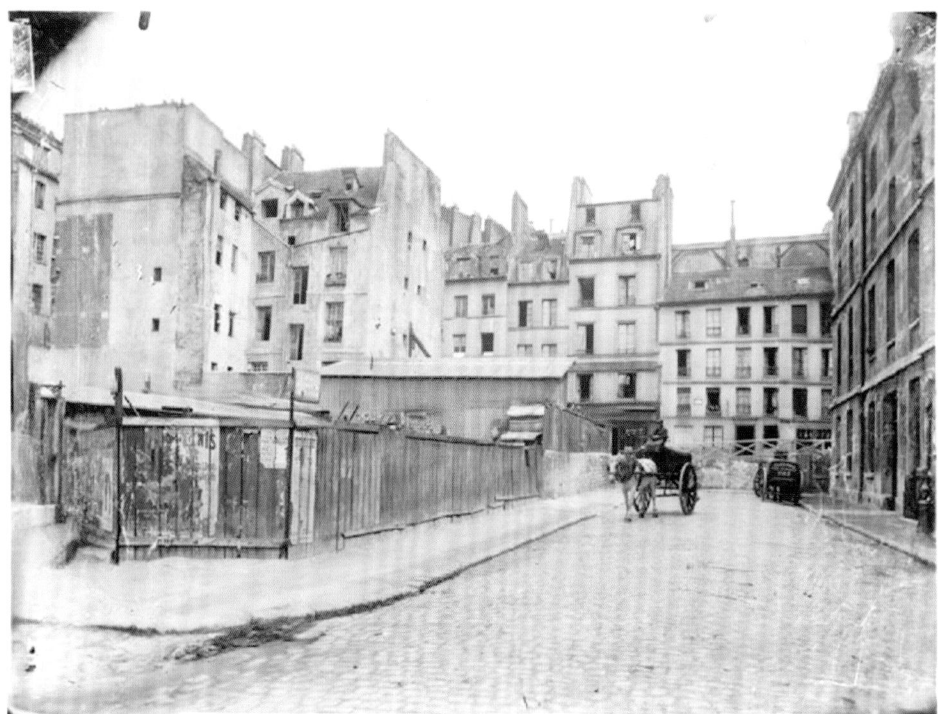

FIGURE 5.45

Let's remove the scratches and clean it up some more.

7. With the top layer selected, create a composite layer by pressing Alt+Ctrl+Shift+E/options+command+shift+E (Windows/Mac).

You will see a combined layer on top (**FIGURE 5.46**).

8. Choose Filter > Neural Filters.

9. Turn on the Photo Restoration filter with the blue switch (**FIGURE 5.47**). **Note:** The first time you use a Neural Filter, you will have to click the icon to download it.

10. Choose the lowest settings that give the result you want.

11. Click OK.

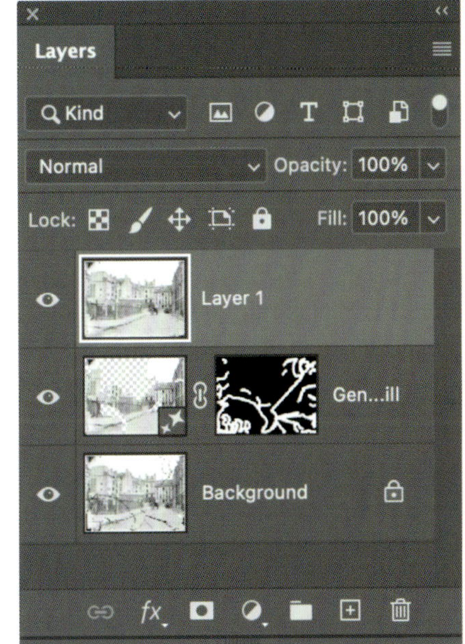

FIGURE 5.46

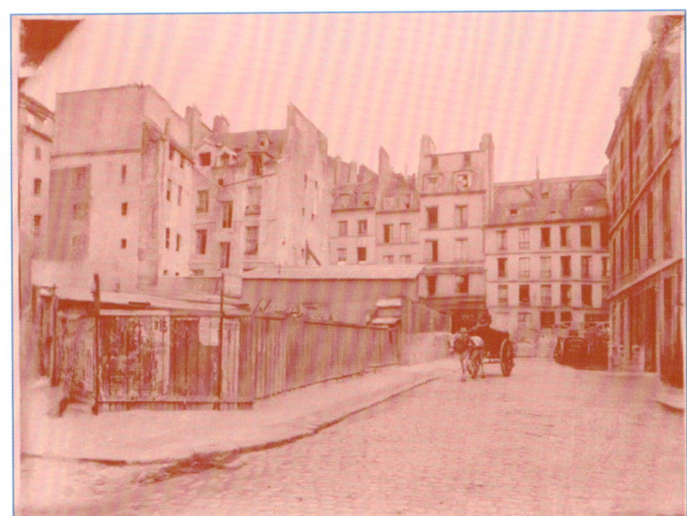

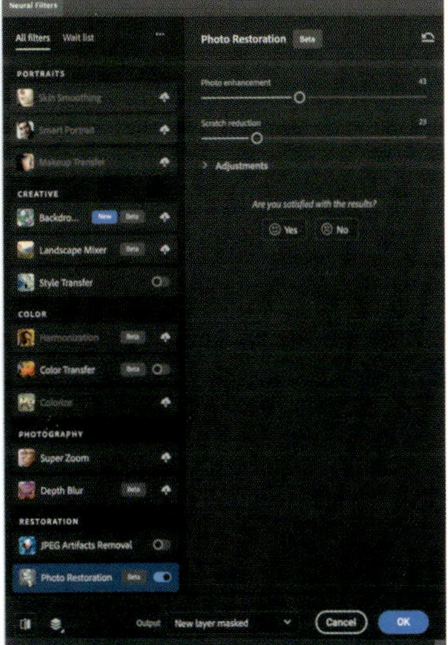

FIGURE 5.47

Now the image looks a lot cleaner (**FIGURE 5.48**).

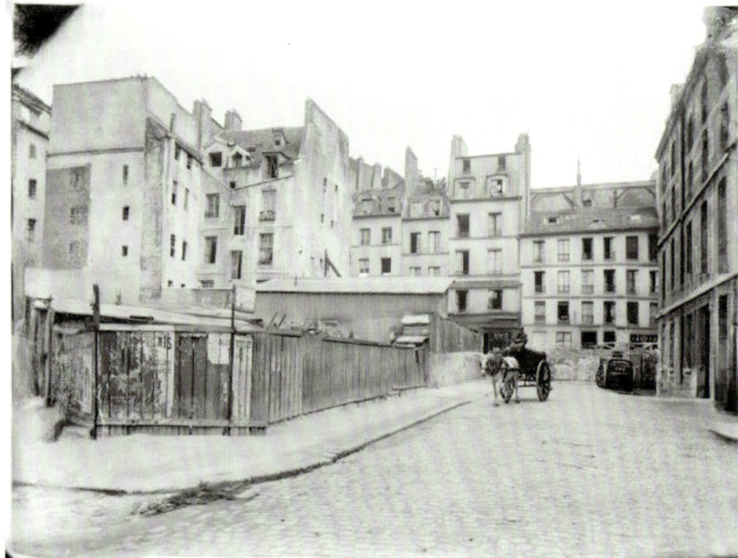

FIGURE 5.48

You can take it a step further by colorizing the image.

1. Choose Filter > Neural Filters.

2. Turn on the Colorize filter with the blue switch and click OK (**FIGURE 5.49**).

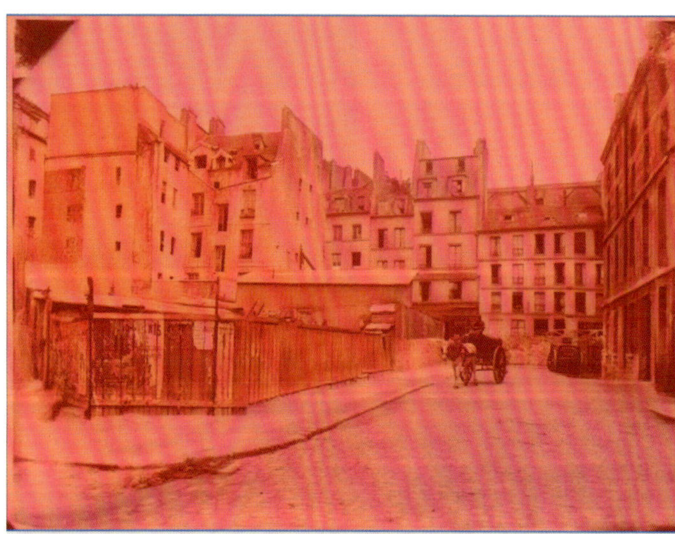

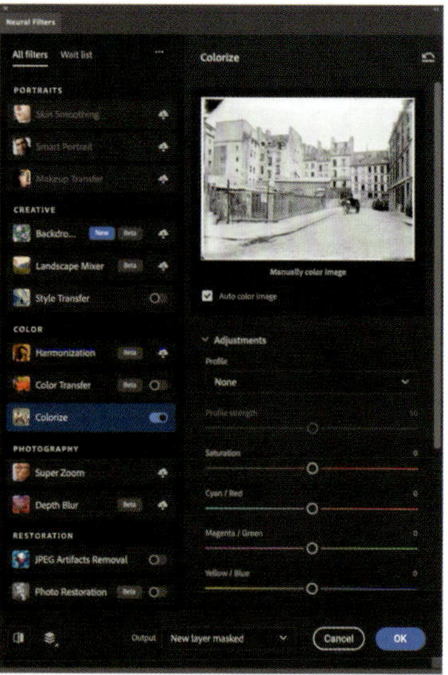

FIGURE 5.49

Now the AI-powered Filter will change the black-and-white photo to color (**FIGURE 5.50**).

I actually like the rough edges of the image borders, but if you want to clean them up, simply crop the image and use Generative Fill to touch up the corners.

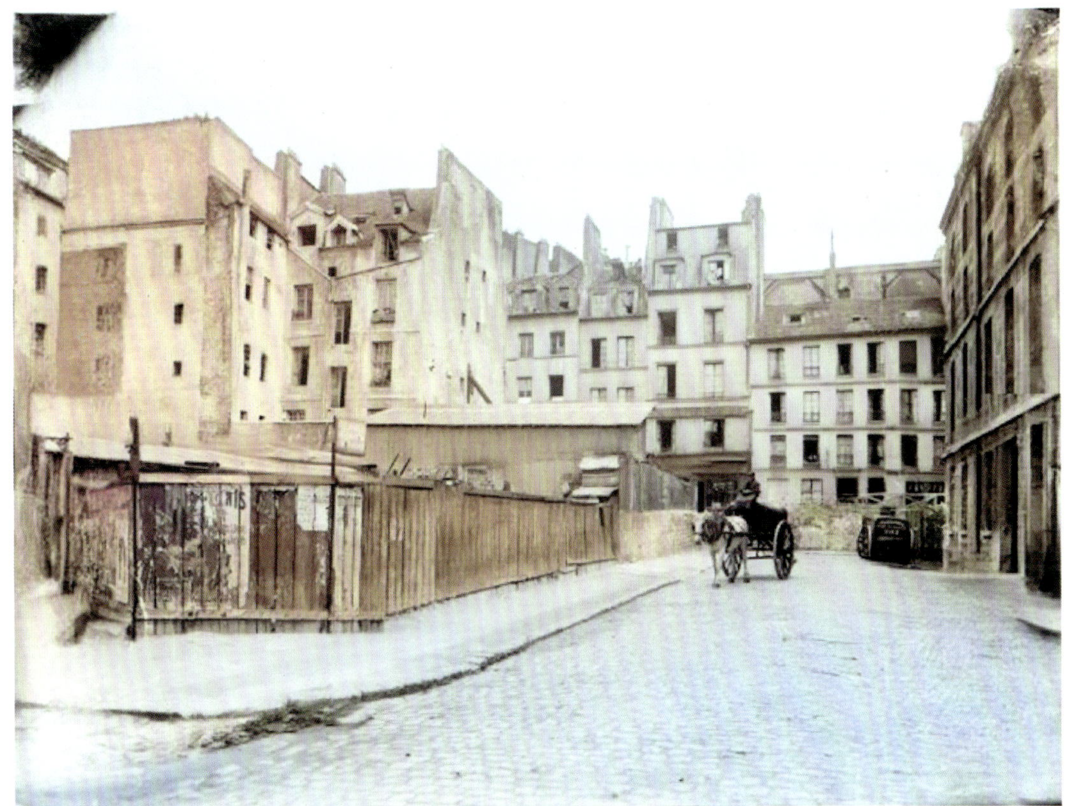

FIGURE 5.50

Transforming a Landscape

Let's do an exploration transforming an environment with Generative Fill.

The idea behind **FIGURE 5.51** was to shoot a starting place for an *Alice in Wonderland*—themed image. We found a location and shot the initial image, and now we will use Generative Fill to tell the rest of the story. Let's start by adding some pathways.

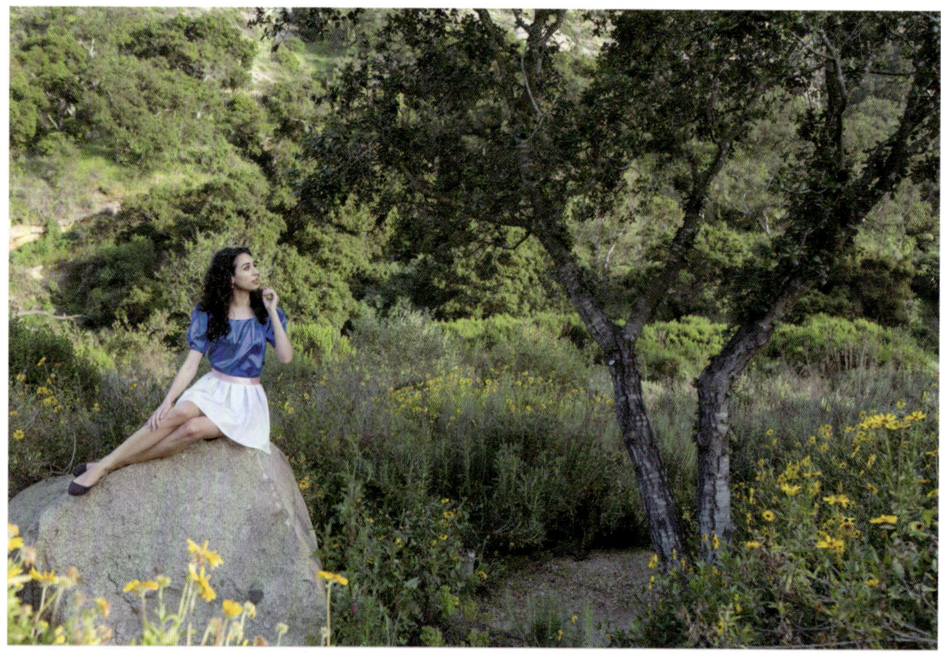

FIGURE 5.51 © Colin Smith

I tried to make a selection around the entire pathway, but it didn't work. I learned that sometimes you need to build things up piece by piece.

1. Choose the Lasso Tool from the Tools panel.

2. Make a selection in the clearing under the tree (**FIGURE 5.52**).

FIGURE 5.52

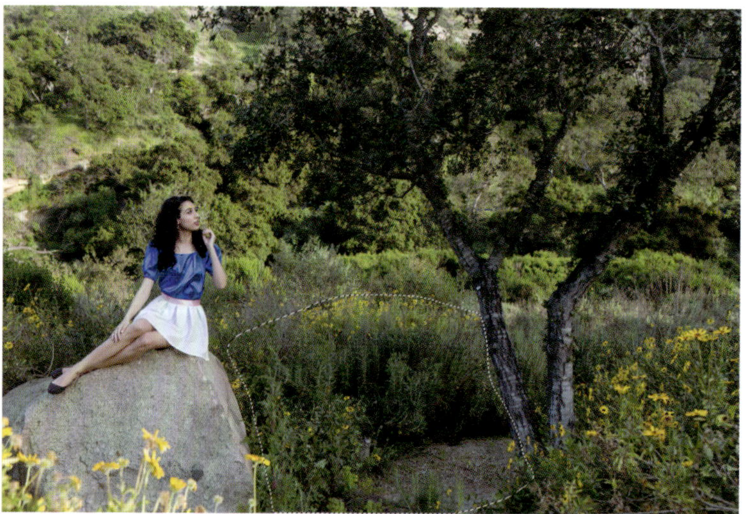

3. Click on Generative Fill in the Task Bar and enter "paved patio" for the prompt.

4. Click Generate.

5. Choose the best variation in the Properties panel.

FIGURE 5.53 was the best variation, but I don't like the post to the left.

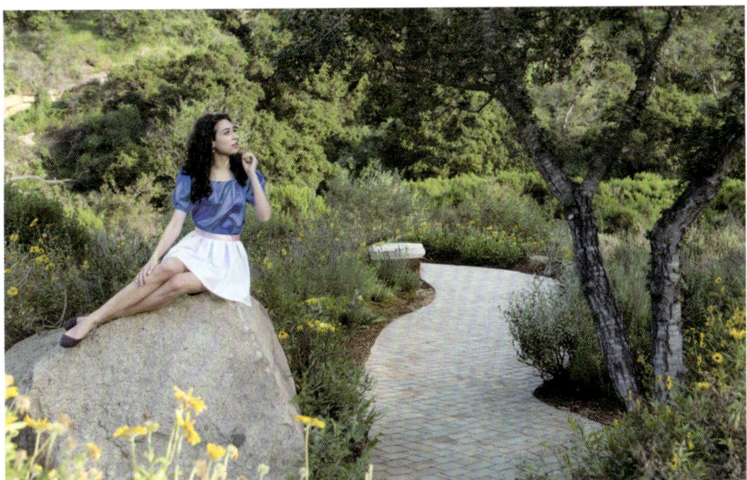

FIGURE 5.53

6. Remove the parts you don't like by making a selection around them and by applying Generative Fill with the prompt box empty (**FIGURE 5.54**).

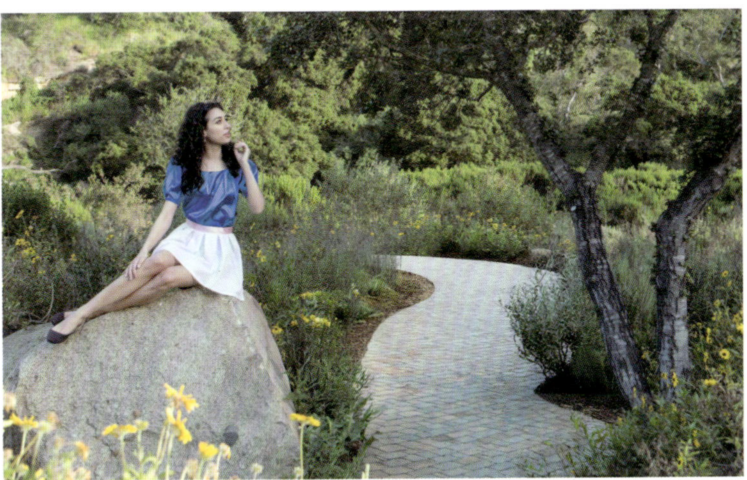

FIGURE 5.54

Let's add a fork in the path and continue it off the image to the right.

7. As you make the selection, you don't have to worry about trying to avoid things like the tree trunk (**FIGURE 5.55**). Generative Fill can work with it.

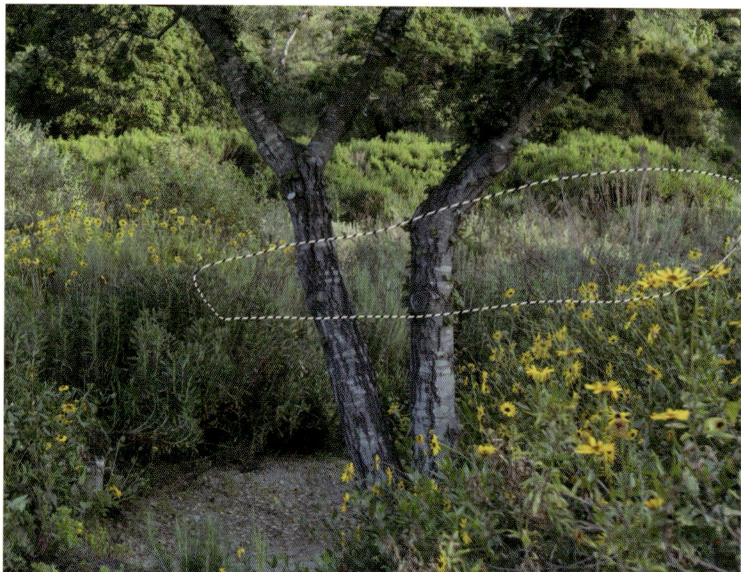

FIGURE 5.55

8. Enter "paved path" into the prompt. You could certainly get more exotic with the prompts, but I'll keep them simple for this exercise. See chapter 1 (page 9) for more on building prompts.

Now we have our fork in the path (**FIGURE 5.56**).

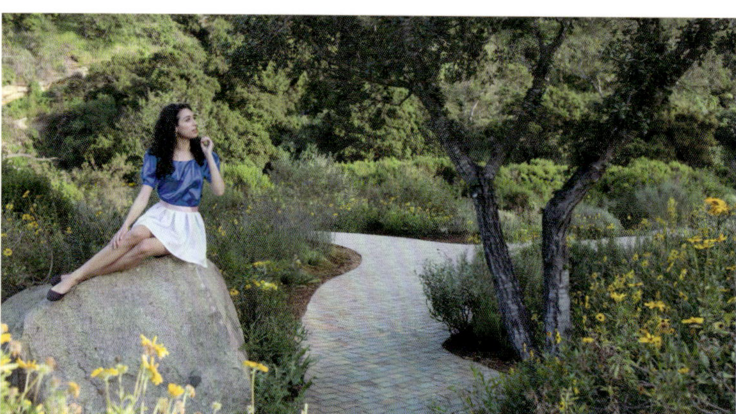

FIGURE 5.56

9. Add a continuation of the path to the left using the same process (**FIGURE 5.57**).

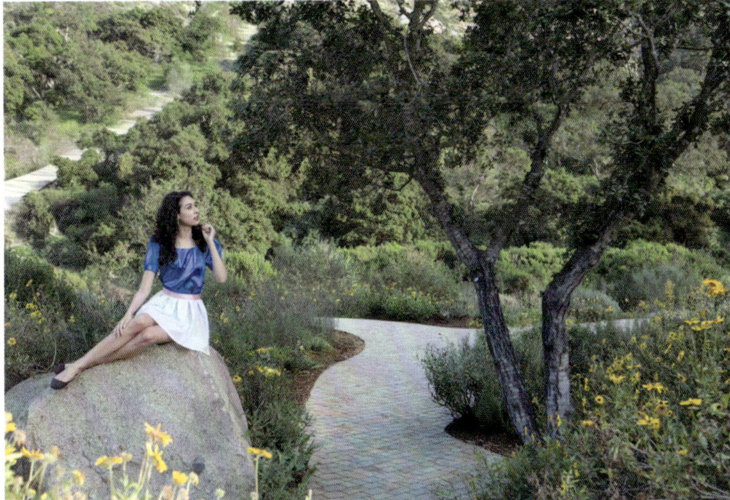

FIGURE 5.57

There is a huge slab of gray visually dominating the left corner because of the boulder.

10. Make a selection around the boulder, click on Generative Fill, and type in "moss" for the prompt. You don't have to type "moss growing on boulder;" Generative Fill knows it's a boulder and this is the logical way to add moss (**FIGURE 5.58**).

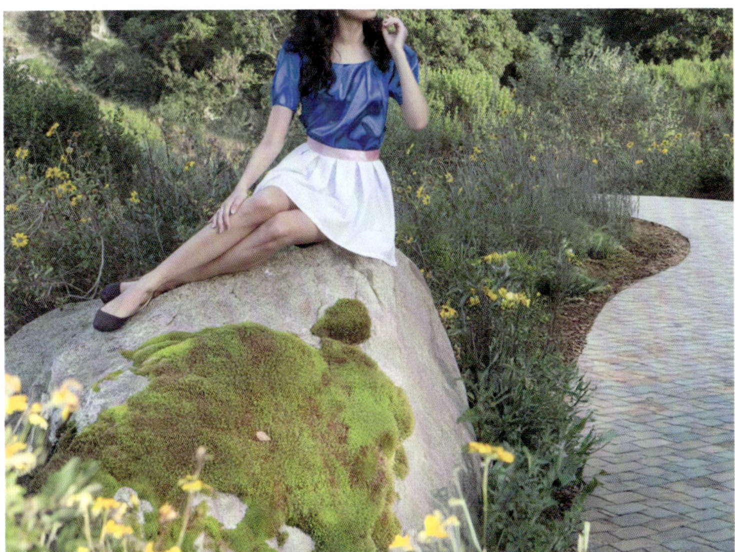

FIGURE 5.58

11. Make a few smaller selections next to the path and use the prompt "colorful red toadstools" (**FIGURE 5.59**).

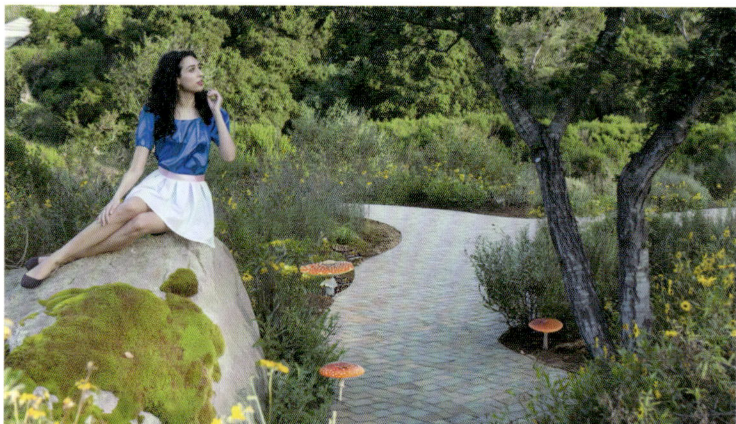

FIGURE 5.59

Now let's build the wonderland theme.

12. Make a selection in the bottom-right corner of the image and use the prompt "heart shaped hedge" as a nod to the Queen of Hearts (**FIGURE 5.80**).

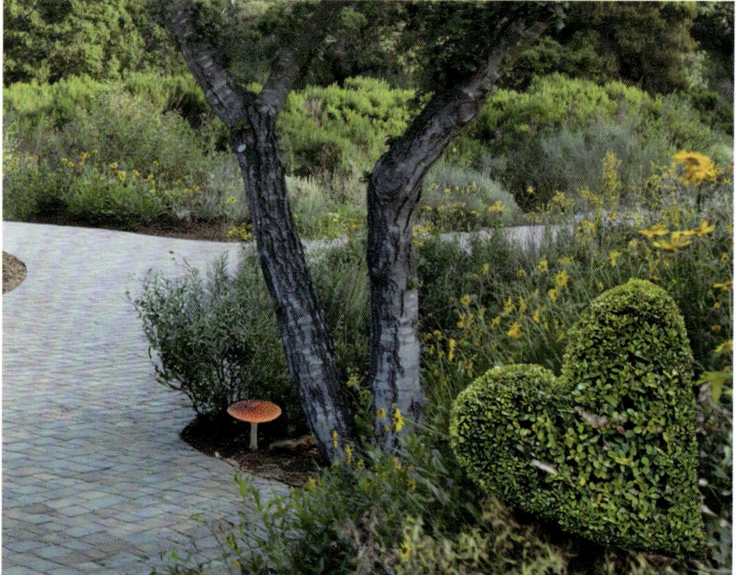

FIGURE 5.60

13. Make another selection and generate the white rabbit (**FIGURE 5.61**).

Now we need the Cheshire Cat on the branch.

14. Make a selection in the shape of a branch coming off the left side of the tree (**FIGURE 5.62**).

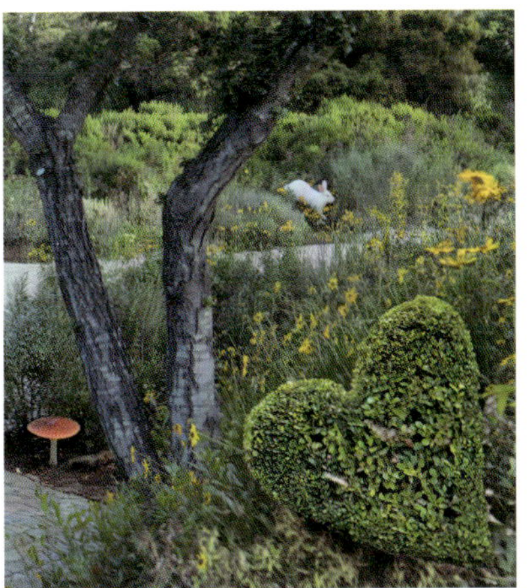

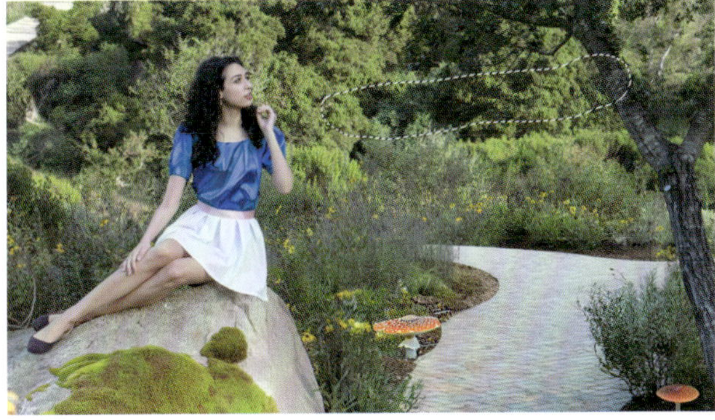

FIGURE 5.62

FIGURE 5.61

15. Enter "tree branch" into the prompt and click Generate (**FIGURE 5.63**).

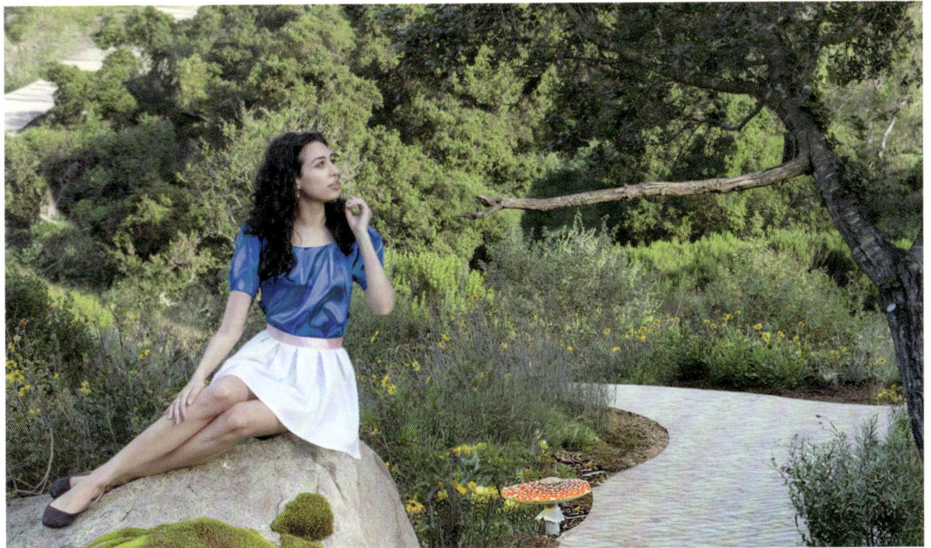

FIGURE 5.63

16. Adding the cat was actually quite a challenge. After trying various prompts and getting plenty of cartoonish-looking cats (even with the prompt "photo-realistic"), "grinning fat furry cheshire cat" worked the best (**FIGURE 5.64**).

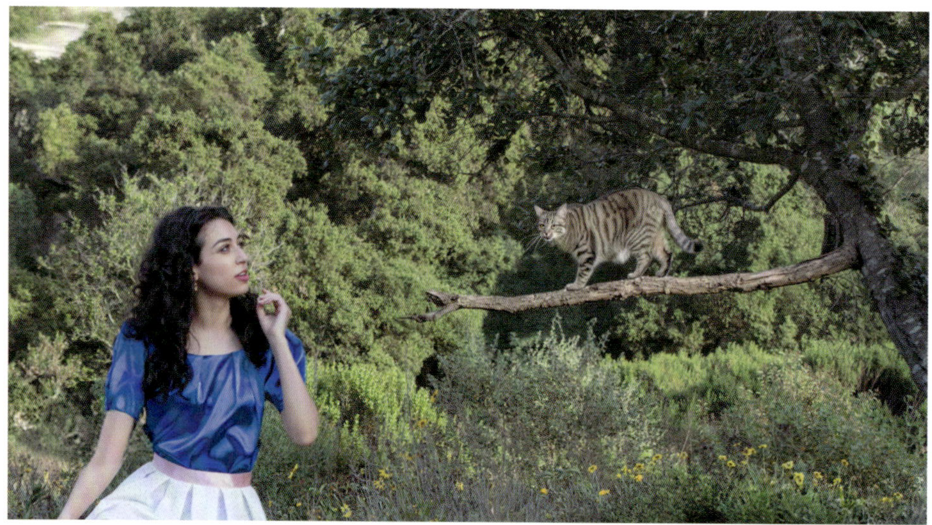

FIGURE 5.64

The scene still looks a little barren, so let's add a body of water.

17. Make a selection over some of the bushes (**FIGURE 5.65**).

18. Simply use the prompt "lake" (**FIGURE 5.66**).

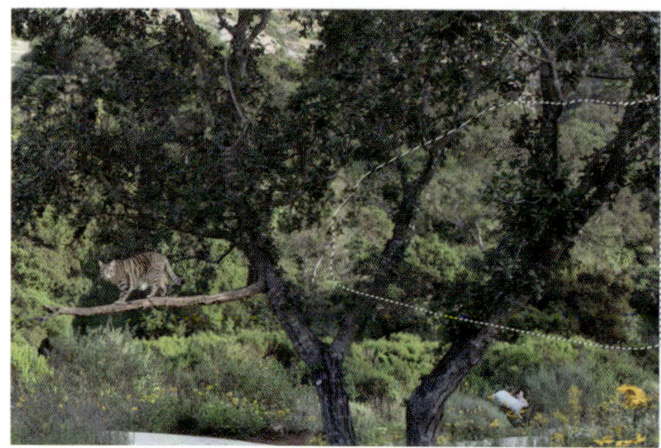

FIGURE 5.65

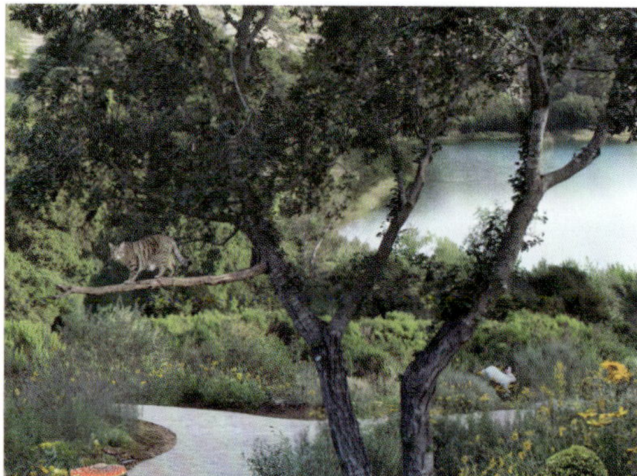

FIGURE 5.66

We have transformed a basic photo into our own *Alice in Wonderland*, without getting too over the top. If you want to make it a little more surreal, adding saturation and warming up the color temperature will do the trick (**FIGURE 5.67**).

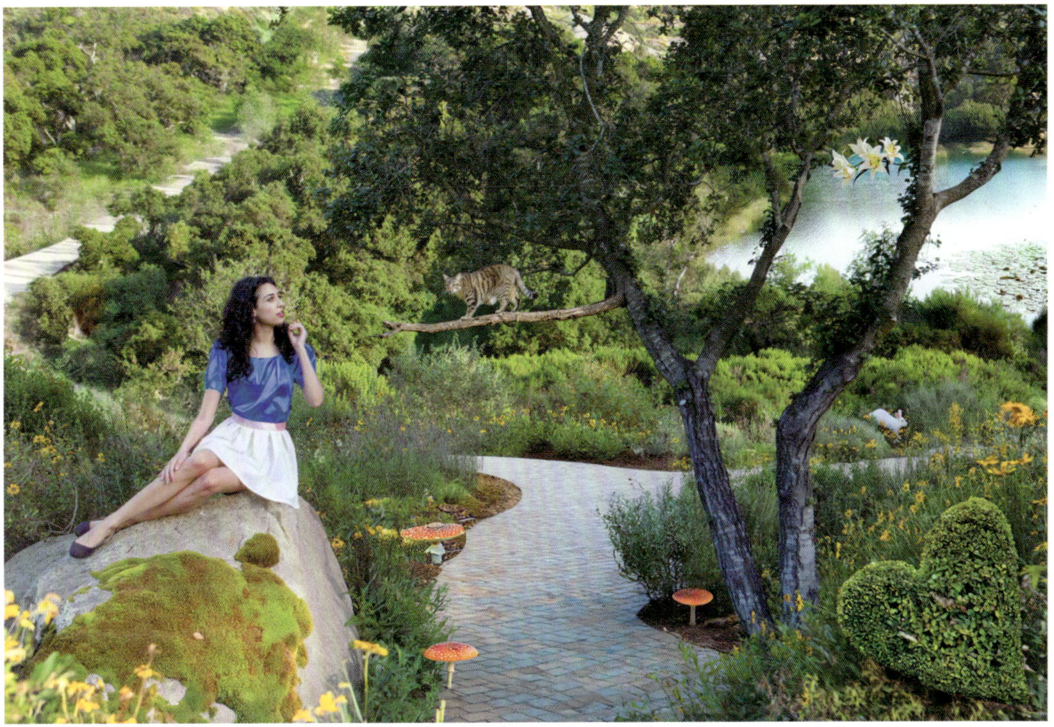

FIGURE 5.67

In this chapter, we learned that we change almost anything in a photo with Generative Fill.

In the next chapter, we will explore the art of combining different images together using Generative AI.

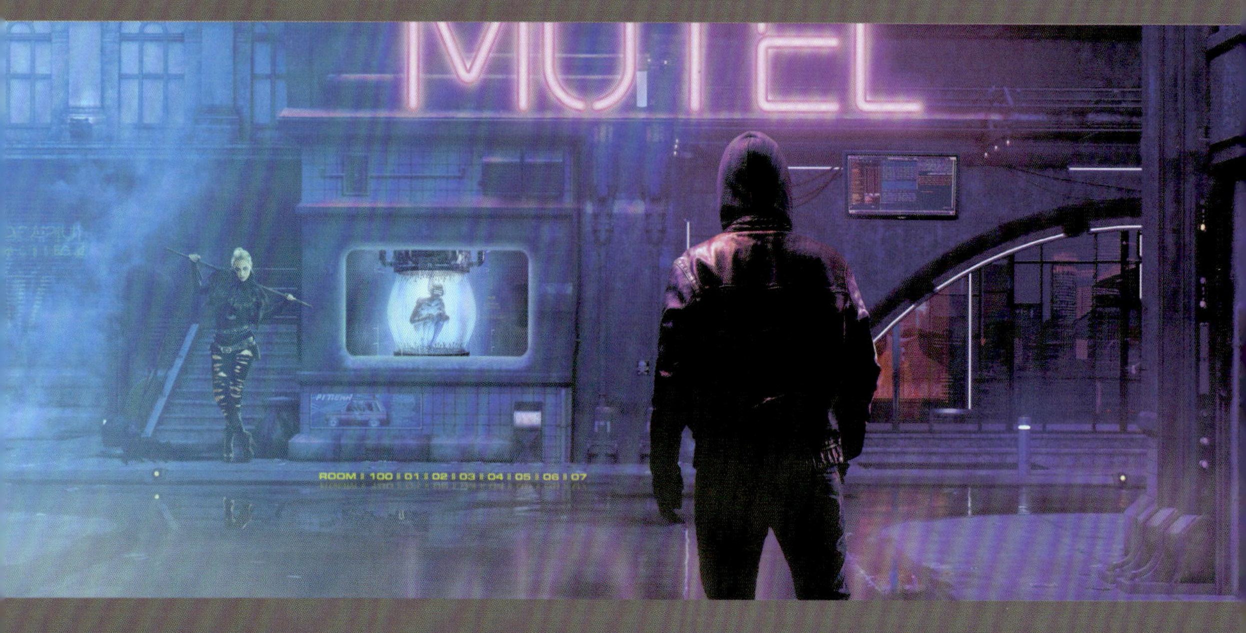

MOTEL
ROOM | 100 | 01 | 02 | 03 | 04 | 05 | 06 | 07

6

COMBINE

In this chapter, we are mostly working with our own "non-AI" images, using the powerful tools in Generative Fill to help us combine images together. We will also wrap up with a fun project and add some finishing touches to a complex composite that was all done by hand. Let's see what we can add to enhance the result without making it look AI-generated.

Combining Images with Generative Fill

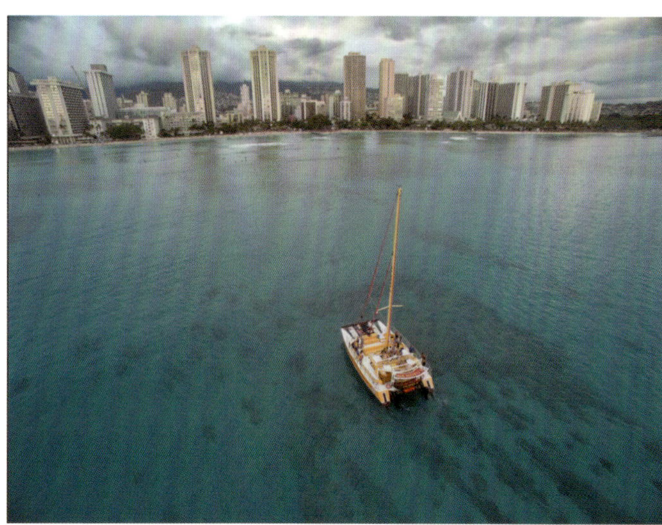

FIGURE 6.1 © Colin Smith

Generative Fill excels at combining different photos together. Let's take two of my drone photos and make a little magic. In the first photo we see a catamaran sailing into Waikiki beach (**FIGURE 6.1**).

If we were to pan the camera to our right, we would see the famous Diamondhead Crater. Instead, I have photographed it from a different angle (**FIGURE 6.2**). We are going to turn this panoramic shot of Diamondhead into an island, and instead of heading toward the beach, the boat will be heading to the island.

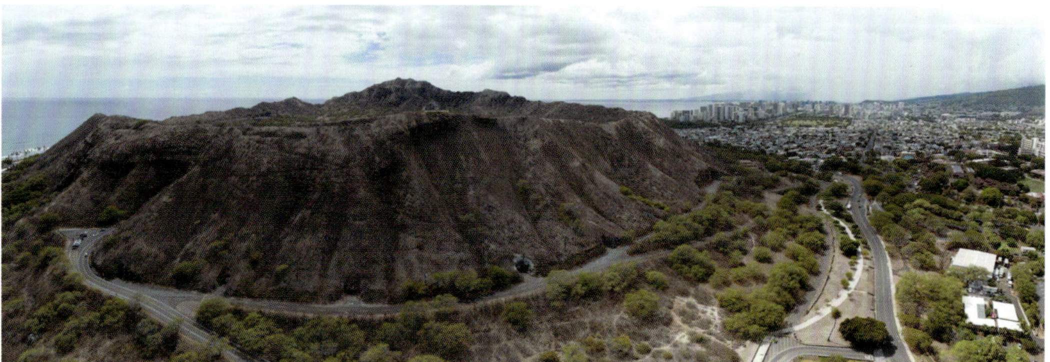

FIGURE 6.2 © Colin Smith

To start, we need to get the two images into the same document.

1. Choose File > Open and open both of the images in Photoshop.

2. With the Move Tool, click in the middle of the first image and drag it up to the tab of the second image (**FIGURE 6.3**). While still holding down on the mouse, pause a couple of seconds and the second image window will open.

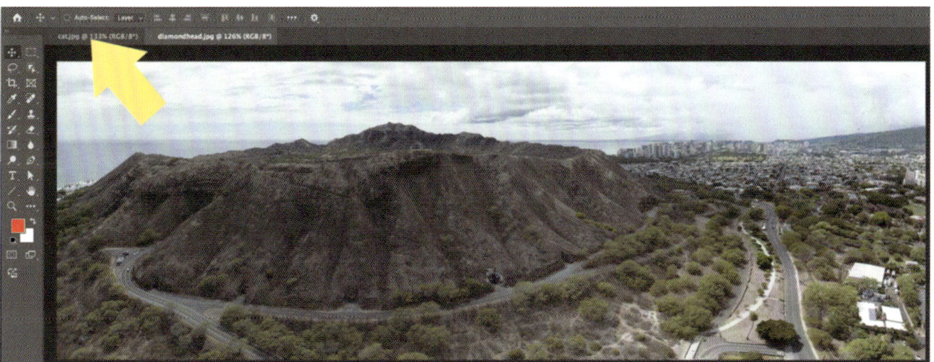

FIGURE 6.3

3. Move your curser into the center of the destination image.

4. Hold down the Shift key and release your mouse. You should now have both images in the same document. The Shift key centers the image.

5. With the top layer still selected, press Ctrl+T/command+T (Windows/Mac) for Free Transform. This will allow you to resize the Diamondhead layer to fit the size of the catamaran layer underneath. To resize, drag the corner handle with your mouse.

6. Drag the top layer and position it above the tip of the mast on the catamaran. Part of the image will not be visible because it's beyond the canvas size (**FIGURE 6.4**).

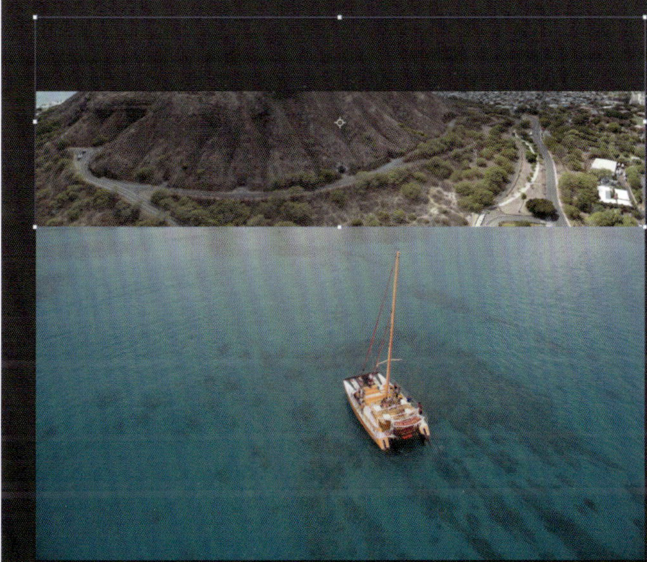

FIGURE 6.4

7. Choose Image > Reveal all.

The canvas will resize and you should now see the entire image.

Next, we need to blend the two layers together, while making the top layer an island (**FIGURE 6.5**).

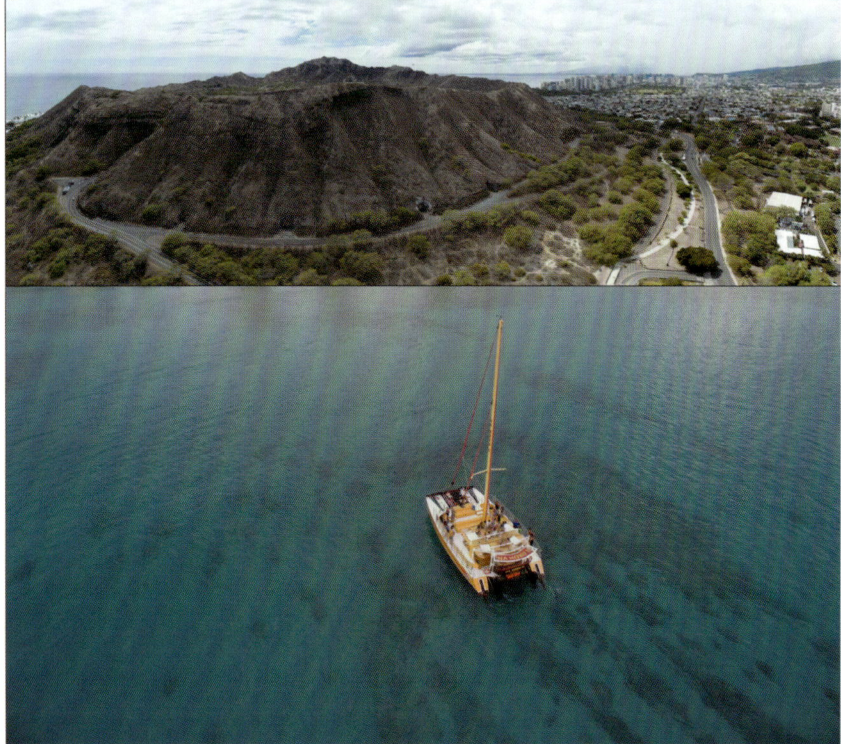

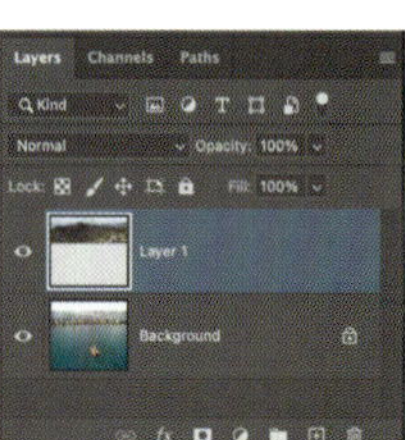

FIGURE 6.5

8. Grab the Lasso Tool from the Tools panel (**FIGURE 6.6**).

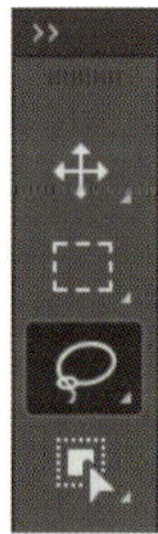

FIGURE 6.6

9. Carefully make a selection of everything around the bottom of the mountain. The selection should include all the land and extend into the water image, as shown in **FIGURE 6.7**.

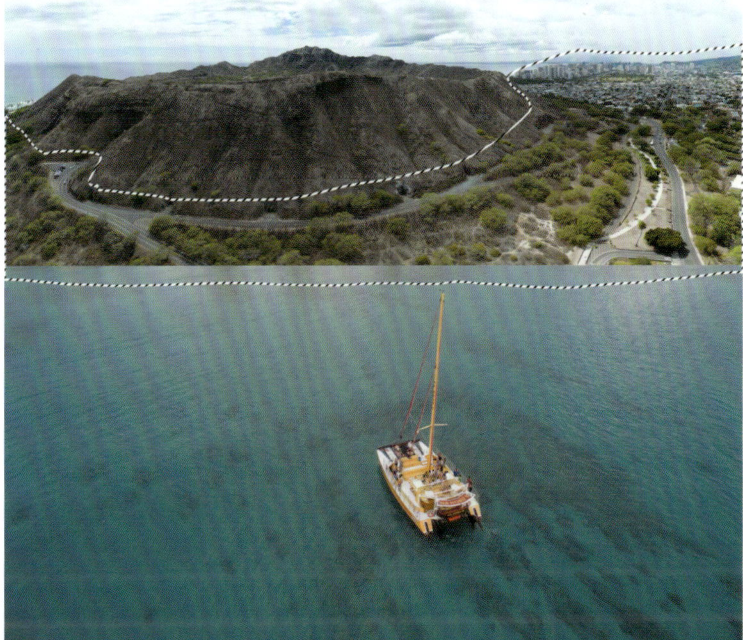

FIGURE 6.7

10. Click on Generative Fill in the Task Bar (**FIGURE 6.8**).

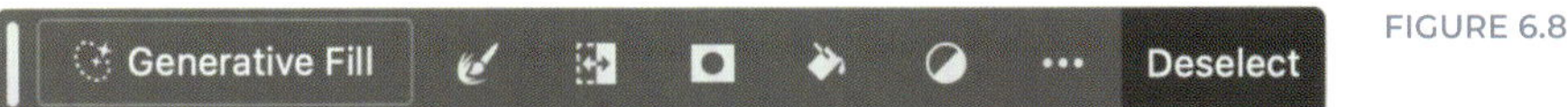

FIGURE 6.8

11. Enter "ocean" into the text prompt field and click Generate (**FIGURE 6.9**). In this case, we don't leave the prompt blank because we want to generate something specific.

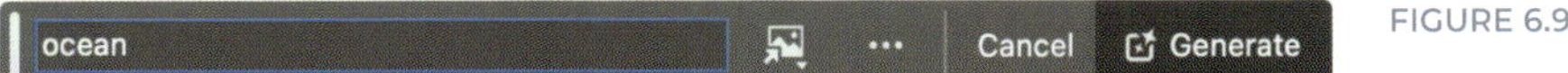

FIGURE 6.9

12. Choose the best variation in the Properties panel (**FIGURE 6.10**).

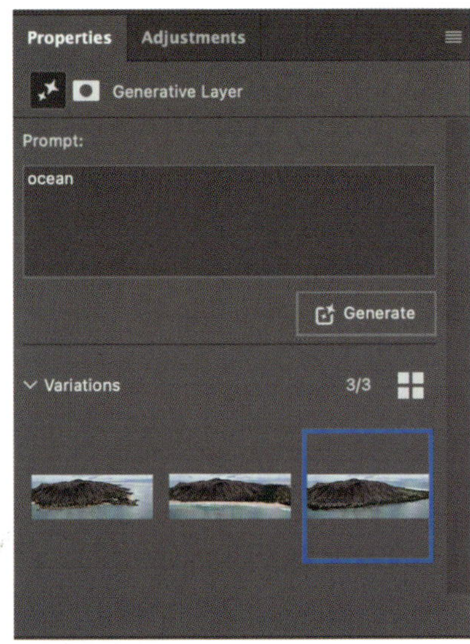

FIGURE 6.10

We have successfully made our image (**FIGURE 6.11**).

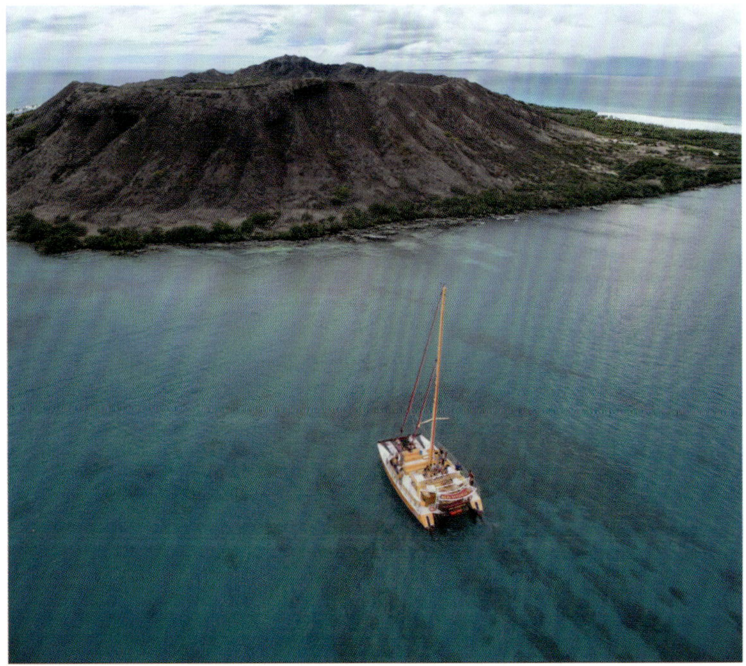

FIGURE 6.11

Joining Images Together

There are different reasons you may need to join images together. Maybe they were scanned from a book and there was a seam down the middle. Maybe they were scanned from a very large photo in pieces and need to be recombined. Perhaps you were shooting a panorama and there are pieces missing or you didn't create any overlap. Generative Fill is the perfect tool for the job!

In this example, we have two photos that almost meet, but there is a gap (**FIGURE 6.12**). In the past, you would have to do a lot of reconstructive retouching to fix this issue, or you'd just abandon the image altogether. You can also use this technique for overlapping images that don't quite match.

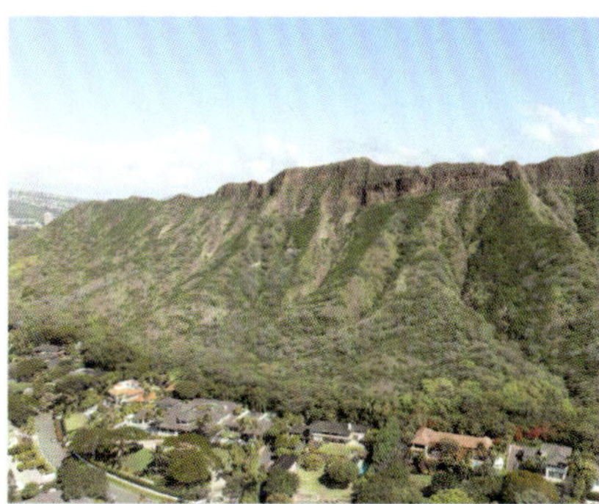
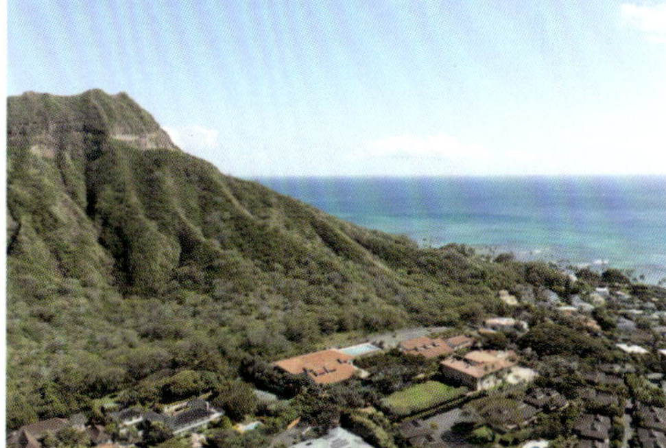

FIGURE 6.12 © Colin Smith

The two images are on different layers in a single Photoshop document. If they were flattened on a single layer, this would work the same way.

To open two images into the same document, simply follow steps 1–5 in the previous section.

Now let's work on combining the images.

1. Click on the top layer in the Layers panel (**FIGURE 6.13**).

2. With the Move Tool selected, position the images where you want them to be relative to each other.

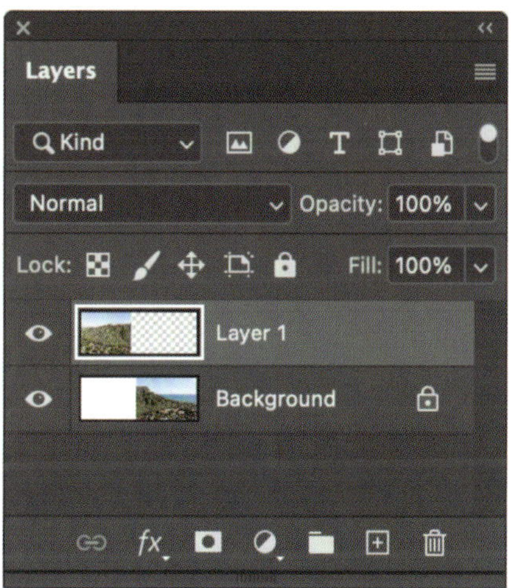

FIGURE 6.13

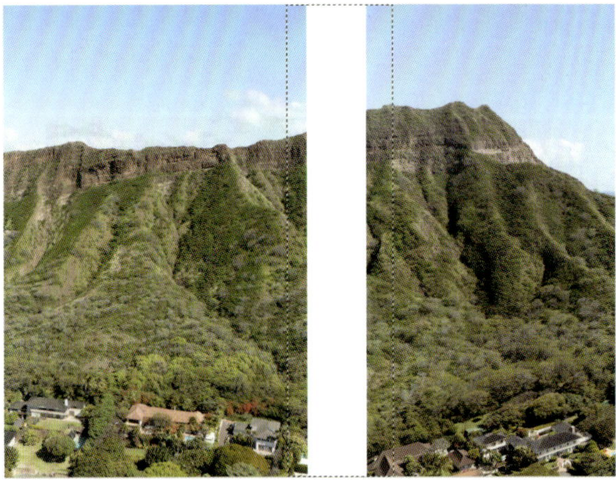

FIGURE 6.14

3. Choose the Rectangular Marquee Tool from the Tools panel.

4. Make a selection overlapping both of the images (**FIGURE 6.14**). Extending the selection into each image a bit will give Generative Fill room to produce a more convincing blend.

5. Click on Generative Fill in the Task Bar.

6. Leave the text prompt field blank and click on Generate.

7. Choose the best variation, and you are done (**FIGURE 6.15**)!

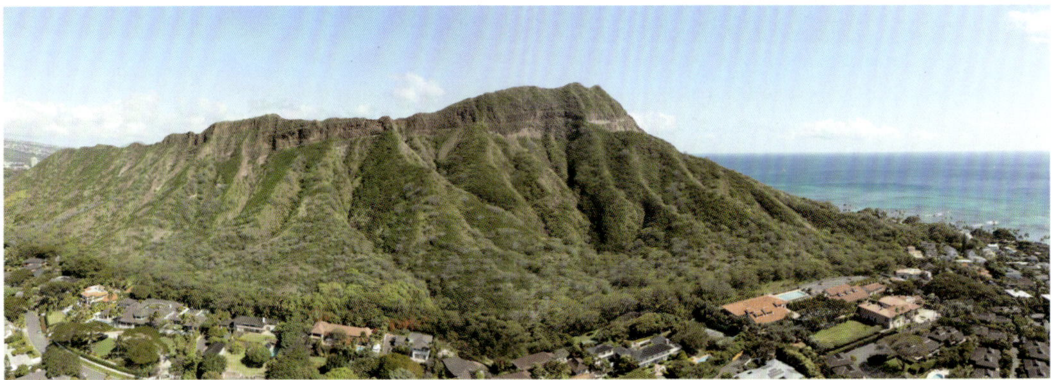

FIGURE 6.15

Enhancing a Composite

The main way I use Generative AI is to integrate it into my existing workflows and use it as another tool. I rarely use fully AI-generated images in my commercial work. More often, I work with the tools in Photoshop and use AI to save time. Sometimes I generate pieces that will be added to the composite.

FIGURE 6.16 is a multilayered composite I made in Photoshop. Most of these elements are from Adobe stock and other sources, and some I created from scratch.

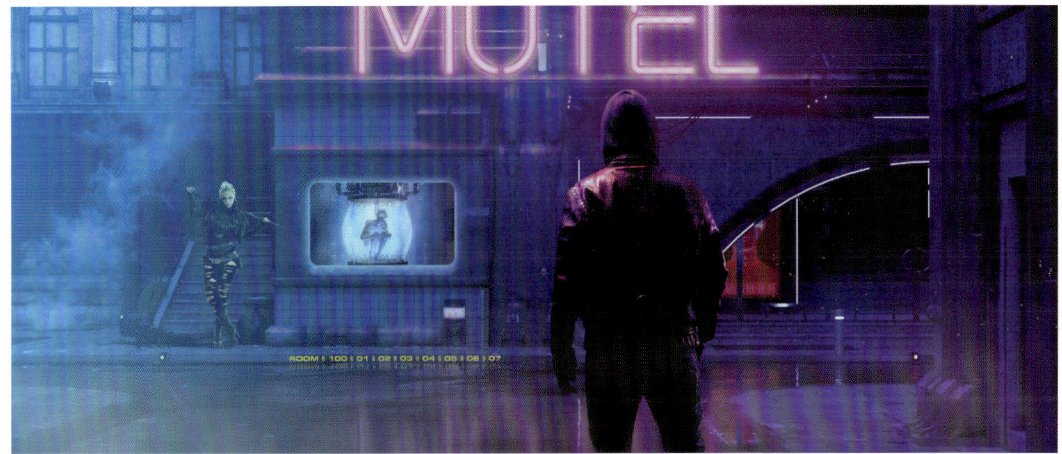

FIGURE 6.16 © Colin Smith, some elements from Adobe Stock and Pixabay

In **FIGURE 6.17**, you can see there are quite a few layers involved in this composite.

Historically, it has been difficult to create realistic reflections in post-production. Sure, we can easily cheat and flip part of the image over and blend it in, but there is a big problem with that: You are essentially looking at the same angle. A trained eye will know that a real reflection will show a different angle.

Say you are looking down on an object with a puddle underneath it. You will be looking at the top of the object, and the reflection will show the underside of the object. In the past, this was very difficult to achieve in Photoshop. However, Generative Fill does a fantastic job of generating reflections at the correct angle. Let's try it.

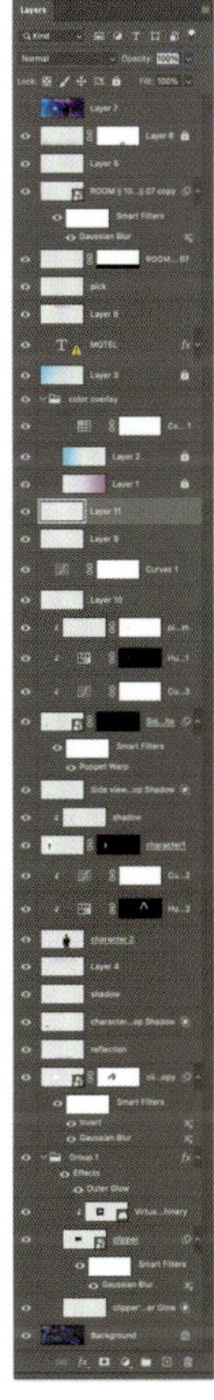

FIGURE 6.17

Adding Reflections

1. Grab the Lasso Tool and make selections around the areas where you want to add reflections (**FIGURE 6.18**).

2. Click on Generative Fill in the Task Bar and type "reflective puddle" or something similar into the prompt field, and you get realistic reflections (**FIGURE 6.19**).

Before we create a different type of reflection, let's do some set dressing with Generative Fill.

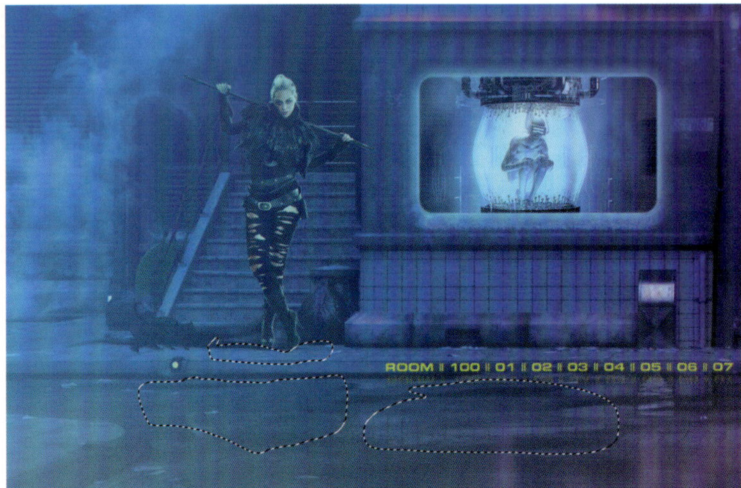

FIGURE 6.18

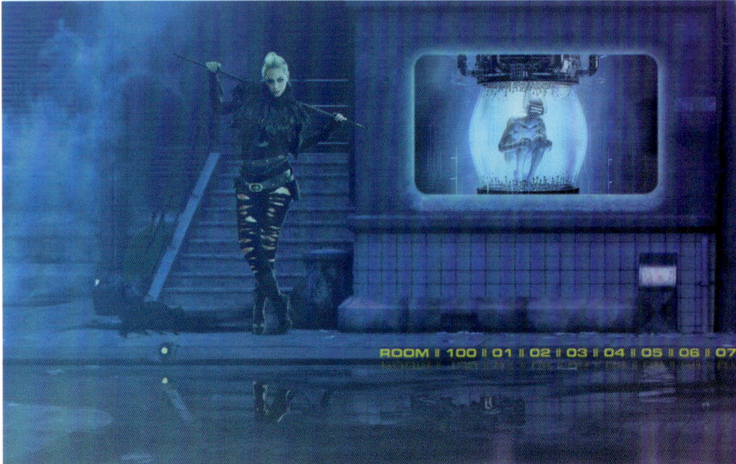

FIGURE 6.19

Adding Visual Detail to Images

1. Make a rectangular selection on the wall (**FIGURE 6.20**).

2. Choose Generative Fill and type in "computer screen with graphics."

Now we get a screen (**FIGURE 6.21**). This is a lot quicker than creating one from scratch or hunting for hours through image assets.

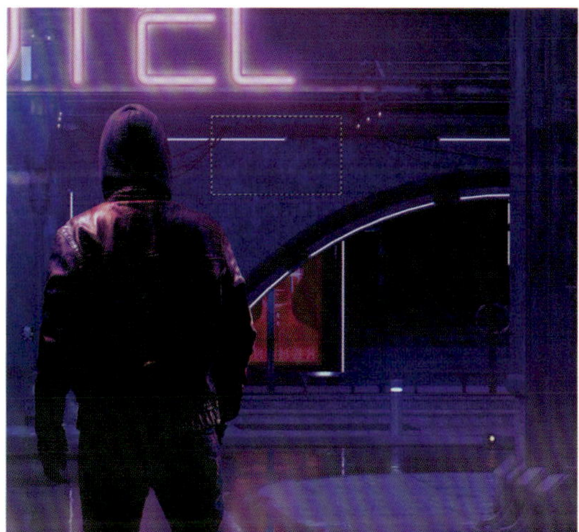

FIGURE 6.20

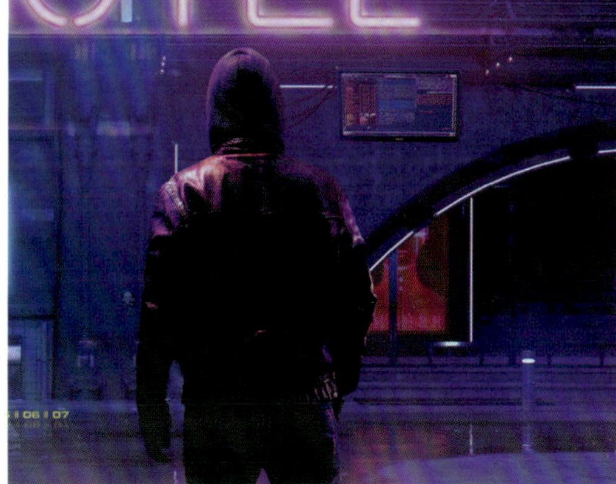

FIGURE 6.21

Add Specific Reflections on a Window

We have a great cyberpunk scene, but we can add to the big-city vibe by adding a reflection in the window.

1. Grab the Quick Selection Tool, or the selection tool of your choice, and make a selection around the glass (**FIGURE 6.22**).

2. Click on Generative Fill in the Task Bar. For the prompt, use "reflections on glass, cyberpunk dystopian city."

Now we have reflections of the city in our glass, and the colors match the colors of the scene (**FIGURE 6.23**).

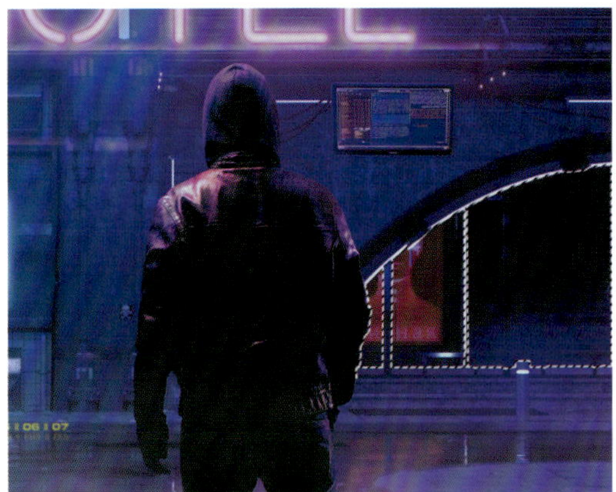

FIGURE 6.22

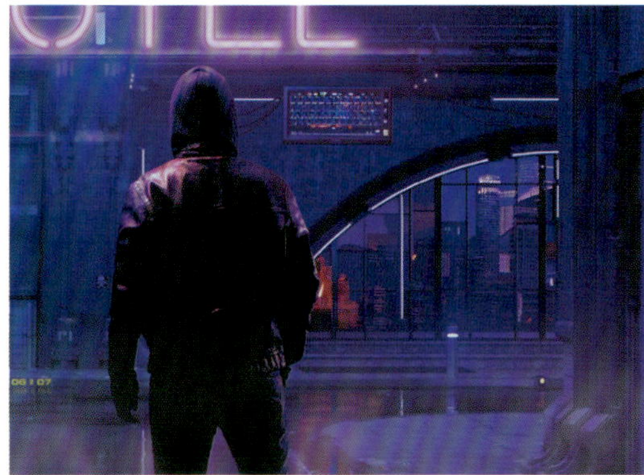

FIGURE 6.23

If you want to make it more subtle, go to the Layers panel and reduce the Opacity of the generated layer. Now, just a hint of the city will register in the viewer's subconscious without it dominating the scene (**FIGURE 6.24**).

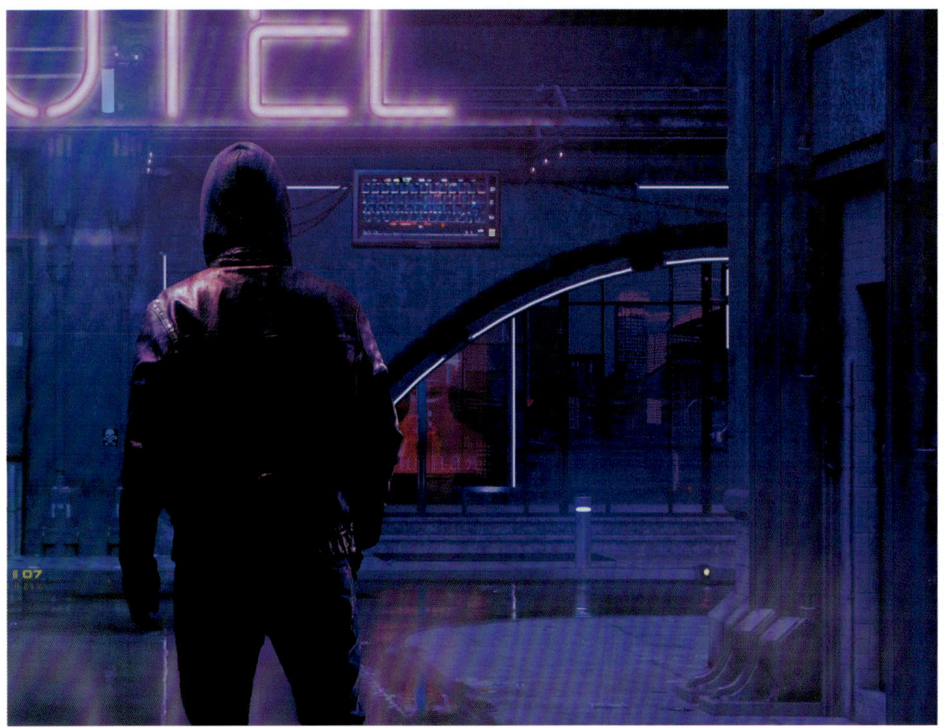

FIGURE 6.24

As you can see, this is still human-created art, but we are using Generative Fill to enhance the image and add some finishing touches. I also added some vents and piping, as well as posters and random details that are subtle, but add to the overall look and feel (**FIGURE 6.25**).

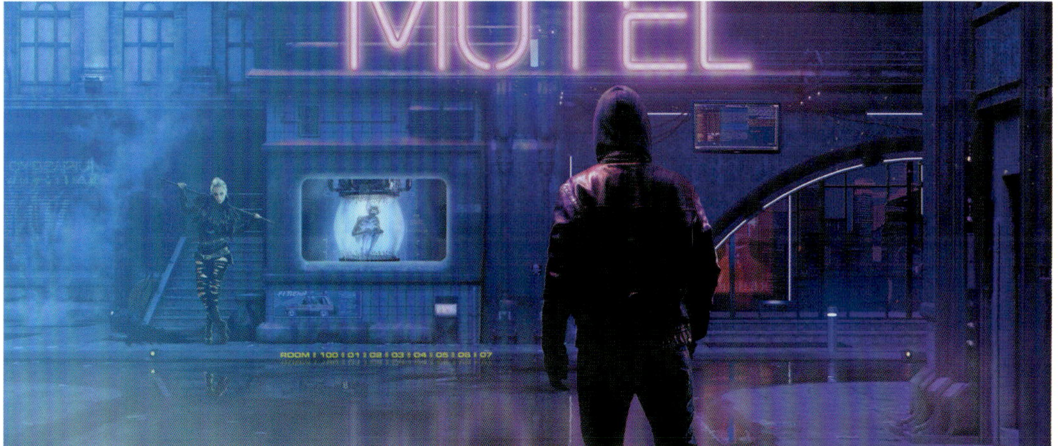

FIGURE 6.25

Compare the final image to my original composite (**FIGURE 6.18**). It's subtle, but all of the enhancements add to the overall feel of the final image.

Go Forth and Experiment

I really hope you found this book useful and that it expanded your scope of what's possible with Generative AI in Photoshop. This technology will be changing fast, so I encourage you to check out my website and follow me on the socials @PhotoshopCAFE to stay up to date on the latest changes.

Now, the rest is up to you! I encourage you to experiment for yourself and see how Generative AI can fit into your workflow and help you bring what's in your imagination to life.

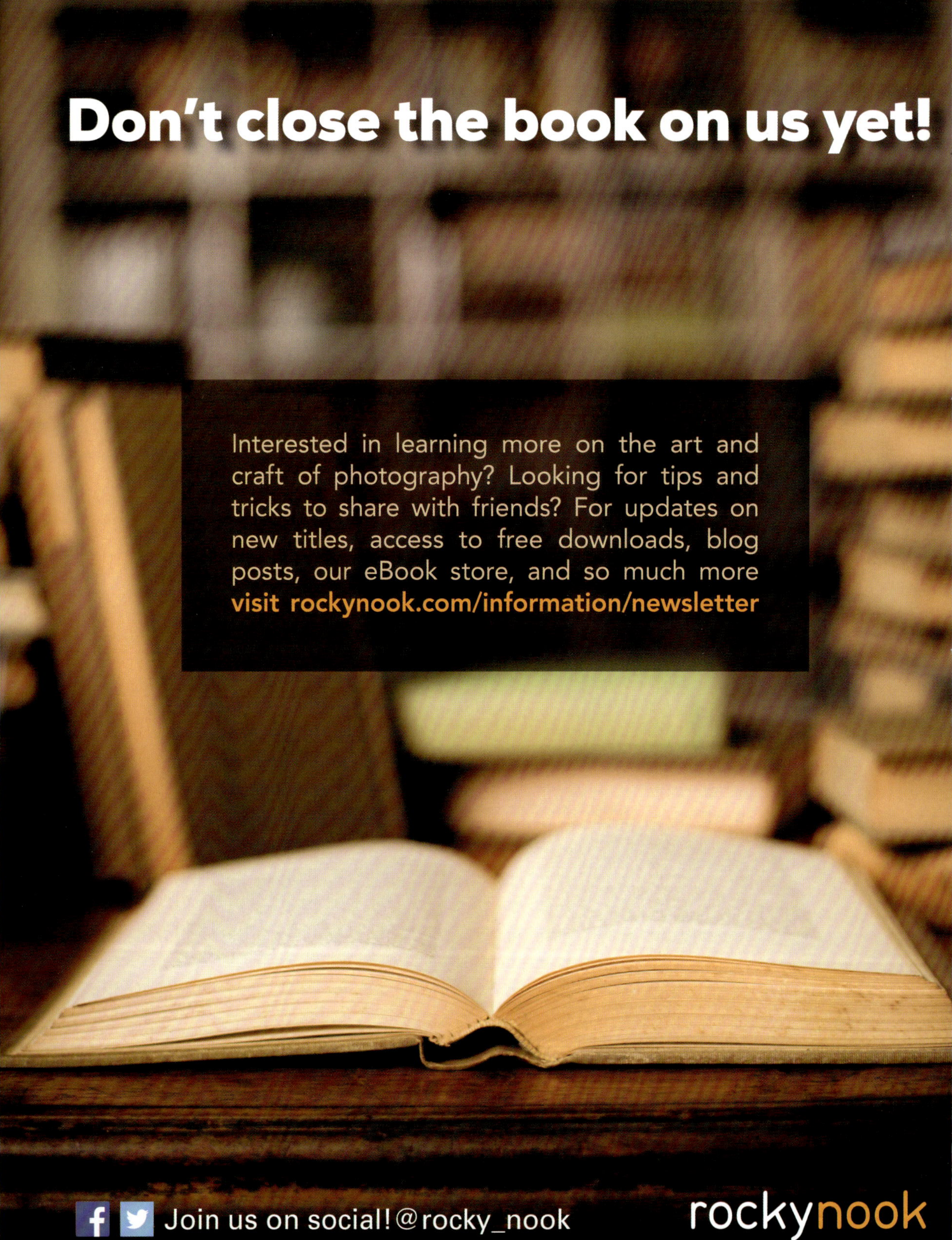

Don't close the book on us yet!
Interested in learning more on the art and craft of photography? Looking for tips and tricks to share with friends? For updates on new titles, access to free downloads, blog posts, our eBook store, and so much more visit rockynook.com/information/newsletter
Join us on social! @rocky_nook
rockynook